SOUTH ASIA—from India to the Philippines—has, almost overnight, become one of the most crucial areas of the world. Americans looking at world affairs are impressed by the significance of the struggle between the Atlantic powers and the Soviet bloc. The decision may lie, not in Europe or America, but in Asia.

This collection of lectures provides an analysis of the social forces emerging in South Asia and of the problems which its leaders, as well as the leaders of the Western nations, must solve. Nationalism, political independence, Communist propaganda, population pressure, and the striving for rapid political and economic advance, now that the colonial ties are broken, provide the pattern in which South Asia's future shapes itself.

The contributors to the volume are experts who either are natives of South Asia or have spent many years there as travelers or residents. They all speak with a full understanding of local conditions and of present difficulties and complexities. They provide an integrated picture of the contemporary and prospective political and social dynamics of this important, but in the United States rather neglected, area, which holds a quarter of the world's population.

SOUTH ASIA IN THE WORLD TODAY

EDITED BY PHILLIPS TALBOT

SOUTH ASIA IN THE WORLD TODAY

HENRY BRODIE
KINGSLEY DAVIS
CORA DuBOIS
JOHN EMBREE
J. S. FURNIVALL
WILLIAM L. HOLLAND
HAROLD ISAACS
KARL J. PELZER
B. M. PIPLANI
CARLOS P. ROMULO
MILTON SACKS
SOEDJATMOKO
DANIEL THORNER
JUSTUS VAN DER KROEF

THE UNIVERSITY OF CHICAGO PRESS · CHICAGO

THE
NORMAN WAIT HARRIS MEMORIAL FOUNDATION

The Twenty-fifth Institute

THE Harris Foundation Lectures at the University of Chicago have been made possible through the generosity of the heirs of Norman Wait Harris and Emma Gale Harris, who donated to the University a fund to be known as "The Norman Wait Harris Memorial Foundation" on January 27, 1923. The letter of gift contains the following statement:

The purpose of the foundation shall be the promotion of a better understanding on the part of American citizens of the other peoples of the world, thus establishing a basis for improved international relations and a more enlightened world order. The aim shall always be to give accurate information, not to propagate opinion.

Annual Institutes have been held at the University of Chicago since the summer of 1924. The lectures delivered each year have been published in essentially their original form in a series of volumes of which this is the most recent.

THE UNIVERSITY OF CHICAGO PRESS, CHICAGO 37
Cambridge University Press, London, N.W. 1, England
W. J. Gage & Co., Limited, Toronto 2B, Canada

PREFACE

A VARIETY of considerations led the committee of the Norman Wait Harris Memorial Foundation to choose South Asia as the subject of its twenty-fifth annual Institute, which was held at the University of Chicago, May 25–29, 1949. The area is inherently important. It holds a quarter of the world's population. It is the seat of ancient cultures. It has been a prime producer of the world's tropical products, a market of no mean size, and a major prop to the western European standard of living.

During the decade of World War II, South Asia underwent drastic convulsions whose consequences are significant to itself and to the outside world. Politically, the conjunction of maturing nationalisms with contracting European power, coupled with American withdrawal from the Philippines, has resulted in independence for five countries and exhausting struggles in two others. The reins of power have fallen from alien colonialists into the hands of indigenous leaders. This by itself has transformed the position in South Asia. But economic and social changes have been even more profound. The colonial-tropical pattern of production and trade, so laboriously built up under European control, has sustained severe shocks. Agrarian revolts and labor unrest suggest an unfinished economic revolution, likely to be enhanced by social restiveness.

These developments posed serious questions. Where would the new nationalisms find vigor to weather the storms that buffeted them? Were the difficulties so great that their peoples would turn to the Communist solution, especially at the application of pressure from Communist China?

Then, again, what were the prospects for South Asian regionalism, of the sort envisaged by such spokesmen as Nehru and Romulo, who had predicted that South Asia might become a neutral third force interposed between the contending great powers? How would the new position in South Asia affect the

PREFACE

Atlantic community and the United States? What was America's new role since the recession of European influence in the area? Where would the Truman Point Four program fit in?

To consider such issues, some fifty specialists participated in the Harris Institute. Including Americans, Europeans, and Asians, they represented universities, business firms, journals, and government agencies. The public lectures presented during the Institute, and some of the papers read at round-table sessions are contained in this volume, along with excerpts and summaries of the discussions.

For the sake of precision, South Asia was defined as the belt of countries along the southern fringe of Asia from Pakistan to the Philippines, where colonialism has been a common characteristic, although Siam was included. Specifically, the countries that were considered are Pakistan, India, Ceylon, Burma, Siam (now, again, Thailand), Indochina, Malaya, Indonesia, and the Philippines.

The book is divided into five parts. In the first, J. S. Furnivall sets forth the background and the proportions of the problem of South Asia in the world today. Mr. Furnivall is one of the very few Britishers invited by Burman government leaders to remain in their country and give counsel after independence. He brought to the Harris Institute not only the experience of a lifetime of service in South Asia but also a completely fresh report of conditions in the region, which he had left only a few days previously.

In Part II specialists address themselves to the cultural and social aspects of South Asia. Fundamentally, who are these people? Do their religions, their languages, their nationalist revivals and ambitions, draw them together into common and regional consciousness, or do these basic forces serve to divide them? What predictive value as to the course of events in South Asia—with regard to Communist pressure, for example—lies in a study of cultural characteristics? Anthropologists Cora Du Bois and John Embree and the Indonesian student, Soedjatmoko, consider these questions.

Part III deals with economic ramifications of South Asia's nationalist and regional aspirations. Mr. Furnivall, in an over-

PREFACE

all view of the plural societies of the area, outlines a difficult but possible alternative to the Communist program for the abatement of the people's ills. In detailed analyses of individual sectors of the economic front, Kingsley Davis makes a demographic examination of the position in India and Pakistan, Karl J. Pelzer considers the resources of Southeast Asia, Henry Brodie describes trade patterns, and B. M. Piplani looks at agricultural and industrial planning by the South Asian countries. Daniel Thorner summarizes the round-table discussions on economic matters.

The political contours of South Asia are investigated in Part IV. H. E. Ambassador Carlos P. Romulo of the Philippines submits that non-Communist governments in South Asia can band together and strongly resist Communist pressure, especially from China. This is possible, he argues, in spite of what he calls America's equivocal and stifling policies in Asia. Harold Isaacs poses the dilemmas that confront the national movements *after* they have won political independence. An appraisal of Communist policy and activities in the area is the work of Milton Sacks. Part IV also includes excerpts of the round-table discussions, as does Part V.

The final section, Part V, is devoted to an examination of America's stake in South Asia. Harold Isaacs calls for a new and bold American policy in the area, while other participants urge different facets of a strategic concept. In the last contribution, William L. Holland sums up the discussions held on political problems and America's interest.

The 1949 Harris Institute marked not only the twenty-fifth year of this series of forums on international relations but also the quarter-century mark of Professor Quincy Wright's supervision of the Harris Foundation. I am grateful for his guidance. I am also indebted to Professor Bert Hoselitz for his ready cooperation, both in planning the Institute and in seeing this volume through the press during my absence from the country.

PHILLIPS TALBOT

UNIVERSITY OF CHICAGO
October 1949

TABLE OF CONTENTS

PART I. THE PROBLEM

SOUTH ASIA IN THE WORLD TODAY 3
 J. S. Furnivall

PART II. SOCIAL FORCES IN SOUTH ASIA

CULTURAL FACETS OF SOUTH ASIAN REGIONALISM 27
 Cora Du Bois

A CASE STUDY IN CULTURAL CONTACTS: THE MALAY LANGUAGE . . 45
 Soedjatmoko

Rapporteur's REPORT OF ROUND-TABLE DISCUSSIONS ON SOCIAL FORCES 51
 John F. Embree

PART III. ECONOMIC FORCES IN SOUTH ASIA

CO-OPERATION, COMPETITION, AND ISOLATION IN THE ECONOMIC SPHERE 63
 J. S. Furnivall

THE ECONOMIC DEMOGRAPHY OF INDIA AND PAKISTAN 86
 Kingsley Davis

THE RESOURCE PATTERN OF SOUTHEAST ASIA 108
 Karl J. Pelzer

THE POSTWAR PATTERN OF TRADE 119
 Henry Brodie

AGRICULTURAL AND INDUSTRIAL PLANNING IN SOUTH ASIA 134
 B. M. Piplani

Rapporteur's REPORT OF ROUND-TABLE DISCUSSIONS ON ECONOMIC
 FORCES 142
 Daniel Thorner

PART IV. POLITICAL FORCES IN SOUTH ASIA

NATIONALISM, COMMUNISM, AND REGIONALISM 153
 Carlos P. Romulo

PROBLEMS OF NATIONALISM 161
 Harold R. Isaacs

ECONOMIC ORIGINS OF INDONESIAN NATIONALISM 174
 Justus M. van der Kroef

COMMUNISM AND REGIONAL INTEGRATION 202
 Milton Sacks

EXCERPTS FROM ROUND-TABLE DISCUSSIONS ON COMMUNISM IN SOUTH
 ASIA 211

TABLE OF CONTENTS

PART V. AMERICA'S STAKE IN SOUTH ASIA

A POLICY FOR THE UNITED STATES 221
  Harold R. Isaacs
EXCERPTS FROM ROUND-TABLE DISCUSSIONS 229
Rapporteur's REPORT OF ROUND-TABLE DISCUSSIONS ON POLITICAL
  FORCES AND AMERICA'S STAKE 235
  William L. Holland

APPENDIX

LIST OF PARTICIPANTS, TWENTY-FIFTH HARRIS INSTITUTE 247

INDEX

INDEX 251

PART I
THE PROBLEM

SOUTH ASIA IN THE WORLD TODAY

By J. S. FURNIVALL[1]

SOUTH ASIA of today is the child of revolution, of destructive energy, in contradistinction to the South Asia of yesterday, the child of the Suez Canal and the outcome of constructive effort. Its natural resources are still abundant, but the accumulated capital has been destroyed, and the labor diverted from production. The men of business, who formerly developed the material resources and out of their profits set aside the capital for further progress, and the officials, who maintained the public order essential to economic progress, represented the heart and brain of the prewar social system; they provided the driving force and co-ordinating genius. Now the structure which they erected has collapsed, and they are buried beneath the ruins. On the other hand there are signs of a new dynamic spirit among masses that were formerly inert. Why did the prewar structure crash? Should we—can we—patch it up again? How, if at all, can we replace it with a new building on more secure foundations? What part, if any, remains for those who erected the old building? How far will the new dynamic spirit suffice to equip the people with the capital and labor requisite for the development of their resources, and what can be done to help them? These, in general terms, are some of the chief questions relating to South Asia. But vague questions invite vague answers. We must try to frame exact questions in appropriate terms. This demands an exact knowledge of the circumstances and a firm grasp of general principles. It is with that end that I venture to submit the following remarks. They relate mostly to Burma; partly because I am best acquainted with the circumstances in Burma and partly because the course of affairs in Burma seems to me, for reasons that I shall explain, especially instructive and the present situation there especially important.

1. Adviser to the government of the Union of Burma.

BURMA

a) UNDER BURMESE RULE

Burma, cut off from the outside world by mountains and the sea, forms a natural political and economic unit. It has been peopled by successive migrations from central Asia by tribes almost exclusively of Indonesian or Mongoloid origin. Some have never got farther than the border hills or have been driven back into the hills after settling in the lowlands. The most important hill tribes are the Karens, Chins, and Kachins. Their social organization is tribal and not territorial, and the chain of authority is based on the personal relations between chieftain and dependent. In agriculture they have barely advanced beyond shifting cultivation. Their religion is the complex of ritual and superstition usually termed "animism," but many have adopted Buddhism, especially among the Karens and Chins; the Karens, too, have taken readily to Christianity, which has also made some progress among the Chins.

Often reckoned with the hill folk are the Shans, close cousins of the Siamese—Shan and Siam are different pronunciations of the same word. They are Buddhists; they have made some progress toward substituting a territorial social organization for one based on kinship, and many have settled down to permanent cultivation. The other chief peoples are the Mons, who long disputed Lower Burma with the Burmese, and the Burmese themselves, for nine centuries the ruling race. They are also Buddhists and agriculturists who have definitely crossed the border line between tribal and territorial social organization. Burmese, Mon, and Shan, all from time to time made contact with Indian Buddhism, and on this basis they built up in seclusion from the outer world a common Buddhist civilization with many attractive features, notably the absence of caste, freedom of the women, a wide diffusion of the elements of literacy, and harmony between church and state. The Burmese king was not only the political suzerain of the hill peoples but the center of the only civilization which they knew and which they tended gradually to absorb. Yet he ruled them indirectly through their own chieftains, and one critical factor in the social evolution of

Burma has been the imperfect assimilation of the different racial elements.

Another feature of importance is that even among the Burmese the vestiges of a tribal organization had never been finally eliminated. The supreme authority was vested in the king, regarded with superstitious awe, but assisted by a council of elders which, in practice, might hold the reins of government. There was an elaborate central administration, organized on quasi-tribal lines; but this came into contact with the people indirectly through hereditary local chieftains, who represented government to the common man and whose authority over their dependents was personal and, superficially, had some resemblance to that exercised by a feudal lord over his vassals. It was the circle or township under this local chieftain, comprising some fifteen to fifty villages, which gave permanence and stability to the political organization. The chief bond of social union was the conservative influence of the Buddhist religious order, with the crown as patron and with a representative in every village. The religious order observed what might be termed "canon law," but Burmans never reached the stage where civil and religious law were sharply differentiated. The whole chain of authority was based on personal relations, regulated by custom, which had the sanction of religion. In general, custom sufficed for the maintenance of order. There was no regular army or police force, and there were practically no prisons; yet the sufficient force of custom is demonstrated by the fact that for long periods the country was ruled by hereditary dynasties; from 1050 to 1300, from 1600 to 1740, and from 1750 until the advent of the British. The elements of stability were the religious order, the hereditary personal authority of the local chieftains, and, above all, the general regard for custom. In normal times these were sufficient to maintain social continuity. But the organization was not strong enough to withstand any great shock, and the government was always in a position of unstable equilibrium.

Through successive generations the people had learned the art of living together, and custom insured a wide diffusion of social welfare in a distinctive national civilization. In its economic aspect this national civilization was self-sufficient and complete within itself. Its activities not merely met the daily requirements of the common man for food, clothes, and shelter but also provided the articles of gaudy luxury that gave a show of splendor to the court. It was primarily an agricultural economy. There was little industry or commerce, and the export of goods was discouraged or prohibited. Social welfare would indeed have been imperiled by economic freedom, for it was bound up with the regard for custom. Thus the Burmese social organization protected social welfare, but at the expense of economic progress.

Here, then, are the essential characters of the Burmese social order: the racial elements were imperfectly assimilated; authority was insecurely based on personal relations; and social obligations were regulated by custom with the sanction of religion. It was both unstable and unproductive, and, when challenged by new forces from the West, it inevitably, even if regrettably, collapsed.

b) UNDER BRITISH RULE

The accident of propinquity brought Burma into contact with these forces in the form of British rule in India. In the inevitable conflict it was annexed piecemeal to British India in 1826, 1852, and 1886. British rule was based on the principle of economic freedom under the impersonal rule of law. It was a practical application of the liberalism which inspired contemporary liberal philosophy. But in Burma the results were unfortunate, for it cut at the roots of the Burmese social and economic system. The first concern of the new government was, of necessity, to safeguard the security of British rule, and accordingly it disarmed the people and trusted for support to foreign troops, mainly Indian with a stiffening of Europeans. The subordinate officials had to apply Western methods of administration, and the Burmese officials of the old regime were therefore replaced by new men, also from India. Official business was conducted in English (or at first in Persian), and even the clerks and menials had to be brought over from India. Burmans knew nothing of Western medicine or engineering, and here again Indians had to be employed. Whatever was not English in the new administration was Indian. Not only the administration but the whole economic structure was entirely foreign in practice and in personnel. European, Indian, and Chinese merchants poured in, to take advantage of the new opportunities for making money; and Burmans, driven from the towns and from industry and commerce, became, even more than before, mere cultivators. In course of time the government found it expedient to employ Burmans in subordinate posts in the interior, but otherwise there was practically no occupation open to them but agriculture, while various groups of foreigners similarly specialized in occupations for which they had particular aptitude or opportunity. Thus, merely by the working of economic forces, there came into existence a plural society, comprising many distinct racial elements, differing in culture, and performing different economic functions and with nothing in common but the desire for gain. What had formerly been a national society was converted into a business concern.

Three factors—one political, one economic, and one social—contributed mainly to the rapid diffusion of economic forces and the disintegration of Burmese social life. The political factor was the transformation and eventual abolition of the hereditary local chieftains. These were at first transformed into nominated officials of the central government; then in 1886, after the third war, they came to be suspected as centers of resistance and disaffection, and the historic circles and townships were broken up into their constituent villages. The political structure disintegrated. Hitherto custom, embodied in the person of the local chieftain, had served to stem the flood of economic forces, but now that barrier was destroyed. The economic factor was the method of development. Most tropical dependencies are developed by Western planters, and the people continue to cultivate for home consumption. But in Burma rice, the chief export crop, was cultivated by the people themselves, who were thus brought directly into contact with the Western market and within the sphere of Western law. This entailed the disintegration of the village community, and "atomization," a characteristic disease of tropical society under Western rule, was especially virulent in Burma. Another result was that many people fell into debt and lost their land to moneylenders, who for the most part were Indians with no interest in land except as an investment. The social factor in disintegration was the decline in the influence of the monastic order, a natural consequence of foreign rule.

These conditions, however, prevailed only in the plains. In the hills, where cultivation yielded no surplus for the market, the people were left, as in Burmese times, under their own rulers. Whereas Burma proper was brought under direct administration on Western principles, the hill folk were governed indirectly. Moreover, the hill tribes were recruited for the army, to protect the government against the large Burmese majority. The natural result of governing the hill tribes separately on a different plan and admitting them to the army, while excluding the Burmese, was to accentuate the racial divisions that formerly had tended to disappear. It was especially unfortunate that, at the instance of the Christian missionaries, Karen Christians were recruited to suppress the Burmese rebellion in Lower Burma in 1886 in connection with the third Burmese war, as this fostered civil and religious discord which time has failed to heal.

Almost from the earliest days of British rule, however, it was found possible to recruit the Burmese for civil administration. For a generation or more the Burmese magistrates and judges received no formal education beyond that given in the monastic schools, and few except Karens attended the Western schools established by the Christian missionaries. These Western schools, however, opened up better chances of promotion, and, as the Burmese demand for Western education grew, the government met it by providing lay schools. This was in line with the general trend of Western philosophy during the nineteenth century in the direction of socialism and self-government. Here again Britain may claim to have been a pioneer in colonial administration. But here again the results were unfortunate. The new system of education accelerated the decay of the monastic order; the brighter and wealthier lads deserted the monastic schools for the lay schools, which offered better prospects of advancement. The official organization gradually grew more elaborate until in 1923 it was crowned with a local university. Meanwhile, however, the alienation of the monastic order proceeded so far that during the later years of British rule one of the chief problems of government was clerical disorder and disaffection. Alongside education, the government endeavored to promote public health and other aspects of social welfare. There was no barrier to the advancement of Burmans, and not a few rose to the High Court, while one even officiated as governor. But outside civil administration the environment was unpropitious. There was no opening for them in the sphere of industry and commerce and therefore no demand for a training in natural science or economics. Hardly any Burmans entered either of these two gateways to the modern world, and there were hardly any Burman engineers or doctors.

They were, however, given a place in the seat of government. Beginning in 1897, they were represented in a small legislative council, and in 1923 a quasi-democratic form of government was devised, with popular election on a wide suffrage. But in a plural society Western forms of democratic government serve only to aggravate racial and sectional antagonisms, and, by weakening the executive, they allow still greater freedom of economic forces; instead of promoting the reintegration of society, they accelerate disintegration.

In the purely economic sphere, however, British rule clearly demonstrated its superiority over Burmese rule. The country poured forth a growing abundance of rice, timber, oil, and minerals, and all those concerned, as officials or nonofficials, looked with legitimate pride on a notable achievement. In this rapid economic progress, however, Burmans, except as cultivators, played a very minor part, while even as cultivators they were declining from a peasantry into a landless proletariat. With every new extension of economic forces into the native world, the first result was an increase in material prosperity, but, where economic forces have free play, the weakest goes to the wall, and the secondary effect was gradual impoverishment.

The whole process naturally engendered a reaction against British rule, although for many years this did not appear above the surface except in occasional sporadic outbreaks of national sentiment among the peasantry. Not until 1905, with the Japanese victory over Russia, did the men who had been educated in the Western type of school venture to voice their discontent and the modern nationalist movement take shape. The leaders of this movement had absorbed the prevalent liberal philosophy, of which economic freedom was one aspect. At first they looked to Western education as an instrument of liberation. But, in a plural society as in other forms of social organization, the educational system is conditioned by the environment, and Western education did not help them. At a later stage, on the introduction of constitutional reforms, they thought to gain their freedom by using their large numerical majority to weaken the executive. This hope also proved vain, for what the country needed was a strong government able to control and direct economic forces. In the economic sphere liberalism leads naturally to capitalism. Burmans, however, failed to recognize the connection and, while pressing for further liberal political reforms, began to denounce capitalism as responsible for their economic disabilities. When confidence in liberal reforms was shaken, the modern Fascist and Communist reactions against liberalism encouraged the younger generation to look to Japan for aid and to Russia for guidance. Meanwhile, communal tension between Burman, Indian, and Chinese was growing more acute, and the relations between the people and the government more embittered. Each side blamed the other for maladies which were, in fact, merely the logical result of the unrestrained activity of economic forces. These could be brought under control only by the operation of some motive transcending the economic sphere which all could recognize as of superior validity. The only motive that all could accept was nationalism. But nationalism could not easily be reconciled with capitalism. Thus, under British rule, as formerly under Burmese rule, the political and social organization of the country was in a position of unstable equilibrium. British rule was more effective than Burmese rule as an instrument of economic progress, but the neglect to develop the human, as distinct from the material, resources of the country contributed to its political instability. On the first challenge by the Japanese the whole structure collapsed.

c) UNDER THE JAPANESE

The Japanese made a sharp break with the liberal tradition. On their first arrival in 1942 they ruled the country through a nominated governor, Burmese, however, and not, as under British rule, a stranger. Then in August, 1943, they recognized the independence of Burma under its own president. Although he had the assistance of an advisory council, he ruled the country on authoritarian lines. On the British evacuation, practically all the Burmese officials stayed behind. These were reinstated in their charges and carried on the administration very much as they had done under the British. But the authority of government rested on the Japanese army and secret police. With their assistance and using methods that no British government would have tolerated, the new regime was conspicuously successful in suppressing violent crime. It re-established order.

In many ways Japanese rule contributed to the political, cultural, and economic advance of Burmans. By granting at least a show of independence, it appealed to popular sentiment as British rule had never done. For the first time Burma had its own foreign minister and its own representatives in those foreign lands to which the Japanese had access. Although its foreign policy had to be aligned with Japanese requirements, Burmans were for the first time enabled to gain some experience in the handling of foreign affairs. Burma had its own minister of defense and its own army, which was no longer, as under British rule, mainly composed of Indian troops who would support the government against the people, along with a few detachments from the tribal hills to foster racial particularism. For the first time Burmans were at least nominally responsible for their own defense, and for the first time since the final collapse of the Burmese power in 1886 Burmans were given a real chance to acquire experience of arms and military service. And also for the first time the whole administrative personnel from top to bottom, general and judicial, was wholly Burman; the Japanese were content to occupy the position of advisers—though in most matters, of course, involving any conflict of opinion, their advice had to be taken. Burma had not only the show but in a very considerable degree the substance of political independence.

In cultural life it was not only the practice but the deliberate policy of the Japanese to foster close relations with Burmans. They did not, like the British, stand aloof from the people but mixed freely with them in social intercourse. This had the paradoxical result that Western ways of life made greater headway among Burmans under the Japanese than under British rule.

Economic conditions were likewise favorable to Burman progress. The evacuation of Indian landlords and moneylenders cured most of the agrarian trouble, and many cultivators, with no creditors to worry them, resumed possession of their land. At the same time the shortage of imported goods and the absence of foreign competition stimulated and enabled Burmans to engage in industry and commerce.

Yet Burmans found the new order more irksome than the old. Inflation robbed the traders of their profits. Local manufacturers could not meet the shortage of clothing and other imported goods. Men preferred unemployment to compulsory labor in the Japanese "sweat corps," and the harsh discipline enforced by the secret police contrasted unfavorably with the personal freedom enjoyed under the rule of law. And, although Burmans had formerly complained that British officials were aloof and arrogant, they did not fear them as they learned to fear the suave politeness and calculated brutality of the Japanese. One result of the Japanese occupation was to increase the Burmese impatience of authority and to add the term "Fascist" to the vocabulary of political abuse alongside "bureaucrat," "capitalist," and "imperialist." A result of still greater consequence was that Burmans were encouraged in the belief that they could do much that they had never previously had a chance to do. This strengthened their resolve to maintain and consolidate the independence which the Japanese had granted.

Perhaps the most significant feature of the new order was the unification of the plural society that had grown up under British rule; the former alien elements vanished, and domestic differences of race and class were forgotten in common opposition to the new authoritarian discipline. On the other hand, the war sowed the seed of future internal tension, for it divided those of common stock who fought on opposite sides. The Burmese army included Karens and others but was in the main Burmese, whereas most of those who fought in the Allied armies came from the hill tribes. The Burmans remembered that in 1886 Karens had helped the British and now suspected them as traitors to the cause of freedom. During the early disorder consequent on the collapse of civil rule, some Burmans in the Delta turned savagely on the Karens and thereby inflamed passions that defied subsequent attempts at reconciliation.

Another consequence of Japanese rule was also pregnant with future trouble. From the very earliest threat of Japanese invasion the Communist leaders were stalwart in resistance and even while still detained in prison by the British government urged the other political prisoners to support the Allied cause "without reserve." By thus taking the lead in national resistance to the Japanese, they taught the troops, the militia, the underground army, and the common man to identify nationalism with communism.

SOUTH ASIA

Formerly in Burma numerous racial elements were imperfectly assimilated in a quasi-national society exhibiting a complex of tribal and territorial types of social organization, though in all cases the chain of authority was based on personal relations which were regulated by custom endowed with the sanction of religion. This elaborate social organization was *unstable* because its stability depended solely on the regard for custom; and it was *unproductive* because economic progress would involve a breach with custom on which the social fabric rested. These conditions seem to have been much the same over the whole of Southeast Asia, and much the same also in India, though more so, for in India custom had hardened into caste. If this view is generally valid, we have dug down to the foundations of South Asia in the world today. It is on these old foundations that a modern Western superstructure has been erected.

This superstructure was erected under Western influence on Western principles. Traders from the West who came to buy and sell found that they could not do business on Western lines unless the lands were ruled on Western lines. Scattered throughout the region there were already foreign orientals, but under Western rules these multiplied, and in every country there came into existence a plural society dominated by economic forces. The conflict of economic interest was in itself a cause of racial division, and Western rulers instinctively, if not deliberately, fostered racial particularism. Even in the native group the imperfectly assimilated racial elements tended to fall apart, and this process was stimulated by selective recruitment for the army of occupation. In this plural society there was nothing to withstand the unceasing pressure of economic forces attacking social life on all sides, and, as these forces spread through ever widening circles, native cultural life declined, and the native social order was broken up into a crowd of individuals, reacting against this system and demanding national independence; but a plural society can never be a nation, and every fresh encroachment of economic forces rendered the community less capable of independence. Although *productive*, the social organization was still *unstable:* crime, disorder, and unrest increased; the tension between the component elements grew more acute; and the relations between rulers and ruled were subjected to increasing strain. Here again conditions seem to have been much the same over all the colonial dependencies in South Asia.

What gives special significance to Burma is that here the liberal theory of colonial rule was applied most unreservedly in all its aspects and carried most deeply into native life. In other countries of South Asia, for various reasons and in various ways, the free play of economic forces was halted more or less effectually at the threshold of the native world. Yet the same forces were at work throughout the whole region, even in politically independent Siam. Burma, however, would seem to typify the manner of their working and to demonstrate most clearly the result.

Finally, in the third stage, when the plural societies built up under Western rule collapsed before the onslaught of the Japanese, it seems that elsewhere, as in Burma, attempts to build up a new national society gave some promise of success. But this new society had to be adapted to Japanese requirements and depended on the Japanese army and police system for support. With the defeat of the Japanese, South Asia was brought once more into political and economic contact with the Western world; the new experiments came to a dead end, and the old problems came up for solution, but with new complications in a far more difficult environment.

SOUTH ASIA TODAY

With the defeat of the Japanese we reach at last the subject for discussion: South Asia in the world today. One fact was obvious—that at the end of the war the whole of Southeast Asia was in ruins, and nowhere was the devastation greater than in Burma.

But there was a choice of plans, in Burma as elsewhere, for reconstruction: either to reconstruct a new building on the old model or to erect a different building on a new plan and on more secure foundations. Under Western rule peace had been maintained; the people had increased in numbers; new cities had sprung up; agriculture, trade, and industry had flourished; and elaborate provision had been made for education, public health, and other welfare services. The former rulers did not see how they could have served the people better or more faithfully, but they saw very clearly that prosperity could not be restored without their help. The demonstrations of welcome for their assistance in driving out the Japanese encouraged them to expect popular co-operation in reconstructing the old building.

This, however, was a vain imagination. Life under the Japanese had confirmed the people in their dislike and distrust of foreign rule. Siam had prospered as an independent state and, by being able to choose its own policy, had suffered least damage from the war. Moreover, the progress of formerly dependent peoples in industry and commerce since the collapse of foreign rule encouraged them to believe that they could manage their own affairs quite well enough if left alone. The stage was set for a sharp conflict between the old order and the new; between imperialism and nationalism, capitalism and socialism; between economic progress as a key to human welfare and human welfare as a condition of economic progress. The capitalists knew that capital would be needed for rapid reconstruction, and they thought to get their own terms for providing capital. But the nationalists did not know what help they wanted or how much they needed help, and they were chary of accepting foreign capitalist help on any terms. The issues, however, were by no means clearly cut. Capitalist and nationalist alike could appeal to liberal principles; and the measures needed to restore authority and order could be denounced with equal plausibility and fervor as Communist and Fascist. Thus, as men trod warily, but blindly, along the narrow path leading to the goal of human freedom, rising gales from either side threatened to engulf them in the bottomless pit of anarchy.

In Siam the foundations of social life were most secure, for it had never lost its independence and had been least disturbed during the war. In Indonesia and Indochina the weakness of the Dutch and French encouraged the nationalists to take up arms. In the former British and American dependencies, however, the forces of occupation were too strong to challenge, and there seemed hopes of a peaceful settlement. In the Philippines the United States had made arrangements before the war for an orderly withdrawal; in Malaya racial divisions cut so deeply as to preclude the growth of any common nationalism; and only in Burma were the opposing forces nicely balanced. The British government on its return from Simla expected Burman cooperation in reconstructing prewar Burma, but Burmans looked to the British Labour government, with socialist ideals and nationalist sympathies, to grant them independence.

For two years Burmans had, nominally at least, been managing their own affairs; the Simla government assumed that they were incapable of doing so. The administration had been wholly Burmese from the president down to the office boys; now the old officials returned to take the higher posts, accompanied by a crowd of new subordinates who knew nothing of Burma or of administration. Naturally, the Burman politicians and officials were disgruntled. The Simla plans for economic reconstruction appeared to Burmans, not without reason, as plans to reinstate foreign private enterprise with public funds. Foreign enterprise was cautious about investing new capital. Most of the so-called "foreign" capital in Burma before the war represented the accumulated profits of foreign enterprise in Burma; now this would have to be replaced by outside capital, freshly raised on the security of prospective profits, and foreign enterprise insisted, therefore, on safeguards for an adequate return. But the two fatal blunders of the new government were the attempt to reinstate Indian moneylenders and other absentee landlords in the possession of their land and the neglect to provide employment for the many thousand young men who had joined the Burmese guerrilla army during the war. This provided the Communist leaders with propaganda and recruits. In these and other ways the Simla government soon wore out its welcome. The Labour government in England had to choose between facing a nation-wide rebellion and granting Burma independence. The former alternative offered no prospect of success and would certainly give a new stimulus to communism. The Labour government chose the lesser risk and granted Burma independence.

But nothing had ever been done to train the people for the responsibilities of independence. The whole stock of capital and the machinery of industry and commerce were in foreign hands, and the rehabilitation of agriculture would require an agricultural revolution involving the reintegration of social life from the village upward. It was certain that the new government would need a strong army to support it, but it had no army on which it could rely with confidence. Trouble began almost as soon as the Burmese flag was hoisted.

Burma was in sore need of funds. But within a few days it was faced with claims from foreign firms on account of war damage, for which the Burmese government denied responsibility, involving huge sums, which it could not possibly disburse. Quite apart from these claims, capital was needed for rehabilitation and development. Burma had to raise this capital either by domestic loans, which would necessitate compulsory saving, or by finding some expedient for raising foreign capital on terms that would not endanger its national independence. Moreover, if Burmans were to find a place in industry and commerce, the state would have to show the way, and the nationalization of natural resources and various industries was contemplated. This raised delicate and knotty problems with regard to the payment of compensation, and tension between the government and foreign enterprise grew more acute.

Far more serious, however, was the domestic friction in connection with the land problem and unemployment. The two main pillars supporting the government were the Cultivators' Union and the People's Volunteer Organization, the former comprising the occupants of land, the latter mainly consisting of men without land or cattle. Between these two sections there was some conflict of interest. The Communists were bidding for the support of both sections with promises of land for all, free of rent or revenue, and the government had to counter these inducements by pushing on as rapidly as possible with agrarian reforms. Unfortunately, it could not provide land for all the landless; the reforms told in favor of the cultivators and tended to alienate the ex-soldiers.

It was, indeed, impossible to promote welfare in any direction without arousing some opposition from interests adversely affected. This put the liberal government in a quandary. It professed democracy and was averse to all forms of compulsion; at the same time it claimed to be socialist and to favor strict control over all forms of economic activity. The brand of socialism which it favored had affinities with communism in recognizing the peasants and workers as the ruling and only class and differed from communism chiefly in trusting to peaceful reform rather than violent revolution, in placing more faith in Buddha than in Marx, and in being more suspicious of Russia and less suspicious of the Western powers. Ideological confusion, however, was not the chief reason for its tolerance of opposition. It was not strong enough to be intolerant. Under British rule the Burmese had been debarred from military service. The Communists had been the spearhead of resistance, and the Burmese element in both the army and the People's Volunteer Organization was largely Communist in origin and sympathy. When the government reluctantly decided that the Communist menace must be suppressed by force, the People's Volunteer Organization seceded, and before long took up arms against the government. Action against the Volunteers led to the mutiny of their sympathizers in the army. This left the government largely dependent on the Karen regiments for the maintenance of order. The commander-in-chief of the combined military forces was a Karen, and so also was the head of the air force, and there were other Karens in high positions in both these services and also in the navy. Karens were represented in the government and on the board of directors of the Central Bank, and there were Karen magistrates in charge of districts where Karens were numerous. But some Karen leaders incited their people to rebel. Thus within a year of attaining independence the country was involved in a desperate struggle against insolvency and anarchy.

The issue of the struggle would seem to be of more than local interest. I have suggested that the case of Burma is of particular importance. It is only too probable that similar troubles will develop in the other countries of South Asia, or at least of Southeast Asia, and for much the same reasons. If we can help Burma to solve its problems, we can hope for a satisfactory issue elsewhere. But if anarchy gains the upper hand in Burma, it is likely to spread over the rest of South Asia. Then what will happen in the other center of colonial rule, the great continent of Africa? And with uproar in Asia and Africa, what will happen in Europe? Burma is a remote and insignificant country, but is it wholly fantastic to see in the issue of the present struggle a critical turning point in world affairs?

ISMS IN SOUTH ASIA

Once again I feel apologetic for talking all about Burma. But have I been talking merely about Burma? I hope not. It is through the welter of "isms" in Burma that I have been trying to blaze a track, and these isms are much the same throughout South Asia. Let us recall them in much the same order as they have forced themselves on our attention: animism, tribalism, racialism, Buddhism, imperialism, capitalism, materialism, individualism, liberalism, nationalism, socialism, communism. Going outside Burma, we might add Hinduism, Moslemism, Confucianism, and perhaps Christianism and humanism. Is not this a list of the forces which in varying degrees of intensity are boiling and bubbling over throughout South Asia in the world today? They have made South Asia—one might say that they *are* South Asia—and the bare list of them summarizes its problems and the solutions attempted in the past. Even if each ism in succession has been found to lead down a blind alley, it is instructive to ascertain what checked further progress.

The fundamental problem, I have suggested, is to develop the human and material resources of the region for the greatest welfare of the world. This statement of it carries two implications. One implication is that we are all living in one world. Now it is true enough that, apart from a few remote and backward peoples, we are all living in one economic world, but we are very far as yet from success in building up one social world. If we are to achieve that, we must incorporate the peoples of South Asia as citizens of the modern world. This carries the further implication that, to solve the problem, we require the assistance and active consent of the people. Mere acquiescence will not suffice; it has been tried and failed. With mere acquiescence we may develop the material, but not the human, resources.

Consent implies some manner of popular control over government by the people; it implies some form of democracy. But this need not mean the introduction or imitation of Western forms of democratic machinery. Experience has demonstrated repeatedly that, although democratic institutions on a Western pattern fortify still further a strong social organization, feeble societies collapse under the strain. Only too often Western democratic forms of government have been adopted in the hope that they would function on democratic lines, and the result has been very different from that intended. Gradually, however, it is coming to be recognized that, in social, as in civil, engineering, form does not determine function, but function determines form. That is a principle which demands close attention in those parts of South Asia where subject peoples have just attained or are on the point of attaining independence. Under foreign rule the people thought to direct economic forces in their favor by control over the government through Western political institutions, but in practice these institutions served only to weaken government and allow still greater power to economic forces.

At the present time the countries of South Asia need a strong government in order to build up a new social organization on stable foundations; the people rightly hold that government cannot be strong or stable unless based on popular consent, but few have yet appreciated that in the circumstances of South Asia democratic institutions in their Western form are incompatible with either stability or strength and that they must design their own pattern of democracy, looking to function rather than to form. Unfortunately, many in the West who sympathize most warmly with such aspirations and ideals are themselves heirs of the great liberal tradition and fail to appreciate its limitations in a social environment other than their own.

In Burma, and I think in other parts of South Asia, men look to liberal forms and catchwords as a means of achieving socialism. This is rather like taking a ticket from Chicago to New York and setting out in the direction of San Francisco. It may seem to be very much what has happened in England, where socialism has developed out of liberalism. But socialism of this type demands an instructed electorate with a strong social sense, and in South Asia these prerequisites are absent. Socialism in the West implies conferring greater power on the state as the organ and image of society. But in South Asia it implies the reintegration of a disintegrated society. For so formidable a task leadership is essential, and socialists in Burma tend therefore to favor government by one party that shall instruct and lead the people. Again society needs to be rebuilt from its basis in the village, the commune. Thus in an Eastern setting socialism tends to absorb the more constructive elements of communism. Much of the so-called communism in the East might, in fact, be more appropriately termed "communalism" and, if called by that name, would be robbed of half its terrors. This, however, is a matter which will come up for discussion in one of our round tables. Here in this preliminary survey it is enough to note that in the East neither socialism nor communism has the same connotation as in the West and that in dealing with the problems of South Asia we must have regard to facts and functions rather than to words and forms.

Among the isms that we have noticed, racialism is a fact, and nationalism is a fact. Both represent a reaction of the human spirit against the purely material economic conception of life, implicit alike in capitalism and in communism. But racialism divides; nationalism unites. It is important to note that in South Asia nationalism *does* make for social unity. Racial ties help to hold society together, but they exclude strangers as out-casts. A social organization of the territorial type, based on common residence, provides much richer material for social evolution. In the West nationalism is suspect, partly because it is often confounded with racialism and partly because it sets up a barrier against a still higher form of international social co-operation. Nationalism, then, like socialism and communism, has different connotations in the East and West. Even in the West national units may still make a valuable contribution to-ward a world society, and in the East it is difficult to suggest any motive other than nationalism that everyone can admit is of superior validity to purely economic motives. The peoples of South Asia are turning instinctively to nationalism for protec-tion against the disintegrating influence of foreign capitalism and against the devastating attack of foreign communism; they desire passionately to achieve and maintain their national inde-pendence. They need our help, and, if the conclusions indicated by this preliminary survey are valid, they deserve our help; for it is only on the basis of nationalism that we can develop the human and material resources of South Asia for the greatest welfare of the world. Doubtless, special cases will require special treatment—backward peoples, for example, and cities like Singapore. But it should not be impossible to weave these into one general design. How, then, can we set about building up a new world in South Asia on the principle of nationalism? It is a stupendous problem, and we are unlikely to achieve success if we set about it by drawing blueprints of political machinery before deciding what the machinery will have to do:

> For forms of government let fools contest,
> What best performs its function is the best.

What, then, are the conditions of national independence in the modern world, the conditions without which political inde-pendence is a mere shibboleth? The first condition is that the nation shall be capable of military independence; it must be able to maintain its independence against all probable external aggression and able also to maintain an adequate degree of internal security and order without the support of foreign troops, except possibly such troops as it may hire. Second, it must be capable of economic independence. It must be able to exist without foreign doles, except possibly as a temporary measure; and it must be able to develop its human and material resources without foreign capital, apart from loans on fair terms that it will be able to repay, and without foreign aid in the management of economic enterprise or in the provision of technicians and of skilled and unskilled labor, except on terms compatible with its political independence. Third, it must maintain such a minimum standard of human welfare, especially in the control over infectious disease among men, cattle, and crops, as the conditions of the modern world require. Finally, but most important, there must be adequate provision for ascertaining and giving effect to the common social will of the community so far as this is consistent with ordered social and economic progress.

If we translate these conditions into concrete terms, the task may well seem impossible. How can a new state replace the former army of occupation with home forces on which it can rely? How can it raise the capital it needs without imperiling its independence? What is to be done about the foreign capital with which it has hitherto been developed? Where is it to obtain the guidance necessary to help it develop its resources and the necessary supply of managerial skill and technical assistance? What about labor to replace the former immigrant or imported foreign labor? How can we establish a government on popular consent to maintain standards of welfare that the people do not appreciate by methods in which they do not believe? How can we provide the element of continuity in government that in the West we take for granted and that must in some way be created if government is to be effective or even to survive? How can we adapt democracy to such conditions? How, above all, can we convince popular leaders who know little of the modern world and little perhaps even of their own land that these and other like conditions are indeed conditions of maintaining national independence? One might go on asking such questions almost indefinitely, but the people concerned do not, for the most part, even recognize that there is any need to ask them. Siam, they say, is independent; then why not Burma, Indochina, Indonesia? India, again, although so long dependent on Britain, now appears capable of independence; then why not other countries of South Asia? But in Siam the crown provides the necessary continuity; modern India grew up with the modern world and has been held together by the protective bond of caste. In these two countries social and economic progress on democratic principles may possibly be immune against the vote-catching slogans of the demagogue; elsewhere conditions are more difficult.

Here, then, are some of the tangled problems that are common to the whole of South Asia. From this it would follow that some form of international co-operation between the various countries of the region is required to deal with them. How far is such co-operation possible, and what part can India play as a major partner in such a combination? And this perhaps is as far as I can venture in this preliminary survey.

PART II

SOCIAL FORCES IN SOUTH ASIA

CULTURAL FACETS OF SOUTH ASIAN REGIONALISM

By Cora Du Bois[1]

THE cultural factors making for, or impeding, South Asian *rapprochement* should, I am sure, in your minds as they do in mine, suggest a scholar of great amplitude —a person versed in Hinduistic, in Sinitic, and in Islamic cultures. I can claim not one of these aptitudes, much less the necessary three. My only possible escape from this dilemma is to give culture the meaning usually ascribed to it by my fellow-professionals, the anthropologists, and therefore to consider my topic not as a cultural one in the narrow sense of the word but rather as an evaluation of some of the forces, traditional and current, in the South Asian scene which may work for or against the formation of regional ties. Since political and economic factors are to be stressed by other speakers, they are to a large extent deliberately omitted. Also it should be stressed that I am not attempting to discuss the area as an anthropologist applying the concepts current in this discipline. This, I am afraid, would serve only to reveal our ignorance of the area and to open up research problems rather than to provide an appraisal of such meager data as we now possess.

Social and cultural forces operating for or against the formation of a South Asian regional *rapprochement* might be considered in terms of historic depth. We might consider, in turn, the animistic tribal substrata of the region, the early historical period of Hindu cultural expansion, the later period of Islamic influence, and, finally, the period of European expansion in its earlier mercantile phase and its later colonial administrative phase.

It is my personal conviction, however, that the modern world

1. Chief, Southern Areas Branch, Division of Research for Far East, Department of State.

is less well understood in terms of systematic chronology than by a selection of conflicting forces to which historic depth is then added.

South Asia comprises that vast area of the world from the subcontinent of India to the Philippines. In the grossest cultural terms this region can be divided into the following groups: the Hindu bloc of India; the Buddhist bloc of Ceylon, Burma, Siam, and Indochina; and the broken Moslem bloc of Pakistan, Malaysia, and Indonesia. On the western periphery lies Pakistan and on the eastern periphery is the Philippines archipelago.

It is difficult to find another region of the world in which a more heterogeneous group of great cultures flourish. One is hard pressed to discover a single consistency throughout the area. I shall therefore discuss the differences within the area. These are grossly apparent. But as each difference is raised, I shall attempt to assess the degree to which it is an important divisive force and what counterforces of unity may also be discovered within the context of the difference.

Geographically, the region varies from the semiarid interior of India to the lush tropical islands of Indonesia. Yet it lies predominantly within the monsoon belt. The formal transportation facilities of the type studied by strategists form no binding network between the countries of South Asia. Nevertheless, the very logic of geography helps to bind together this region, which protrudes on three sides into vast ocean areas and which is hampered to the north by mountains and jungle from direct and easy access to China. There is therefore a certain geographic pressure to turn inward.

Racially, the Caucasian Indians and the predominantly Mongoloid peoples of the rest of the area are members of two distinct stocks. In addition, there are innumerable minor racial variants of these main themes. Race, like geography, is not, strictly speaking, within the purview of this discussion, but attitudes toward racial differences *are* legitimately within our scope. First of all, we must be careful not to project Euro-American attitudes toward racial differences upon the peoples of South Asia. Ethnic particularism does exist, but these peoples have not rationalized their prejudices in terms of body forms. Therefore, the varieties of physique have not yet been used to express antagonism. The racist virus of Europe has so far infected the region only minimally. I would not predict that racial prejudices will not develop; but, if they do, I suspect that they may be directed toward whites and possibly toward the Chinese in the area rather than toward each other. Racism, like all symbol formations, has a quality of irrationality. Just as we are full of inconsistencies in this respect, so I would expect that South Asians might learn to dislike whites but not the light Indians or to abhor the Chinese but not the Mongoloid Siamese. There is no use in speculating at this juncture on such an unpleasant contingency. It is useful, however, to point out that the marked physical diversities observable among the inhabitants of South Asia have not yet been used to rationalize antagonism which may be rooted elsewhere in social relationships.

Linguistically, the variations in South Asia exceed those commonly faced even in Europe. The Indo-European and Dravidian languages of India alone profoundly divide that subcontinent. That variation is further emphasized by varying scripts. As we progress eastward into Southeast Asia, basic linguistic stocks multiply. Burma, Siam, Indochina, and Indonesia are divided between at least two linguistic families: Sinitic and Malayo-Polynesian. These profound language differences are further complicated by a borrowing of scripts which bear no relation to linguistic families. Just as national entities may bear no relationship to linguistic classification—as in trilingual Switzerland—so writing in South Asia cuts across languages. Siamese, for instance, which is related to Chinese, is nonetheless written not ideographically like Chinese but in a modified phonetic script like the totally unrelated languages of India. The Malayo-Polynesian language of the Malay Peninsula is written in an alphabet devised for a Semitic language.

South Asia, unlike Europe, therefore has no highway to easy linguistic communication. In England or Italy a minimal knowledge of the structure of your own language will cut a wide swath in learning cognate European tongues. On the other hand, a knowledge of Hindi is no entree to Siamese, Annamese, or Malay. To acquire these additional languages means entrance into a wholly new world of linguistic order and concepts, as well as of vocabulary. There are, however, some words of Sanskrit origin which have spread throughout the region.

These traditional linguistic barriers were re-emphasized to a lesser degree in the European languages introduced during the colonial period. English, French, Dutch, Spanish, Portuguese, and, of course, Chinese have all had varying impacts on the region. The postwar leaders of South Asia are fully cognizant of the problems which they face. They realize that, if reason were to dictate the answer, English might well provide a common medium of communication. It is, of course, already the most widely known second language of the region and has been the chief medium of communication in conferences like the Asian Relations Conference in 1947, the New Delhi Conference on Indonesia in 1949, and in such international bodies as the Economic Commission for Asia and the Far East. However, whatever rational judgments the leaders may hold, there is never any insurance that reason will prevail where national sentiments are concerned. Peoples in the throes of developing national status are forced frequently to rely upon emotion and conviction, to summon traditional symbols, rather than to depend upon the cooler virtue of reason and efficiency.

Nevertheless, it is perhaps indicative of the present direction that the eagerness to learn English among the young people of Indonesia since the war has been frequently commented upon. Their remarkable success is equally praised. In the Philippines the attempt to introduce Tagalog as a national language in the schools seems well on its way to being forgotten. In Bangkok there is talk of teaching English in the Buddhist monasteries devoted to advanced training for the monkhood. The widespread desire to attend American schools and learn American know-how may also help to swing the area as a whole toward English.

Furthermore, the difficulty, the cost, and time required to translate textbooks into South Asian languages has already proved a real obstacle. This is particularly true in rapidly changing scientific subjects. When Urdu was made the official language of Hyderabad, teaching in Urdu at Osmania University was required. The cost and difficulties of providing texts alone was a clear demonstration of the practical problems involved in shifting to another language. Despite the use of Urdu as the official language for over twenty years, English was still used for teaching purposes in technical subjects. Thus the very real barrier to intra-regional linguistic communication may be overcome by the adoption of a common second language, which may well be English.

And on the subject of education we have another factor to consider. Where are South Asians to turn today for the advanced work in technical disciplines that they realize they so urgently need? Certainly, the United States has much to offer in this respect, but our colleges are crowded, dollars are in short supply, and local training is often inadequate to meet the entrance requirements of our graduate and undergraduate schools. Parenthetically, I should like to insert the hope that our large universities would apply themselves to this problem—not only in terms of fellowships but also in special courses and special counseling, perhaps in their extension services, so that there might be provided an additional preliminary year to compensate for deficiencies in subject and language training. Simultaneously, the new arrivals might serve as assistants in departments of oriental languages, of anthropology, of sociology, or in Far Eastern area programs.

In any event, many South Asians will have to gratify their desires for advanced training in less expensive and more accessible institutions. India and the Philippines offer the most promising opportunities, now that Japan and China are no longer in the running. But these two countries also have their problems. In both countries higher educational institutions are overcrowded and understaffed. In India housing and dietary restrictions are often additional difficulties. In the new quarters of the University of the Philippines at Diliman the local disorders are a source of concern. In addition, the high exchange rate of the Philippine peso offers difficulties. In Batavia the Indonesians are boycotting for political reasons competent Dutch faculties. The scientific facilities of Indochina are inaccessible and deteriorated. The Siamese faculties are inhibited by local difficulties both political and economic, yet Bangkok has a good school of agriculture and might attract South Asian students. Civil war has temporarily closed down the University of Rangoon. The new University of Malaya is only now beginning to take shape, but the Medical School has a good reputation and vigorous leadership.

Despite handicaps, it seems probable that India, the Philippines, and eventually Singapore may come nearest to offering intra-regional facilities for advanced education and that South Asian students will have more opportunities to know one another in the future than they have had in the past. In fact, there has recently been established a Southeast Asia Association at the University of Manila which comprises Philippine, Siamese, Korean, Chinese, Indonesian, Malayan, and Indian students.

Everywhere one turns, differences and difficulties are of the essence in South Asia. Yet for each difference and difficulty some small countering symptom can be discovered if one is determined to find it.

As I have previously indicated, the recent colonial experiences of South Asia have served in many ways to emphasize old differences and develop new ones. The nine major countries of South Asia in at least the last four centuries have experienced the expansive impact of eight nations whose cultures and patterns of colonization were as different as those of Portugal, Spain, the Netherlands, France, England, the United States, China, and, most recently, Japan. During the last century alone these South Asian countries have been tied by separate cords to distant and different nations. India, Pakistan, Burma, and Malaysia through varied channels have been oriented to the United Kingdom; Indochina to France; Indonesia to Holland; and the Philippines to Spain and the United States. The Westernizing influences, the languages in which these influences have been transmitted, and the institutional and administrative forms which have been introduced not only have been varied but have profoundly altered the indigenous cultures and often subtly diversified the direction of the countries to which they were applied. Land could be preserved for the local cultivator, transferred to foreign enterprise, or lost to immigrants from other Asian areas. New occupations emphasized the coolie rows of plantation agriculture, the urbanization of factory work, the profits of moneylending and of small enterprise. This process everywhere undercut, but did not entirely eliminate, traditional artisans. Legal systems might be based on Roman, on common, or on local customary law. The Dutch, for example, were particularly scrupulous in their study and observance of native customary law. The diversity and complexity of these varying legal systems have done much to preserve ethnic differences among the Indonesian peoples. Despite instances of this sort, traditional behavior and needs have not been profoundly revolutionized everywhere in South Asia. Nowhere, however, did they go unscathed. The countries of South Asia for over a century have experienced a profound ferment and an ever accelerating rate of change, but each nation has been manipulated by a different puppeteer. Thus the indigenous leaderships which developed were oriented to several different European nations and not toward one another. Before the war it was the rare Indian leader who knew Bangkok or Batavia as well as he knew London or Paris. The educated Indonesians were better acquainted in The Hague than in Saigon or Rangoon.

However, to counterbalance slightly, but only slightly, this type of division, another Asian nation, Japan, has most recently appeared on the scene and given great impetus to that desire to turn toward one another which we find in South Asia today. The Japanese military occupation afforded the first reasonably consistent administrative overlay which Southeast Asia, at least, had experienced. Peoples were moved by the hundreds of thousands from their traditional home environments. The overt aspects of Westernization made marked advances under the Japanese. But, most important, Japan fathered ideas and slogans which took root, however much the Japanese themselves came to be disliked. "Asia for the Asiatics" and the "Co-prosperity Sphere" are ideas which had deep appeal even though the Japanese interpretation was repugnant. Ever since 1945 travelers in South Asia who have interviewed the leaders of national movements report consistently the interest that these leaders express in one another and the problems which they are mutually facing. Taruc inquires about Ho Chi-minh; Pridi is interested in Sjahrir; Nehru wished to meet Soekarno and Hatta; Datu Onn wanted to know what manner of men led the Philippine republic.

Just before the outbreak of World War II, Romulo mentioned the desirability of a Pan-Malayan league. Even earlier, the Indonesian Communist, Tan Malakka, propounded his regional union which he called "Aslia," since Australia was also to be included. A short-lived unofficial association called the "Southeast Asia League" was established in Bangkok in 1947 with a central executive committee consisting of Siamese, Viet-Namese, Laotians, Cambodians, Malays, and Indonesians.

In January, 1949, nineteen Asian nations gathered in New Delhi to support—within the framework of the United Nations —the cause of the Republic of Indonesia. Romulo conferred with Nehru during these meetings and, subsequently, at Lake Success, gave leadership to those UN nations which had participated in the Delhi meeting.

It is the young Burman leader, Aung San, who has been credited with first suggesting the Asian Relations Conference which was finally held at New Delhi in 1947 by invitation of the Indian Council of World Affairs. Nehru in the inaugural address of that conference stressed the isolation of Asian nations during the period of imperialism, stating that the countries of Asia even culturally looked toward Europe "and not to their own friends and neighbours from whom they had derived so much in the past." He then continued with his usual eloquence: "Today this isolation is breaking down . . . the walls that surrounded us fall down and we look at each other again and meet as old friends long parted." It appears, therefore, that the separatism of the colonial era is being combated consciously and actively by the new leaders of South Asia. I should like to add that these leaders, preoccupied as they are with internal difficulties, are showing if not a powerful, at least an unprecedented, interest in their common problems. It was this sense of common problem which seemed to dominate the minds of some two hundred and thirty delegates from twenty-eight Asian nations who gathered at the Asian Relations Conference. It also dictated the organization of the round-table discussions.

Obviously, political freedom and the rationalization of their economies took a high place. Since these do not come within the scope of this paper, I shall confine myself to listing briefly some of the social and cultural questions which were discussed. Although these questions by no means represent the full array of common problems, they nevertheless are of particular interest as a guide to the preoccupations of the Asians themselves.

In the field of education the desire for adequate scientific research and equipment was stressed, but largely in terms of practical needs for a competent technical corps. The need, as I have already indicated, is urgent indeed. The Technical Assistance Program suggested in the President's inaugural address has aroused expectations in South Asia that it behooves us to implement quickly before the opportunity is lost to us. The vast illiteracy of the region, which ranges from 90 per cent in Indonesia to 51 per cent in the Philippines, was mentioned, and hopeful suggestions were made by various delegates for guidance from the U.S.S.R., which has reportedly done so much so quickly in reducing adult illiteracy. So far as I know, the U.S.S.R. has not responded to these appeals.

The status of women was a vigorously discussed topic, although their status was closely linked with the need for social services, including medical care, public health, and housing. Such programs, if implemented, should reduce death rates. Since it has been estimated that birth rates are in any event at the maximum biologic level, a decrease in death rates could make nothing short of catastrophic the over-all population increases statistically foreseeable, unless technological and social adaptations are made along many lines quickly and simultaneously.

Lastly, the Asian Relations Conference was seriously concerned with what it termed "Racial Problems and Inter-Asian Migrations." Essentially this was the problem of the overseas Chinese, although migrant Indians were also mentioned with some acrimony by the Burmese delegation. We have so far made no mention of this facet of South Asian regionalism, yet it is an important one. The overseas Chinese in the area number some six million. They have been singularly impervious to acculturation and tenaciously loyal to political issues in their homeland. In addition, they have been, on the whole, more adaptable to the European economic demands than many of the indigenous peoples of Southeast Asia. Need I add that they are widely distrusted and often disliked. The dangers of a serious minority problem are real and recognized by the leadership of the southern countries. The recent turn of political events in China cannot have lessened their concern.

Despite these discussions of common problems, it is true, of course, that the leaders of South Asia are today greatly preoccupied with the tremendous internal difficulties facing their own countries. Leadership is limited and must spread itself thin. And, lastly, these emergent nations are naturally sensitive about the dignity of their countries. Nevertheless, when these countries turn outward, I would expect them to be enthusiastically international in their foreign relations. There are many reasons for this supposition. For one thing, political nationalism in South Asia is not an indigenous growth of many centuries, as it is in Europe, but a recently imported concept whose principal dynamic has been, or still is, resistance to political and economic exploitation. Second, the weakness of these emergent nations would also suggest affiliation with the outer world. And, lastly, the natural aspirations of South Asia are appearing on the international forum in a period of history which has tacitly admitted that aggressive nationalism is—or at least should be—moribund. The United Nations is an experiment in reducing rampant individualism among nations. Regionalism is in the air. As for communism, whatever its immediate tactical gains from the encouragement of nationalism in underdeveloped areas, it is fundamentally international in philosophy and, wherever possible in practice, antinationalistic—at least for non-Soviet countries.

Even tactically the U.S.S.R. has vacillated during the last year and a half in the kind of national aspirations and national leaders that it will support in South Asia. This vacillation, reinforced by the successes of Communist China, have revealed to moderate South Asian leaders more clearly than ever the dangers of Stalinist communism and the wisdom of seeking common support. The unpopularity of Chinese minorities in Southeast Asia may afford additional support to consolidation. There is some evidence that Thakin Nu's government in Burma may see some virtue in forgetting old grudges toward the Indian Chettyars in favor of closer contacts with the government of India.

However, if these emergent nations find themselves in a world which demands that they take sides between two opponents and in which war will soon be their lot, it seems to me that their impulse will be to say "a plague o' both your houses" and that they will try to find their affiliations among likeminded neighbors. Soetan Sjahrir has already clearly expressed this viewpoint and was supported in it by his Partai Sosialis Indonesia.

It is not my function to discuss political matters in any detail; but, since political forms are but one expression of cultural forces, I should like, very hesitantly, to make some suggestions concerning the temper of religious philosophy in South Asia, which I believe is not totally unrelated also to the developments which can be anticipated in its political forms.

I realize how vague and inaccurate are broad generalizations about so heterogeneous an area. I confess the imprecision of phrases like "religious and philosophic temper." Nevertheless, for our purposes it seems to me that there may be some use in reminding you that the major *indigenous* religious philosophies of the area have been characterized as inclusive rather than exclusive.

The two great proselytizing religions, Christianity and Islam, are essentially exclusive in mood. The Christian or Moslem must cling for his salvation exclusively to his faith. The temper of Hinduism and Buddhism is to absorb and reconcile differences of faith, not banish them. In South Asia there are approximately two hundred and thirty million Hindus, fifty-two million Buddhists, one hundred and sixty-three million Moslems, and twenty-four million Christians. The animists probably outnumber Christians, but these peoples, still essentially tribal in their mode of life, represent only a series of disparate and minor factors in the main stream of cultural forces now shaping South Asia.

In these figures members of the inclusive indigenous religions outnumber members of the exclusive religions in a ratio of about three to two. Furthermore, the weight of the Christian population lies in the eastern periphery of the area in the Philippines, while the weight of the Moslem population is largely on the western periphery of the region in Pakistan. However, Indonesia, which is so important in the South Asian region and in which the Moslem faith is in the vast majority, forms a solid Islamic bloc in the center of the South Asian area. It should be noted, however, that the Moslems of the Malayan world, faithful as they are, have less fanaticism and austerity than the Arabs of the Moslem heartland.

In addition to a considerable body of scholarly studies supporting this thesis, there is the conciliatory statement of a Malayan delegate to the Asian Relations Conference when discussing religious education in schools. It was the Malayan delegate's opinion that the common principle and points of agreement between all religions should be stressed. Love for the ultimate and the universal is the common basis of all Asian religions, he said, and, by pressing this point home, it should be possible to create mutual understanding. It is as though long contacts with the traditional Hinduistic and Buddhistic worlds had somewhat softened the edges of Moslem exclusiveness.

Furthermore, if we may judge from the writings of recent great figures in India, the inclusive spirit of India, at least, is still strong. Rabindranath Tagore has said that it was India's obligation to offer to others the hospitality of her best culture and India's right to accept from others their best. Sir Shri Ram in the welcoming address of the Asian Relations Conference in 1947 said: "India in particular . . . has been an important meeting ground . . . of different cultures and has made her own unique contribution in synthesizing seemingly antagonistic cultures. Where an extraneous element could not be absorbed into or grafted on the local cultures, India has generally shown great tolerance to the element and allowed it to exist side by side, and survive, if survive it could, on its own merits."

CULTURAL FACETS OF SOUTH ASIAN REGIONALISM

Certainly in our survey of divisive forces in South Asia, the great religious antitheses might seem an insuperable barrier to union. A superficial glance at the recent communal riots of India might seem to reinforce the impression that there can be no unity in such diversity. Yet with the Pan-Islam movement moribund, with the renascent vigor of an inclusive India, and with all the other factors which we have considered and shall consider tonight, it seems possible that the inclusive quality of the indigenous faiths may prevail. If this quality of inclusiveness should persist and succeed in pervading the South Asian scene, it may well affect national solutions also. It has, in fact, been specifically voiced in respect to nationalism by Nehru, who said: "We seek no narrow nationalism. Nationalism has a place in each country and should be fostered, but it must not be allowed to become aggressive and come in the way of international development."

We have so far mentioned and weighed factors which are, at face value, divisive. I should like to continue with a series of factors whose face value is unifying. There is a complexly interwoven fabric of extremely old traditional affiliations in the midst of the many divergencies of South Asia. And I should like to stress at the outset that the admiration for, as well as the strength and persistence of, tradition is greater in South Asia than among ourselves. We have admired change and have given it a positive value-judgment which we call "progress." The South Asian leaders, while recognizing the need to adapt their countries to a Western-dominated world, have prized, but by no means slavishly, their own ancient and consciously held values and are today ready to re-emphasize traditional cultural bonds. This emphasis is not phrased in terms of imperial aspirations but in terms of mutuality. Let us examine briefly the nature of these ancient bonds.

India, with the beginning of the Christian Era, was expanding its cultural influences in Southeast Asia. It carried the whole complex of vigorous Hindu culture, including Visnavite, Saivite, and Buddhist cults, which flourished side by side or alternately in Burma, Siam, Cambodia, and Java. Although Buddhism today has all but disappeared in India, its basic traditions, like those of Hinduism, have their roots in the Upanishads and the more ancient Vedas. Traditional Indian epics, particularly the *Ramayana*, *Mahabharata*, and *Panchatantra*, are still part of the sacred and folk resources from India to Bali. These themes and their heroes every village child hears and sees in the folk drama and arts. Indifferently, he shares them as a common Buddhist or Hindu tradition with the majority of South Asians. Rabindranath Tagore said of Siam that it had preserved what India had lost. The aptness of the statement could be extended to all the Hinayana Buddhist countries. And yet it is a statement of only partial difference, since through Buddhism the Southeast Asian peoples are firmly rooted in the universalist philosophy which underlies diverse Hindu sects.

The spread of the Buddhist and Hindu traditions was accompanied by relatively small, but profoundly influential, movements of Indian population. Traders settled on the coasts, married the daughters of local chieftains, and established dynasties of city-states whose conquests and whose decline constitute the historical chronicles of the region. It is evident that not only the religious philosophies but also the architecture, sculpture, language, and political concepts of India were diffused. For almost a millennium the *mission civilisatrice* of Indian culture dominated Southeast Asia. Under its influence these areas themselves developed philosophic schools greatly admired by Chinese scholars.

While India was continuously influencing these areas, the Indianized states themselves launched on their imperial adventures. The Srivijaya Empire of Sumatra in the eighth century extended for a time its suzerainty over Cambodia. Warriors from the kingdoms of East Java not only invaded Sumatra but twice raided Ceylon in the thirteenth century. The last of the great Javanese empires, the Madjapahit of the fifteenth century, dominated not only Sumatra and Borneo but also the Malay Peninsula. Siam, Burma, and Cambodia expressed in their frequent wars keen awareness of one another. The first European observers testify to the cosmopolitan character of the court of Ayuthia in Siam, where even Japanese mercenaries were to be found.

CULTURAL FACETS OF SOUTH ASIAN REGIONALISM

Although the historic contacts between Indianized states should not be overstressed for their bearing on the modern scene, it is well to remember that such contacts have not ceased, nor have the traditions which they left died out. For example, Ceylon, although a Buddhist country, not only is culturally and linguistically predominantly Indian but at the same time maintains its long, intimate religious ties with the theocracy in Burma and Siam. A visit to any of the great shrines of Buddhism in these three countries will testify to the extent of intra-regional pilgrimages which still occur. Treasures in the Temple of the Tooth at Kandy have been presented by devout travelers from Burma and Siam. Similarly, not only is Burma today bound to Ceylon and Siam by religious ties, but we must not forget that as recently as 1936 it was also tied administratively to India and that Indians formed a large, if unpopular, minority in Burma.

It should also be remembered that there are some six hundred thousand Indians in Malaya, that many Jaffna Tamils from Ceylon served in clerical positions in the Malayan civil service, and that it is not uncommon to find Malay-speaking Ceylonese in Ceylon today. In the Malay-speaking world, Indian immigrants are still often called "Orang Kling," a survival of the name "Kalinga" by which the people of Orissa were known when, from the third century onward, they laid the foundations of Indian and Indianized states in Southeast Asia. The coronation formula of the sultans of Perak is still today in either Sanskrit or Pali, undecipherably transcribed in Arabic characters. The mythical genealogies of the present sultans of Malaya include accounts of Mount Mahameru from Indian cosmology.

In the same fashion that the Moslem Malay aristocracy has created a confused web of Hindu and Moslem traditional elements, so today the ties between Hindu India and Moslem Pakistan cannot be severed by communal riots, political structure, and disputes over Kashmir. The bonds are ancient as well as modern. The Moslem invasion of India began some twelve hundred years ago. The British raj for a time reinforced and extended political union. In 1950 the Commonwealth maintains it.

Some forty million Moslems still reside in India, and some four-teen million Hindus are citizens of Pakistan.

Just as Buddhism, rooted in Hinduism, ties India to some of the Southeast Asian countries, so also Islam has become in-extricably interwoven with Hinduism and, in addition, helps to maintain at least sympathies between the government of Paki-stan and the predominantly Moslem people of Indonesia. So also the Philippines, belonging as they do in tribal roots and lin-guistic affiliations to the Malayan world, are nevertheless allied through some eight hundred thousand Moros of Mindanao to the Moslem tie-in between Indonesia and Pakistan.

These intricately woven and interwoven threads of Hindu and Moslem tradition cross and recross each other in the Ma-layan world. The intricacy of the pattern is, in part, due to the fact that throughout its known history the Malayan culture has had groups of ardent seafarers who have done much to provide cultural contacts between countries. Even today the amount of traffic in small craft of five tons or less is seldom appreciated by persons who do not know the area intimately. The degree of this trade and of these contacts rarely appears in the official sta-tistics and government reports on which political scientists and economists are forced to depend. This does not prevent con-stant contacts between the Sulu Archipelago and Borneo. It does not inhibit the Buginese of Celebes from sailing with the monsoons to and from the ports of the peninsular mainland of Southeast Asia. This trade baffled Netherlands East Indies of-ficials when they tried in 1947 to impose trade controls between Indonesia and the peninsula. The last complete census from Malaya showed that 26 per cent of the Malays in what is now the Federation were either Sumatrans or Malaysians from other areas.

Avowedly, this complex web of traditional ties and of current contacts between the little people of the area does not add up to a convincing factor in tough Western minds accustomed to deal-ing with the generalizations of economic and political systems or with immutability of power politics.

We have so far considered a series of overtly divisive factors—geography, race, language, colonial tradition, nationalism, and religious philosophies. In each case it was possible to indicate that the fragmentation implied was not necessarily insuperable. We have reviewed as overtly unifying factors the intricate web of current and traditional ties. We have stressed the growing interest that Asian leaders evince in one another, their sense of common problem, and the emergence of South Asian nations into a world predisposed toward international affiliations and the formation of regional ties.

If one judges with the mentality of *Realpolitik*, the cultural forces drawing together the nations and peoples of South Asia would appear weak indeed. From such a viewpoint the narrow interpretation of cultural factors making for South Asian regionalism are of no account whatever. Even the broader interpretation of cultural factors which I have allowed myself is not of great significance. And therefore from this viewpoint I have not had a significant topic to which to address myself. Perhaps both you and I by now share that feeling.

However, the dangers of such ethnocentric judgments must always be guarded against. In appraising cultural developments and international relations, it is essential to understand clearly not only one's own position and motives but also the motives and position of those with whom one deals. It is not without significance that international affairs, in their active aspect, are referred to so frequently as "relationships." The essence of a relationship is the interaction of two or more nonequivalent factors. Modern scientific thought clearly indicates that actuality lies in a study of relationships and that projections into the outer world of one's personalized structure does not give a complete picture of reality.

Therefore, it behooves us, in judging the South Asian scene, to try to stand outside our own skins; to try to understand the value-systems and patterns of sentiments meaningful to peoples whose motives and goals may not be identical with ours. I suspect that, if one speaks from the viewpoint of the values and sentiments of some South Asian leaders, the forces making for a South Asian regional unity will in the next decades be irresistible. And, certainly, sentiments today are nearer the surface in the East than in the West. Leaders speak more freely in idealistic and emotional terms. They are planning for the future. They hope for a cultural renascence which will be neither an arid revival of their own past achievements nor a sterile imitation of the West. It is in intent rather than in fact that their strength lies. Perhaps that is why they seem to have the ring of youthful vigor, of men who are going somewhere, and why all the middle-aged forces of disillusionment and reasonable experience feel challenged to weigh their plea.

A CASE STUDY IN CULTURAL CONTACTS
THE MALAY LANGUAGE

By SOEDJATMOKO[1]

MALAY is one of the Indonesian languages, a group which forms a branch of the Malayo-Polynesian linguistic family. This family covers the territory extending from Madagascar in the west, through the Indonesian archipelago, across the Malay Peninsula to the borders of Burma and Siam, to the Philippines and Formosa in the north and across the Pacific to Melanesia and Micronesia, even to distant Hawaii. It comprises, apart from the Indonesian language group, the Polynesian, Melanesian, and Micronesian languages. The Indonesian group is the largest branch of this group. Malay, a member of this group, is the language originally spoken in middle and southern Sumatra and later in the states on the peninsula of Malaya.

The interinsular trade which flourished in the fourteenth century brought about the extension of the use of this language to the coastal areas of the islands in the entire Indonesian archipelago; and, when new foreign influences came to the Indonesian archipelago, the Malay language automatically became the medium for the expansion of these influences. Three times it was the language used in such a process. First, by the Indian traders who brought the Islamic religion with them, then by the Portuguese with whom the Malays of Malaya first came into contact, and, finally, by the Dutch. The situation is now such that the Malay language is spoken and understood everywhere on all the islands of the archipelago except for the most remote rural areas In many sections it has even replaced the original native tongues, as in West Borneo, Batavia, and most of the islands of the Moluccas between Celebes and New Guinea. It became the language spoken in the ports and the bazaars of the Indonesian

1. Member of Indonesian Delegation to the UN Security Council.

archipelago, the medium of the Dutch colonial administration and of the Islamic and Christian missions. The enormous expansion of the use of the Malay language outside the regions where it was originally spoken cut it off from the continuous rejuvenation enjoyed by a language which finds its roots in the vernacular of a people. At the same time, subjected to the impact of foreign users, it became removed from the classical Malay as spoken in the courts and literary circles of Malayan feudal society. Thus, with its original basis lost, the Malay language as the lingua franca of the Indonesian archipelago reached a very chaotic state, to the extent that the Dutch linguist, Berg, refused to consider the Malay language as a language but preferred to call it a "language-like phenomenon."

The development of the nationalist movement in Indonesia, however, greatly strengthened the position of the Malay language and definitely set the pattern of its development toward a fully adequate cultural medium. The Indonesian nationalist movement, which was born in its modern form in 1908, had, by 1929, finally overcome the more or less separatist and regional elements of its initial growth. In that year it emerged as a culturally and politically unitarian movement comprising the entire territory of the Dutch East Indies. At the same time it adopted the Malay language, thereafter called the "Indonesian language," as its national tongue. Nationalist propaganda and agitation and nationalist political education from then on were almost exclusively carried out in the Indonesian language. This was generally accepted by the Indonesian people, despite the fact that thirty million of the seventy million inhabitants of the archipelago spoke a language which in many respects was better developed and had a longer cultural past, that is, the Javanese language.

It was this decision which gave the development of the Malay language a tremendous impetus. It was this which changed Malay from its status of an unorganized handmaiden for all foreigners and for widely varied ethnic groups, an ancilla used rather loosely without a strict observance of either its classical grammar or its idiom, to a modern language which had to serve as the medium between Western culture and the nationalist renaissance. Rigorous adaptation and development were necessary in order to make the language a suitable vehicle for the expression of modern political and social thinking. Furthermore, in the literary field, the nationalist renaissance created the desire among the people to free themselves from the frozen and rigid forms of literary expression, from the epic and from the pantun, the Malay quatrain; and it was at that time that the first attempts were made to find new forms of literary expression. The process of individualization which took place as a part of the general nationalist reawakening in Asia was reflected in the emergence of the novel and of modern forms of poetry.

The Japanese military occupation and the consequent discarding of the Dutch language precipitated the full development of the Malay language to a medium which could adequately cover all fields of human activity. It was then that the first language commission was set up, which codified the new developments and became the vanguard of further adaptation and renovation of the Indonesian language. This process was accelerated even more by the fact that, during the Japanese occupation, all education, especially on the higher levels, was shifted overnight from Dutch to Indonesian. The new and sudden requirements, especially in the field of modern science and as a medium for higher education, forced the Malay language to grow too quickly. The process was further accelerated by the fact that the Western-educated intelligentsia started using the Indonesian language, while they did not command the classical Malay. In this situation many elements of Dutch syntax and idiom were brought into the Malay language, sometimes to the extent of corruption of its own grammar. At the same time, however, there grew a strong tendency to check all these new forms and terms against the classical Malay. But this process of adaptation, although it may have corrupted some of the classical purity, brought about a greater flexibility and the larger descriptive power which is so necessary for an adequate medium for modern culture and science.

The Indonesian revolution confirmed this development, and, since this revolution expressed the self-assertion of the people, actually of a new people and their assertion of a new life and a new sense of living, this modern Indonesian language emerged as the medium of expression of this new sense of life. The alien elements and changes in structure and substance were accepted in their own right. Conformity with the structure of original Malay was no longer considered obligatory, since the Indonesian language was to become a new language, the language of a new nation now in the process of being born. The revolution, in terms of the development of the Malay language, means a breach with the past in this respect as well as in so many others.

The literature created in this revolutionary period reflects the attempts of the younger generation to define their newly discovered individuality, their newly discovered "I." In our modern poetry the search for that definition of the uniqueness of the individual and his relations in life and society, a search reflected in the poetry of men like the Dutch poets Slauerhoff and Marsman, is the central theme. It may also account for the popularity of T. S. Eliot. Thus it is clear, merely from a superficial examination, that the Malay language, especially the Malay language as spoken in the Indonesian archipelago, is a reflection and even an expression of the nationalist development. Therefore, its role is closely connected with the political development of Indonesia.

The question then arises, since the modern Indonesian language is an expression of Indonesian nationalism, What will its role be in any regional thinking in Southeast Asia? In order to clear the way for a consideration of this question, it should be remembered that outside Indonesia the Malay language is spoken in the Malay Peninsula and in British West and North Borneo and that Tagalog, one of the Philippine languages, is a member of the Indonesian linguistic group. Apart from small Malay-speaking minorities in Burma, Siam, and Indochina, the languages of the countries around Indonesia have no relationship to the Malayan language. It is possible to go even further than that. Several of these countries have not solved their own linguistic problems. In Indochina there are three totally different languages: Viet-Namese, which is the most widely spoken; Cambodian; and Laotian. In Burma there are also three languages: Burman, Karen, and Shan.

It is equally important to realize that colonial nationalism and, therefore, Indonesian nationalism have only a limited objective and only a temporary and interim character. Colonial nationalism has no aims beyond the attainment of political freedom as the only possible basis for a life of human dignity. Certainly, colonial nationalism has no claim whatsoever for a universal application of those values and standards, spiritual and political, by which its adherents live. In that respect it differs fundamentally from the kind of nationalism which arose in some of the free countries of Europe in the twentieth century. In short, colonial nationalism as such has no political or cultural expansionist elements. It is a rejection and a reaction, and thus it can be expected that, after having attained its political aims, colonial nationalism will die down and the other elements of revitalized energies of the peoples will come to the fore. Therefore, a deliberate expansion of the Malay language beyond the boundaries of the former Dutch East Indies is out of the question. It remains possible, of course, that as a result of Indonesia's emergence as a free nation the Malay-speaking territories outside Indonesia will seek closer ties with Indonesia. This may prove to be the case, particularly for the Malayans in Malaya who would like to safeguard their position in their own country, especially vis-à-vis the Chinese. It is even theoretically possible that, with the necessary stimulus from the Philippines, the dream of several leaders in those areas of a pan-Malayan federation will be revived. Current thinking in regional terms, however, is much more along the lines of Southeast Asian regional alignment.

In fact, regional alignment is a constant preoccupation of the leaders in Southeast Asia. The solution to many economic and political problems and even the answers to the question as to how much political strength can be generated by the entire Southeast Asian region as a whole will depend on the ability of these newly emerged and emerging nations to approach these problems on a regional basis rather than a national one. On the other hand, apart from the fact that the interest of the people of the entire area is for the moment focused on their own individual national problems, there remain strong potential elements of political and economic isolationist thinking. It is impossible to say at this stage what direction the developments in these countries will take. In any case it is likely that a development will take place on the basis of political and economic factors pertinent to the individual situation in each country and to the mutual relationship within that region and the position of Southeast Asia as a whole vis-à-vis the rest of the world. In working out the mutual relationships in such a regional alignment, the question of cultural relationship does not arise, and certainly language does not figure a priori in this problem. The question of which language will be spoken predominantly throughout these areas, if such an alignment does emerge, will not be determined in the first place by factors of cultural kinship or by a deliberate choice. It will be determined much later by the factors of political and economic development, by factors based on the power relations within such a regional alignment, and even by the changing political scene in Asia outside Southeast Asia.

Southeast Asian regional thinking is a product of modern political reasoning, based on a rational approach to economic and political problems. It is the thinking of the politically articulate leading groups and commercially active parts of the different societies, those groups which have broken away from the past and have in common the modern rational approach to the problems of today. The common cultural elements of the past will most likely play no part in such a development and certainly not for some time to come. The question of a common language or even of a predominantly accepted language, therefore, does not arise.

It should also be realized that, in the development of such regional thinking, the question of language is not of primary concern, at least if no desire for cultural domination exists in any of the nations concerned. This is illustrated by the fact that neither the Congress of Europe nor the Asian Relations Conference in New Delhi raised this problem. Therefore, in the development of regional thinking in Southeast Asia the development of the different languages of the nations concerned and the question of cultural kinship will play no role. It is highly probable that, for the time being, the question will be left entirely to considerations of practicality, that the present situation will be continued, and that the English language will play an important role in cementing the relationships in these areas.

RAPPORTEUR'S REPORT OF ROUND-TABLE DISCUSSIONS ON SOCIAL FORCES

By JOHN F. EMBREE[1]

IN RECENT years anthropology has been concerned with a number of interesting problems. One of these is the influence of culture in personality development, a study of national character structure; another is the problem of the processes and products of acculturation; still another is the problem of cultural evolution. I think that all these researches have some bearing on the problems discussed at this Institute.

During the war a great deal of attention was paid to the character structures of the Japanese and of the Germans. We wanted to know why those people behaved the way they did during the war. I am not one who thinks that you can always transfer a study of culturally conditioned individual behavior to an analysis of national behavior, but still there may well be some connection between the two, and I am sure that in Southeast Asia some analysis of the national character structures of Siamese, Viet-Namese, and of various types of Indians and Indonesians would be of significance.

Acculturation, the study of culture contact, has been referred to before.[2] I think we need to investigate further the processes by which this acculturation goes on and devote a little more attention to an analysis of cultural responses to culture contact. No one, I think, has defined nationalism at this meeting. I am not going to, but under that rubric there certainly is often included one of the products or several products of acculturation: the attempt of a nation or of a culture to reintegrate itself, to re-establish cultural unity in the face of disintegration resulting from initial culture contact. Certainly, some of the phenomena of nationalism in Southeast Asia are of this nature.

1. Associate professor of sociology, Yale University.
2. See the paper by Cora Du Bois, pp. 27–44 of this volume.

Cultural evolution assumes that cultures develop in certain directions and are irreversible. There is a new interest in this subject. In the old days it was discarded because it was too naïve. Then it was assumed that cultural evolution was a simple one-line development from "primitive" to nineteenth-century British. That kind of naïveté in cultural studies is no longer in existence, and there is, instead, an interest in the matter of how cultures develop in diverse ways, what directions they take, whether there are any regular patterns of cultural development which repeat themselves. Attention to such problems in Southeast Asia again is relevant to making predictions as to what is going to happen in the next few generations. I say "generations" because cultural anthropologists think in those terms rather than in days or months or years. I think that any attempts to reorganize these societies from the outside or to try to mold them according to the development of American society are certainly doomed to failure because that is not the nature of the cultural evolution in the area.

Some mention has been made from time to time of "culture areas," but only in passing. I should like to underline here the fact that there is a number of very distinct culture areas in Southeast Asia and in South Asia and that these have a definite political significance. The cultural differences between the Viet-Namese and the Siamese are marked indeed in Indochina, and at the same time there are cultural similarities between the Siamese, the Cambodians, and the Laotians. Taken together with the history of these areas, these facts of culture area are very important and point, for example, to the likelihood of future conflict between Siam and Viet-Nam concerning boundaries. Such conflicts will not be simply political, they will have some of their origin in the very existence of these culture areas.

In this connection I think it is significant that when Mr. Furnivall discusses South Asia he discusses Burma, when Mr. Mandelbaum discusses South Asia he discusses India, when I discuss the area I usually talk about Indochina and Siam. In other words, we usually stick to the regions that we know something about at first hand, and, having casual contact with the other areas, we know the other areas are different. There are, in reality, tremendous cultural differences in the areas of Southeast Asia. The possibility of having this cultural diversity at the same time that an administrative and economic unity is developed has been mentioned. I think an analysis of that is a constructive approach, but I think that to have valid conclusions from such a study of how that diversity can exist within the framework of administrative and economic unity requires more attention than has been given to the very hard facts of cultural diversity.

It has been pointed out by Professor Wright that the philosophy of life of some of the peoples of South Asia is such as to lead them to have fewer material wants than the people of Western nations, particularly the United States. Mr. Isaacs leaped upon this particular statement as a kind of "let 'em eat cake" remark. I would like to refer to an analysis which has been made by Stuart Chase in his book called *Mexico*, in which he discusses some differences between American society and Mexican society.[3] In that book, you may recall that Stuart Chase took two communities studied by social scientists, one a Mexican community called "Tepoztlan" by Redfield, another an American community called "Middletown," studied by the Lynds.[4] In discussing the differences between Mexican culture and American culture, he pointed out what he called the "wantlessness" of the Mexican consumer and what a problem that was to the American in dealing with the Mexican. Both peoples, of course, like to eat; but they like to eat different things; they go about expressing their wants in different ways. It is also possible to make sacrifices—sacrifices of life—in order to maintain certain cultural aspects of your life which you want to keep. In our own society we kill tens of thousands of people every year in traffic accidents. That does not mean that we do not care for human life, but it does mean that, taken collectively, we prefer an industrial life which includes the automobile at the expense of those deaths.

3. Stuart Chase, *Mexico: A Study of Two Americas* (New York: Macmillan Co., 1931).

4. Robert Redfield, *Tepoztlan: A Mexican Village* (Chicago: University of Chicago Press, 1930); Robert S. and Helen M. Lynd, *Middletown: A Study in Contemporary American Culture* (New York: Harcourt, Brace & Co., 1929).

The Mexican comparison to which I referred raises another point which I think is extremely important. That is the fact that we do not have any good community studies from South Asia. In other words, one of the difficulties that we have in talking about culture areas or the ways of life of the people or national character structure is that we do not have the data. The study by Mr. Chase could be made by an outside man coming in and utilizing studies by social scientists in Mexico and the United States. There are no comparable data by which people can go in and draw valid conclusions about Southeast Asia. A possible exception would be the Covarrubias study of the Balinese or some of these special studies like the one on adat law; but, in general, we know very little indeed of a scientific nature about how the peoples of Southeast Asia live their daily lives.[5]

We do have some histories available. History was pretty well ignored in all the discussions, but I think that the traditional enmity of Burma and Siam is not an irrelevant fact in discussing the future of Southeast Asia or the historic Siamese foreign policy of playing one foreign Western power off against another foreign Western power in order to survive. She is carrying on that same policy today and seems more concerned with playing off one foreign outside power against another than with entering into any constructive regional framework within Southeast Asia.

Speaking of history, Professor Wright made a passing reference to an analogy between Southeast Asia today and medieval Europe. There are some points here which might be pursued by those interested. The role of religion in the daily life of the Southeast Asiatic is certainly comparable in some ways to its role in medieval Europe. It is very important in the educational life, or was until recently. The agricultural population is a preponderant group, cities being commercial trade centers and also cultural capitals, foot and wagon travel being the ordinary way of getting about, there being a preponderance of illiteracy but, at the same time, great respect for written material, for learning, and for scholars.

5. Miguel Covarrubias, *Island of Bali* (New York: A. A. Knopf, 1937); on adat law see, for example, P. S. van Ronkel, *Het Maleische Adat-Wetboek van Koetai* (Amsterdam: Noord-Hollandsche Uitgevers Maatschappij, 1935).

I do not think that the medieval analogy should be pushed too far. Dr. Du Bois pointed out in her book *Social Forces in Southeast Asia* that the term "feudal" cannot be used in Southeast Asia in the way it can be used in reference to Europe.[6] There is another difference, that the impact of industrial changes is coming with great speed in the area and that social changes of a different type than those we might have expected in Europe will probably result.

I would like to make a note or two about culture as such as a basis for some other remarks. Culture as the anthropologist looks at it is something like soil or climate or water. You cannot turn it into an "ism" like nationalism or regionalism. This suggests that in terms like "nationalism" and "regionalism" we are thinking about a conscious determinism on the part of people in the country in shaping these things, whereas culture is not something that is ordinarily consciously shaped by the individuals who carry it. On the contrary, it very strongly influences the way of life, the attitudes, and the behavior of the individuals brought up in the particular culture, always granting, of course, that you cannot have culture without individuals to carry it; but culture also has a certain existence, a reality of its own. Another trait is that it is never static; hence any treatment of culture as being static or as being a museum piece is an unreal approach to it. Cultural change is always going on, cultural diversity is always developing, and in any main area, such as most of South Asia, acculturation is a constant phenomenon, not something which happens now and not then. Culture also has a vitality. I think that Mr. Barr emphasized that very well in regard to India. Culture does not suffer the danger of dying off very readily.

When a social structure or a culture is subjected to rapid change as the result of contact with another or as the result of various internal forces, the old structure perhaps becoming too rigid for the new conditions, there is always a reorganization, a reintegration, of the society to fit the new social needs. With the exception of very small communities like some of the Polyne-

6. Cora Du Bois, *Social Forces in Southeast Asia* (Minneapolis: University of Minnesota Press, 1949).

sians, which get swamped by culture contact, this reintegration always takes place and, as a rule, fairly successfully. It may take the form of a revolution. It may take the form of the kind of nationalism you see in Siam today. It may take the form of new religious values being emphasized to bring together new and old elements of culture. Various religious movements are often a reaction to strong cultural change.

Stress on national languages is one of the characteristics today in Southeast Asia, which is a result, I think, of some of these attempts to reintegrate the society in the face of some of the difficult disintegrating factors caused by culture contact. That raises this matter of language, which has already been mentioned several times. I think the emphasis on national languages in Southeast Asia is very significant. Mr. Soedjatmoko treated the Indonesian development in this regard, showed the way in which, first of all, the language itself could readjust to fit new needs and, second, how it spread out to serve the need of integrating Indonesia as a whole with a single language.[7] Tagalog is serving the same end in the Philippines, Burmese in Burma. Language is not just a means of communication, it is a national symbol. But ultimately, while these national languages will serve the short-range function of unification, in the longer-range period these may develop into a rather serious handicap to unity in South Asia as a whole, with this great variety of national languages and with great emotional attitudes attached to the maintenance of these national languages.

Another cultural point which was mentioned, but not very much, was the whole matter of religion in the area. There is a tendency now to regard any serious treatment of religious problems as minor and to be tossed off as simply the machinations of colonialists, but I think that religion is still important and must be considered in the region. The social importance of Buddhism in Burmese life, for example, is one of the very important blocks toward the development of Moscow communism in Burma. The fact that the United States is a Christian country and backs Christians certainly has its political significance in regard to Chiang Kai-shek or, as the French feel, with regard to Bao-Dai,

7. See the paper by Soedjatmoko, pp. 45–50 of this volume.

whose wife is Catholic. That is on the negative side, perhaps. On the positive side there is what Dr. Du Bois referred to as the "inclusive" characteristic of religion in South Asia. This is rather important because it does point up a rather significant cultural difference between religious attitudes in South Asian countries and certain religious attitudes still existing in Christian countries. It makes possible, perhaps, an easier integration on that particular level in South Asia; but we should remember here that the Philippines are Catholic and that the Philippines stand apart from Southeast Asia in this regard.

Coming back, now, to national character structure, I think this is relevant in discussing the matter of "bold new plans" for Asia. Bold new plans, incidentally, sometimes remind me of Aldous Huxley's *Brave New World*—I think we should watch our thinking on that.[8]

The Viet-Namese is an industrious individual, and he has some of the Westerner's attitude in regard to the virtue of work as work and of labor as labor and doing certain things over long periods. Many Viet-Namese have pursued higher studies and have become doctors, engineers, and so on. There is little doubt that, with an opportunity to work out industrialization on their own, they would certainly go ahead with it. Indeed, Paul Mus, who is a Frenchman concerned both with culture and with administration, proposed in 1945 that the best thing for France to do in Viet-Nam would be to establish a series of atomic research laboratories in conjunction with the Viet-Namese, using Viet-Namese technicians and developing them industrially in that way. He was thinking of a culture on which he was as well qualified as anyone to work. To us that might seem a startling proposal. To General de Gaulle it was so startling that it did not get to first base, but it was interesting that Mus made it, and I think that it had some validity and might have worked.

I do not think it would apply to Siam or Cambodia. The people of Siamese culture are not nearly so concerned with work as a virtue. They have other attitudes toward life, and many a bold new plan introduced from the West has failed dismally in Siam, and I think will again in the future. There is a basic cul-

8. Aldous Huxley, *Brave New World* (New York: Doubleday, Doran & Co., 1932).

tural difference right there when it comes to bringing in Western technology.

The matter of attitudes was taken up by Mr. Isaacs. I would certainly suggest that everyone look at his *Newsweek* article on the subject.[9] A study of attitudes is basic, but not just the attitudes of these people as a whole to the United States but also the attitudes of the Siamese in contrast to the Viet-Namese and in contrast to Hindus, etc. The attitude of each of these groups is different toward us; it is also different toward one another. National attitudes within the region have to be considered because these national attitudes are to a degree cultural. Also the attitudes of peoples toward their own governments and leaders are important. The reason Phibun is in control in Siam is because many Siamese think he is a pretty good person. The problem is why they think so.

There is one more point I should like to make. In this matter of cultural differences and cultural unity there is the importance of the elite in the various societies. Very little mention was made of that except to say, negatively, that there seems to be no middle class in many of these countries. The elite, the people you find in urban areas in the upper classes, are rather important in this matter of cultural contact and cultural change in regard to outside countries. It is through them very often that some of these important cultural changes take place. It was through the royal family, for example, that many new things came into Siam. Today there has been a shift, the royal family is out, and there is a new kind of elite coming in—an elite which draws on people in other levels of society but which nevertheless remains a small elite itself. These are important also because there is a certain cultural convergence among them so that, whereas a peasant in Viet-Nam and a peasant from Siam might have some difficulty with each other, a member of the Viet-Namese elite and a member of the Siamese elite could probably talk the same cultural language a good deal better. Mr. Soedjatmoko's passing remark that the leaders in Southeast Asia could work together is, I think, based partly on this cultural con-

9. Harold Isaacs, "South Asia: Where and How America Loses Friends," *Newsweek*, XXXIII, No. 22 (May 30, 1949), 36–38.

vergence of elites. Some remarks in T. S. Eliot's new book, *Notes toward the Definition of Culture*[10] are relevant here.

In coming to a final point I may remark that we here are not concerned and should not be concerned with administration. We are not here as administrators, we are not here as government planners; we are here to analyze the problems involved. The planners are in Washington and Delhi and Bangkok and London and wherever, busy doing their planning and their administrating. That is not our job. Our job is to provide some analysis of the problem so that they can plan a bit less in the dark.

That raises a final question, and that is whether or not individuals can consciously influence cultural change. An anthropologist like Kroeber in his study of the rise and fall of cultures would indicate not.[11] A working political reporter like Mr. Isaacs would insist on an opposite view, I am sure. I would submit to the group an intermediate alternative, not intermediate, really, but off at another angle, and that is this concept that you find in South Asia of karma, the idea that an incalculable series of past acts determines future acts, the idea of the past within the future. By this concept an individual cannot, singlehanded, change the course of history. History is a result of a multitude of collective acts. The individual should not feel frustrated because he cannot turn the stream of history at a right angle, but his small present effort, an effort also determined to a large extent by previous acts of himself and his predecessors—i.e., his character structure—helps to keep the stream flowing, and this, perhaps, is what counts.

10. Thomas Stearns Eliot, *Notes toward the Definition of Culture* (New York: Harcourt, Brace & Co., 1949).
11. Alfred L. Kroeber, *Anthropology* (New York: Harcourt, Brace & Co., 1948).

PART III

ECONOMIC FORCES IN SOUTH ASIA

CO-OPERATION, COMPETITION, AND ISOLATION IN THE ECONOMIC SPHERE

By J. S. FURNIVALL

THE PROBLEM

IT IS the fashion now to remove fear by psychoanalysis. This suggests that if we are to study the relations *between* the peoples of South Asia we must first study relations *within* these various lands. Let us begin, then, with something in the nature of a psychoanalytic study of their economic and social constitution. It is a fascinating subject, which seems to have received less attention from professional economists than it deserves. I am not a professional economist and speak therefore with the natural diffidence of an amateur. But, as an administrator in Burma, I was brought up against problems for which economics textbooks appeared to offer no solution. In puzzling over them, I was driven back to the elementary rudiments, the *ABC*'s of economic theory—the nature of wealth and the fundamental principles governing its production and consumption. Some writers suggest that Western economic theory is not valid for the East, and I hope I shall not trespass unduly on your patience if I recall some of its elementary axioms and maxims. These have frequently cropped up in the course of our discussions. Do orientals recognize our values? What about the acquisitive instinct—do they possess it, ought we to encourage it? I remember scandalizing a group of economists and administrators in Java by suggesting that economic environment conditions population; they were convinced that population conditions the economic environment. We have heard many suggestions to the same effect. Certainly, in Burma everyone wants a fountain pen, a wrist watch, and a bicycle if he cannot afford a car; and casual observation suggested that men wanted much the same things in Java. It is not perhaps exaggerating to say that, given the choice between a wrist watch and a baby, most people would choose the wrist watch. But it is much easier to get a baby. Yet only the other day a modern Burman, a loyal supporter of the government in Burma, explaining how hard it is to make both ends meet now that salaries have been reduced on account of the financial position of the country, remarked that out of what remained he had to support two distant cousins who were on strike against the government. Their attitude is not quite the same as ours, and in attempting an economic analysis of South Asia we should, I think, be rather careful about terms and principles. Ruskin somewhere pokes fun at Mill for saying that it is unnecessary to define wealth because everyone has a sufficiently clear idea of wealth. Modern economists still seem chary of defining it. Does wealth have the same connotation in Asia as in Europe? I think it does. I suppose we may define it as the product of work applied to natural resources in order to produce something that men want and that can be transferred to others.

THE FACTORS OF PRODUCTION

It is common usage to describe land, labor, and capital as the factors of production of wealth. But is this a complete analysis? Conditions in South Asia seem to suggest that one factor has been overlooked. Land, of course, is a conventional abbreviation for all the free gifts of nature, soil, rain, air, rivers, sea, and sun. Labor also is a conventional term including all forms of work, intellectual as well as manual. Anyone who does work expends energy in the production of wealth, just as the mainspring of a watch expends energy in driving the hands. Ordinarily, in doing work a man can produce more wealth than he consumes. He may have no use for the surplus, and in this case so much of his work is wasted. In general, he stores the surplus, and this surplus constitutes his wealth, which may be regarded as a store of his accumulated labor applied to natural resources. He may either store it for future enjoyment, or he may use it for the production of more wealth; and wealth applied to the further production of wealth is termed "capital."

It is, I would suggest, not wholly fanciful and, indeed, helpful to apply in economics the terminology of physical science. We may perhaps regard wealth as an accumulation of economic energy, and we can measure economic energy by the surplus of wealth produced, the store of energy accumulated, over the energy consumed in the form of capital, land, and labor in producing it. Regarded from this impersonal standpoint, economic problems are concerned with production and consumption rather than with supply and demand, the getting and spending characteristic of an acquisitive society.

In some parts of Burma men who have no cattle prepare the soil for cultivation by puddling it with their feet. Most cultivators, however, use some of their surplus produce as capital by investing it in cattle with which they can obtain a larger yield. In the one case the cultivator used labor only; in the other he uses both labor and capital. But in the nature of the work performed there is no difference; in both cases the cultivator is expending economic energy in the production of wealth, but in the latter case, in addition to his own labor, he is using the accumulated store of energy represented by the cattle. From another standpoint, however, there is a great difference between labor and capital. Labor is embodied in the laborer and, except where slavery persists, the laborer owns himself and is free to sell his services. An employer cannot buy the man but only his labor, the economic energy which he embodies. Capital, however, is disembodied economic energy; it is not embodied in any particular individual but can be freely transferred from one man to another and is at the disposal of anyone who owns it. The distinction between labor and capital is valid, of course, in South Asia as in Europe, but the accumulation of wealth in South Asia and the use of it as capital deserve closer consideration.

Scattered about South Asia there are still a few small backward tribes which live from day to day on the herbs and fruit they gather in the jungle and the animals and fish they catch. They produce no surplus because every day they consume all they get, and they remain miserably poor. Some tribes, however, rather more advanced, practice shifting cultivation in hillside clearings and very often, although the land may yield a surplus, they do not trouble to reap more than is sufficient for their needs, so that much of their labor is wasted. Not so very long ago this happened even with settled cultivation in the plains, and I have often been told that in former days, when there was no export market for rice, the surplus produce was left in the fields to be eaten by the rats. Similarly, millet grain is still abandoned to the birds in years when there is a good crop of rice, which men prefer as food to millet. Nowadays, however, most cultivators in the plains store and sell their surplus produce. They have reached a higher stage of social organization than the hill folk, and it is only when men reach this stage that they begin to accumulate wealth. But they store most of their wealth in the form of gold, silver, or jewelry and use only a small proportion of it as capital for the production of more wealth. This is very different from the conditions obtaining in the social organization of the West, where men deposit in the bank any surplus beyond their immediate requirements, so that it becomes available as capital for promoting economic progress.

It is true that work is often wasted in the West. The stock example is the destruction of Brazilian coffee. Even during the darkest days of depression in England, one could read hungrily in the papers of fish thrown back into the sea, and I have myself seen cases of oranges dumped in the Mersey at Liverpool. But in the West such a waste of labor is unusual; in many parts of South Asia it is still usual. It is true also that in the West much of the wealth is expended on display and does not contribute to production directly, if at all; but the proportion so expended is nothing like so great as in the East. As regards both the waste of labor and the waste—if one may call it so—of wealth, there is a significant difference between East and West. But the foregoing outline sketch of social evolution in South Asia shows that it reflects the difference in social environment. In primitive conditions there is no surplus; then a surplus is produced but wasted; in the more advanced oriental communities the surplus is stored as wealth; but only in the social organization of the Western world is any considerable portion of the accumulated wealth applied to production as capital. Surely, then, we must reckon social organization alongside land, labor, and capital as a factor—indeed, the most important factor—in the production of wealth.

It would, of course, be absurd to suggest that economists have wholly overlooked anything so obvious. They have, indeed, from the time of Adam Smith emphasized the economic importance of the division of labor, which is only one aspect of social organization. But they have treated the division of labor as an isolated phenomenon instead of as a process closely linked up with the general course of social evolution. This is due probably to their having assumed as normal the economic structure of the world in which they lived.

CAPITALISM

The system of social organization which most textbooks on economics take for granted is usually termed "capitalism." On the surface at least, there is much to justify this term as a general description of its character; for two outstanding features of the modern Western world are the aggregation of vast masses of capital and the power wielded by the owners of capital, the capitalists, not only in the economic sphere but also in the sphere of politics. Yet if we look below the surface, the term, if not a misnomer, is certainly misleading. The confusion is unfortunate; for it tends to concentrate attention on capital as the essential element in a society and type of civilization of which it is only one, and not the most important, feature. This encourages critics of the system to attribute to the personal activities of capitalists results that are inherent in the working of impersonal economic forces and, on the other hand, allows supporters of the system to claim on its behalf credit for the benevolent activities of capitalists as citizens and not merely as owners of capital. In South Asia today "capitalist" is a term of obloquy, yet it is capitalist America that is conspicuous for such foundations as the Norman Wait Harris Memorial that has brought us all together here to study international relations in South Asia.

One of these unfortunate results is that many people in South Asia have come to regard capital as evil in itself; they condemn not only the use of wealth as capital but even the accumulation of wealth, whether for production or display, and assume that a rich man is a robber. Although those who are more enlightened may advocate merely the transfer of capital from private to public ownership, the great mass of the unenlightened are reckless of destroying capital and wealth in their attack on the so-called "capitalist system." That is a very real danger at the present time. There is a real danger of a relapse into the dark ages. Yet, if I interpret correctly the writing on the wall, the attack, however misdirected by ignorance and envy, is essentially an instinctive human reaction against the control of economic forces, which must be brought under control if civilization is to survive.

Capitalism in its modern form may be regarded as the natural, though not the necessary, result of the economic reforms advocated by the classical economists who did so much to give a meaning to the modern world. It is only one aspect of the great liberal tradition of individual freedom of thought and action, person and property, including the right of individuals to own property and use it for their individual profit. To the economists of the liberal tradition the liberation of economic forces from the control of customary restrictions seemed a master-key to the wealth of nations. This belief was largely justified. Much as the free play of natural selection tends to the survival of the fittest in the struggle for existence, so does the free play of economic forces tend to efficiency in the economic sphere. But natural selection operates by eliminating the unfit, those who cannot adapt the environment to make it fit for them. Ruthlessness is equally a character of unrestricted economic competition. Efficiency may signify either an increase in production or a decrease in consumption and, except so far as economic forces are directed by human will, they tend to reduce consumption rather than to increase production. Unless restrained by human will, they tend to reduce life to its lowest level, to the margin of bare animal subsistence. So far as capital represents pure economic energy, it operates in the same manner; and, although, strictly interpreted, capitalism signifies only a type of social organization, like that of the modern West, conspicuous for vast accumulations of capital, yet in common usage it has come to signify a type of social organization dominated by impersonal economic forces or in which at least economic forces are preponderant. I would say that the preponderance of economic forces is inevitably prejudicial to social welfare, but it is not capital as such that is responsible for the evils attributed to capitalism.

In what may be termed the "precapitalist age," economic forces were restrained by custom. Economic freedom led naturally both to the accumulation of capital and to social disruption. But social disruption was not the necessary consequence of economic freedom. In the West, where economic forces were liberated gradually, they had little effect on the social structure before the industrial revolution. Then, as their activity increased, measures were taken to control them. The men who came forward to defend society against disintegration by economic forces called themselves socialists. After an uphill struggle with defenders of the liberal tradition who rightly valued economic freedom, they forced the stoutest champion of liberalism in England at the end of the nineteenth century to admit "We are all socialists now." It was, however, the capitalist as owner of capital rather than capital as the embodiment of economic forces that presented the more obvious target for attack. Socialists accordingly advocated the substitution of public for private ownership of capital and the control of economic activities by the state as the organ of social will. The mere substitution of public for private ownership is not in itself sufficient to control economic forces; it may result only in state capitalism instead of private capitalism. Thus parallel to and part of the socialist movement was a trend toward democracy as a means of making the state better able to assert its authority over the antisocial effects of economic forces. Both socialism and democracy are still on trial, but it may fairly be said that in the West we are now living in a postcapitalist age in which co-operation is more or less effective in asserting the supremacy of social will as distinct from the capitalist age of unrestricted economic competition, and the still earlier precapitalist age, when economic forces were restrained by custom. What, however, is the situation in South Asia?

DUAL ECONOMY

When Europeans in the dawn of modern capitalism tried to do business in the East, they encountered a society still living in the precapitalist age. Under the local rulers they could not do business on Western lines or even live securely, and in various ways they obtained concessions where they could live their own life in their own way. Each little concession was a fort and a trading station, a capitalist nucleus in a precapitalist world. Yet it was still difficult to conduct business because the people would not trade on Western lines. In the West anyone who wants an additional supply of anything can usually obtain it by offering a higher price. But in the East it often happened that a higher price did not stimulate production. The wants of the people were few and simple, and when these were satisfied nothing would tempt them to produce more. The European merchants, as good men of business, did not want to pay more than was necessary, and they also wanted, if they could, to obtain a monopoly of the European market which would enable them to gain as much as possible.

The Dutch in Java found a solution to the problem. They made contracts with local chieftains who could compel the people to produce the goods wanted by the Dutch and prevent them from selling to outsiders; as the chieftains obtained the produce in the form of revenue, they could sell it on terms very gratifying to the Dutch. With the growth of Dutch power, they superseded the local chieftains and obtained still better terms. But their profit still depended on maintaining the authority of the local chieftains. Out of this arose the tradition of indirect rule. Even until the late nineteenth century the Dutch had no manufactures that they could sell in Asia in a free market, and they wanted more than ever produce, especially sugar and coffee, which the people would not cultivate in sufficient quantities except under compulsion. This produce could be supplied by Western planters. These, however, wanted land and labor which they could obtain on the most favorable terms through local village headmen. Thus the system of indirect rule still survived, though in a modified form. As an economic system it rested on compulsion and not on economic freedom.

The planters, the merchants who bought their produce and supplied their requirements, and the banks which financed the whole process were living in a Western capitalist world. But the people in their villages were still living in a world that, outwardly at least, was a survival of the precapitalist age. There was a capitalist superstructure over a precapitalist base. In the Western capitalist superstructure economic forces acted freely, not even subject to the social inhibitions which still restrain them in the West. In the Eastern precapitalist sector a check over economic forces was maintained by local chieftains, ostensibly deriving their authority from the people as the embodiment of social will but in reality exercising it as agents of the central government, on which they depended for support. These conditions provided some Dutch economists with a theory of a dual economy as a distinctive character of colonial rule.[1]

In tropical dependencies, according to this theory, there are two distinct systems of economy. In the Western sector economic forces act in strict accordance with the economic laws enunciated by the earlier liberal economists; but in the Eastern sector these laws have no force, and Western economic principles are inapplicable. The one sector is ultra-capitalist and the Eastern sector is precapitalist or subcapitalist, with prestige carrying more weight than profit and communal influence restraining the individual desire of gain. Economists of this school attempt to elucidate the principles governing economic relations separately in the two distinct sectors and the relations between the two sectors. Their work has thrown much light on tropical economy, and I personally owe a great debt to them, but their analysis is based on the assumption that Western economic laws do not run in the Eastern world. Elsewhere experience suggests grounds for questioning that assumption. Still in various forms it has found expression in this conference. It may be well, therefore, to glance briefly at some of these elementary principles to ascertain which are valid in South Asia and how far and why others may be invalid.

ECONOMIC LAWS

I have been told that it is a mark of senility to talk of economic laws. I admit the senility but am not to be laughed out of

1. J. H. Boeke, *The Structure of the Netherlands Indian Economy* (New York: Institute of Pacific Relations, 1942), pp. 3–13.

my belief in economic laws. They were, indeed, already out of fashion when I first began to take an interest in economics. Mill had long since restricted their domain to production, and men were beginning to question them even in this branch of economics or rather, perhaps, to assume that on production there was no more to be said. Now we are encouraged to believe that, if any such laws exist, we can override them by an act of parliament or, if in no other way, by a revolution. But *plus ça change.* . . . The British Parliament, it has been said, can do anything except change a man into a woman. But men are not really quite so malleable, and even in an atomic age nature is still nature. We may perhaps classify economic laws as laws of nature, laws of human nature, and laws of social nature, and I would suggest that under each head there are laws no less rigid than the laws of the Medes and Persians and as universally applicable as the laws of motion. They are valid in a precapitalist society no less than in a capitalist society and no less valid in the postcapitalist society in which we live.

If we consider wealth and nature, we find certain laws applicable both to the natural world and to the human world in its economic aspect. It is, for example, a law of nature that all living things tend to increase up to the limit of the food supply. That certainly is a law which applies to a precapitalist society. It is, indeed, one of the chief problems confronting students of tropical economy and practical administrators that efforts to promote welfare in the tropics are frustrated by the growth of the population. "We try," they complain, "to provide food for every mouth, but the only result is that there are more mouths to feed." In the West human will may circumvent the law of population through birth control, but that does not nullify the law any more than airplanes nullify the law of gravity. Again it is a law of nature that effort is exhausting, that energy is diminished in doing work. We may devise means to spur men to greater effort, as, for example, by higher pay for overtime, but nature may still operate to give better results from shorter hours. Or take the law of diminishing returns. This is inherent in the physical character of the soil. Perhaps it is nowhere better illustrated than in very primitive precapitalist society, in which men, scratching the surface of the hillside, must move every year or two on account of the exhaustion of the soil. And in pre-capitalist society the natural law of the survival of the fittest acts quite independently of human volition. In times of famine men have a better chance of survival if they can sustain existence on less food than others. Here, then, are some natural laws bearing on economic relations which operate in a precapitalist society; they act quite independently of human will in conditioning production and are equally valid in the East and in the West. And, unless brought under the control of human will either by custom or by effective legislation, they tend to strip life of its ornaments and graces down to a bare level of animal subsistence, or even below that level to the elimination of the economically unfit. The same laws operate in all stages of social evolution, and it is only the social organization that determines the results.

So much for wealth and nature; how about wealth and human nature? In the West in general and wherever and so far as men are actuated by economic motives, they want to get as much as possible for what they give and to give no more than necessary for what they want. We accept it as common sense, a law of human nature, that no one will give threepence if he can get as good a thing for twopence and that no one will sell a thing for twopence if he can get threepence. Human nature, however, according to the theory of a dual economy, is different in the tropics. Economists of this school argue, with good reason, that in the Western sector of tropical society, economic motives prevail more strongly than in "capitalist" Europe, that men more closely resemble the "economic man" of former classical economists, and that capital is freer from control by social will. But the native in the Eastern sector, they contend, has little regard for economic values. It is, indeed, the general experience of Western explorers and traders on their first contact with new peoples that life is ruled by custom and that the individual identifies himself more closely with the community than in the West. But general experience shows also that the individual self lies very near the surface. Men soon learn to value money and evince a desire to better their position, and the characteristic disease of tropical society under the impact of the West is "atomization," disintegration into individuals. So far as there is any difference between natives under Dutch rule and their Western fellows, the explanation would seem to be that, for good or ill, the Dutch have tried to shelter the people from economic forces and have trusted rather to authority than to the desire of gain to stimulate production. The difference lies in the social environment and not in human nature. I do not wish to say that human nature is the same always and everywhere. In Burma, for example, there is a tribe of which only six families remain because the members are so obstinately celibate that they will marry only under official compulsion. But then in Europe old families die out because of the preference for marrying heiresses who breed only female children. All I am constrained to suggest is that the economic motive of the desire of gain is common to human nature in both East and West and that it is the social organization which conditions its activities.

In this matter another point deserves attention. We have seen that the free play of natural law in the economic sphere tends, in the long run, to bring production to a standstill by cutting down consumption. This tendency is reinforced by human nature. Men actuated by the desire of gain aim at increasing the surplus of production over consumption rather than at increasing the stock of wealth. The easiest method is to cut down costs. Only under compulsion or in a congenial environment do they adopt the more difficult method of increasing output. Self-interest likewise impels them to restrict and monopolize production. Just as the free play of natural law in the economic sphere is prejudicial to social welfare, so also the economic motive of the desire of gain is antisocial, and these general principles are as valid in South Asia as in Europe. They are not only equally valid, but they operate more actively. In Burma, for example, Indian immigrants have a lower standard of living than Burmans. They can afford to pay fifteen baskets of paddy an acre as rent on land where Burmans can afford to pay only ten baskets. Naturally, landlords prefer Indians to Burmans as tenants, and the Burman must either reduce his standard of living or seek other employment. But in the stronger social organization of the West trade-unions protect the laborer against wage cuts and compel employers to increase production so that he can afford to pay high wages.

These considerations point to a law of social nature that also is valid for both East and West. The operation of the laws of nature and of human nature tends to limit the production of wealth and to foster the disintegration of society. In the struggle for survival between different social groups it is the economically strongest society which comes to the front, and only by the operation of some motive strong enough to control antisocial economic forces can any society continue to exist. In precapitalist societies the antisocial effect of economic forces is kept within due bounds by custom. In Western capitalist society the common social will, finding expression in legislation, is a more effective method of controlling economic forces because it allows them freer play without their getting beyond control. But in the dependencies or former dependencies of South Asia, order had to be maintained by foreign troops because these societies no longer possessed sufficient inherent vitality to restrain antisocial tendencies.

Thus in respect of wealth and nature, wealth and human nature, and wealth and society we find that there is no significant difference in regard to the validity of Western economic principles. Yet the same laws acting in a different environment produce different results, and, in attempting an analysis of South Asian economics, we must try to ascertain the nature of this difference. Despite all legislation, despite revolutions, Fascist or Communist, nature remains the same and human nature remains the same. But what we can do by law—and what otherwise will be done by revolution—is to change the organization of society. The great liberal economists, preaching freedom from the bonds of custom and the hampering effect of mistaken legislation, urged that economic activities might be left to nature and to human nature. Time has shown that welfare is not won so easily. In the reaction against liberalism, Socialists looked to legislation, Communists to revolution. Following Marx, the Communists hold that nothing less than revolution will suffice, a desperate remedy and almost certainly worse than the disease. What are we to do about it?

The liberal answer is "Do nothing, laissez faire." Right up to the eve of the late war the abundance of rich treasure which South Asia yielded might seem, on a superficial view, to prove the liberals right. But one could not probe far beneath the surface without asking awkward questions. Marx accepted their economic principles but prophesied that these principles would lead to conflict and disaster. Now, I think, if he could rise from the dead and survey the world around him, he would rub his hands, his skeleton hands, with venomous glee and, in accents no longer prophetic but sepulchral, say "I told you so." Looking at the welter of strife and revolution in South Asia now, who was correct, the prophets of smooth things or Marx? But you may remember that Marx did not insist on disaster as the inevitable result of liberating economic forces; he mentioned England as a land where the social organization might be strong enough to hold out against the strain and a possible exception to the general rule. Can we find any similar exception in South Asia? What about India? Perhaps if we inquire why other parts of South Asia are torn with war and revolution, we shall learn why India is comparatively stable.

It is true, of course, that the war was the immediate occasion of the collapse of the old order. But it was threatened with collapse before the war. Why did it collapse so easily? And why is it so difficult to reconstruct the old order or to replace it by a new order? These are questions that we must answer. One feature that has long been common to the countries of South Asia and is so obvious that it could not fail to impress even the most unreflecting sight-seer is the medley of races. What was almost equally apparent was that the races did not mix. Each race and group had its own quarter, its own temple or place of worship, its club or other meeting ground for social functions, its own liquor shops and so on, its own forms and places of entertainment and recreation. They did not meet in these places but only in the market place—and possibly the race course—to make money out of one another or perhaps, not so often, with one another. They had no common link except in business. What was not quite so obvious was that each race and group had its own special economic function. There was a plural society with its own distinctive and characteristic plural economy.

Typically, a plural society in South Asia comprised three main sections: the Europeans, constituting an upper class; the foreign orientals, Indian or Chinese, constituting a middle class; and the great mass of the native population in the lower class. The Europeans and foreign orientals were temporary residents, strangers to one another or at best casual acquaintances, and the native community was little more than a crowd of individuals. In the relations between the classes there were no social ties to dull the edge of economic competition. Within each class inherited traditions lost their force. East of Suez, said Rudyard Kipling's soldier, "there ain't no ten commandments." Hindus forgot their caste and might even intermarry with Moslems. Society as a whole was divided into groups; each group was merely a collection of individuals, and in each group life was simplified to an economic struggle for existence. Social life was reduced to its economic content, and society was converted into a business concern, and only the foreign army of occupation preserved it from disruption. The essential and distinctive character of a plural economy is that it is dominated by economic forces, and, outside a few partly sheltered oases, South Asia illustrated the capitalist system in its purest form.

SOCIAL DEMAND

This plural society was fundamentally unstable. Economic forces had been liberated from the control of custom but had not been brought under the control of any common social will. It is only as a member of society that man can satisfy those social wants that are distinctive of humanity. Education is a social want, so also is the want for a healthier environment. Civilization is the process in which men learn to live together so as to give effect to social wants, and they do this by the evolution of a common social will. Adam Smith and his followers, living in a stable unitary society, could take social wants for granted; as he remarked, "defence is more than opulence." But, as appeared everywhere throughout South Asia on the Japanese invasion, in a plural society there is no common social will even in a matter so vital to its existence as defense against aggression. The basic problem of Western economics is how best to organize supply to meet demand, and this applies no less to social wants than to individual wants. The same problem calls for solution in the plural societies of South Asia. But in a plural society there is a still more fundamental problem; for such a society has no common social will. The highest factor common to all sections is the desire for individual gain, and the basic problem of economics in the tropics is the organization of social demand.

Education in Burma provides a useful illustration of this problem. Under Burmese rule all the boys obtained at least the elements of literacy in the village Buddhist monastery. There was a social demand for education. It had an economic value, but that was merely incidental; its purpose was to teach boys how to live as Buddhists and as citizens of Burma, and it did not result in the overproduction of lads who could not turn their education to account in the employment market. Under British rule, education in the Western schools was merely an economic asset; it did not teach boys how to live but how to make a living. The schools were, for the most part, managed by missionaries who certainly did not regard education as primarily economic. But the people appreciated only its economic value. The boys crowded into the schools, which soon began to turn out graduates in excess of the demand, and there was a surplus of educated unemployables. This, of course, is true in general of Western education in the tropics. It is transformed from a social into an economic asset. Now the monastic schools decay because monastic education has ceased to be a social asset; it has no meaning in the modern world. To the general rule, however, that Western education is merely an economic asset there is one significant exception. The Christian Karens attend the Western schools for the same reason as Burmans formerly attended monastic schools—to learn how to live. Similarly, nationalism seems to be stimulating a demand for Western education as a social asset, but this must be regarded as a symptom of a nascent social will.

CO-OPERATION, COMPETITION, AND ISOLATION

So far as this analysis of the economic structure of society in South Asia is sound, it leads to conclusions of great interest and of practical importance. It raises problems similar to those so long disputed in political science regarding the will of all, *la volonté de tous*, and the general will, *la volonté générale*. In the West one may perhaps assume that the promotion of individual welfare will result in social welfare; but in South Asia it would seem that, in order to promote welfare, we must aim directly at building up and reintegrating a disintegrated society; for only by this means can we achieve the social welfare which is a condition of individual welfare. On this view we may attribute the comparative stability of India to the Hindu religion, which consecrates the divisions of a plural society and overrides their fissiparous tendency by the common bond of caste. Similarly, in Siam a common allegiance to the crown has hitherto sufficed to hold society together, despite the conflict of economic interests between Europeans, Chinese, and the various groups of the indigenous inhabitants; and at the present moment the problem of restoring welfare in Siam is far less formidable a task than in Burma and other former dependencies of European powers.

PRODUCTION

If we turn from the problem of demand in a plural society to the problem of supply, from consumption to production, we find ourselves on less unfamiliar ground. The basic problem, as in Europe, is how best to organize supply, how to produce the greatest output of wealth with the least consumption of capital and labor in the process. World welfare, no less than the welfare of the people immediately concerned, demands that we shall harness the whole available supply of human and material resources to production. But in a plural society what are the available resources and how can we yoke them so as to pull together?

At present, in South Asia, apart from India, practically the whole supply of capital and sometimes even a great part of the land are owned by aliens. Either we must obtain their co-operation on terms compatible with national welfare, which may conflict with their economic interest in immediate large returns, or we must find some way of dealing with their capital. Confiscate it, say the Communists. But what happens when we try to confiscate it? It disappears, or so much of it disappears that the rest is hardly worth confiscating. Confiscation is attractive but impracticable. Pay it all back, says the capitalist. But can we pay it back? Before the war Burma was exporting goods to about double the value of the imports. If we try to pay back the capital, we shall find ourselves for some years exporting all our produce and getting nothing in return for it. That is no more practical than confiscation. And when capitalists demand that their capital shall be returned, is it really going *back?* Most of the so-called "foreign" capital in Burma, as in the neighboring countries, represents accumulated profits. They were accumulated *in* the country by co-operation between the foreign capitalist and the people and represented as much of the profits as could not conveniently be sent out in the form of dividends. They remained in the country in the name of and as the property of the capitalists. This could in some measure be justified as long as the capitalist used them in developing the resources of the country. But it is a different matter when he asks to take them out of the country. Very well then, prohibit the export of capital. But how does one prevent it? How does one achieve a watertight control over foreign exchange in countries where political experience is as immature and the administrative machinery as inadequate as in South Asia? Again, vast masses of capital have already been destroyed during the war. The capital which formerly accumulated out of profits *in* the country must be replaced by capital newly brought *into* the country. It really will be foreign capital, whereas in the past the capital has only been foreign because in the plural society the managerial function was performed by foreigners. How can we attract it with prospective profits when these will be lower and less certain than under the former colonial regime? Must we then buy out foreign enterprise, nationalize it? But nationalization is not the same thing in South Asia as in Europe. Nationalization in Europe means transferring money from one pocket to another within the same country, but in South Asia it means transferring money from the people to foreigners, sending it abroad, and complying with the demand of capitalists to get "their" money back. And such capital as the government can raise, either by borrowing abroad or from domestic savings, will be better expended on developing the national resources along new lines than in merely taking over enterprises already in existence. All the capital available should be applied to building up new production.

Where, however, is this capital to be obtained? Enterprises already in the country will probably try to replace the capital destroyed during the war, even if they have to bring in fresh capital. Apart from this source, who will risk fresh capital in South Asia when Africa offers a prospect of more lucrative employment and when other parts of the world promise a greater security for investments? Even if these countries can borrow the capital they need, is it prudent at the present time to buy machinery and other capital goods which will have to show a profit when prices have fallen? And can they borrow it without strings, visible or invisible, being attached to it? Moreover, their experience of foreign capitalist enterprise in the past has made them reluctant to seek capital abroad.

The problem of raising capital is, of course, linked up with the problem of obtaining managerial and technical experience and a supply of skilled labor. Expensive machinery is useless, worse than useless, if men do not know how to handle it. As regards foreign capital for large-scale enterprise, some form of partnership seems the only possible solution. Apparently some firms, especially in America, will provide capital goods and at the same time training for a period of years until the local people can take over the management for themselves. That seems a promising solution. But it requires a preliminary investigation as to the proper line of development, such as the International Monetary Fund has recently offered to conduct. In general, however, the conditions suggest that the development of large-scale enterprise must of necessity be gradual and should be linked up in the first instance with the development of domestic and small-scale industries, especially those connected with local agriculture. The development of small-scale industry would require less capital and would yield speedier returns. It would also be more effective in dealing with the problem of unemployment. It is often suggested that rapid industrial development would provide a remedy for unemployment. But the unemployment is mainly seasonal, and it will not be easy to combine large-scale industry with seasonal employment. Unless this is borne in mind, unemployment may grow instead of declining with industrialization.

Even with concentration of small-scale local industries the countries will still need capital; it will be difficult for them to raise the capital abroad on favorable terms, and they are apprehensive as to the conditions which will be attached to foreign loans. What prospect is there of raising local capital? Some, probably a substantial amount, could be raised by a capital levy on foreign enterprises, as, for example, by requiring them to transfer one-tenth of their shares to the government. This would need tactful handling, but, if combined with a plan imposing similar sacrifices on the native peoples, the government might reasonably ask foreign enterprise to co-operate in this way in reconstruction and development. Moreover, it would give foreign enterprise and the government a common interest in industrial development and should conduce to the greater security of capital investment. There is also considerable scope for compulsory saving. We have heard a good deal about the "Hungry Forties" in England, and the difficulty of inducing starving peasants to tighten their belts still more. But we may assume that steps would be taken to relieve the cultivators of the burden of rent and debt under which they have been struggling, and they would still be in a much better position than before, even if required to save and pay into a national development fund a portion of what they have hitherto paid the landlord and the moneylender, while the accumulation of savings in this form would tend to inculcate a habit of saving. It is, in the last resort, from the rent and interest paid by the cultivators that the large surplus of exports over imports has been derived in former years, and the savings would, in fact, come not from a further tightening of the cultivators' belts but out of the surplus of unrequited exports. Again, if capital were borrowed, some would go to pay for labor. But if a levy be imposed on foreign capital and the cultivating and income-tax-paying classes are required to save, then it should be possible to induce the laboring class to make a corresponding contribution in the form of labor. This could be so arranged as to relieve seasonal unemployment.

Thus the chief obstacle to enhancing production in South Asia is not the lack of capital but the difficulty of obtaining and training managerial and technical assistance and an adequate supply of skilled labor. The first condition of giving the necessary assistance is a survey to see how it can be utilized to the best account, and the conduct of such surveys, either by the Economic Commission for Asia and the Far East or by some other competent body, is perhaps the most urgent need for economic reconstruction and development. The actual development of the resources of these countries should, in the long run, be remunerative, but the foregoing analysis of South Asian economy suggests that any plan for their development should be designed with the express object of promoting national reintegration and enabling them to maintain their political and economic independence, in order to contribute to the fullest extent from their human and material resources to the welfare of the world.

CO-OPERATION, COMPETITION, AND ISOLATION

National integration implies a development of national unity, the substitution of a unitary for a plural society. One outstanding feature of new Burma is the growth of national unity. This statement may seem paradoxical in view of the obvious and complicated disunity that fills the news from Burma. Nevertheless, it is a fact. One thing that struck me forcibly on my return to Rangoon eighteen months ago after an absence of some years was that it was no longer, as before, an Indian city but a Burman city. It was not quite so Burman as it seemed at first; there was still a Chinese quarter and an Indian core. And it is, indeed, a collection of Burman villages rather than a Burman city. Still, it is far more Burmese. In the papers one reads that Venketaswami, a Madrasi, or Lim Hock Chong, Chinese, or John Smith, an Anglo-Burman, will in future be known as Maung Maung, Maung Gyi, or Maung Gale. Probably most of these people are half-Burmese, but formerly they took the non-Burman name and remained separate from Burmans; now they adopt a Burmese name and Burmese nationality. In mixed marriages between Burmese men and European women, the men formerly wore European dress, now the women often appear in Burmese dress. There seemed to be fewer Chinese than before. But that was because many had come to dress like Burmans. And one found Burmans in all sorts of occupations that formerly had been reserved for Indians or Chinese. There was a new national unity in both cultural and economic spheres. I do not wish to exaggerate this new development, but it is remarkable and unmistakable; it signifies a new aspiration toward unity.

How far will greater national unity make for greater international diversity? How far will it interfere with the growth of regional unity? The regional unity of Southeast Asia has been questioned. But to me it is beyond question. There is unity in physique. Burmans, Siamese, Malays, Javanese, Annamese, and Filipinos in European clothes frequently mistake a stranger for a compatriot. There is in my view strong regional unity throughout the whole of Southeast Asia; in racial origin, in ethnology, in their food, dress, and general way of life there is much common to the whole region. There is regional unity even though they are for the most part unaware of it. A region defines itself and exists long before it acquires regional consciousness, and now this regional consciousness is beginning to develop. India, of course, differs greatly from all Southeast Asia from the cultural and economic standpoint. But a region has different boundaries for different purposes, and from certain political and economic points of view India may usefully be treated together with Southeast Asia as a common region. This, however, is a digression. The immediate question is how far national reintegration may conflict with regional unity. But I would suggest that the question is not diversity *or* unity. The two are quite compatible. There may well be diversity *in* unity. National unity of the constituent elements, even if it emphasizes their diversity, may and should lead to greater regional unity. In their political and economic problems they have so many difficulties in common, and it is obviously wasteful of effort and money for each people to try to work out its problems by itself.

CO-OPERATION, COMPETITION, AND ISOLATION

Burma cannot afford an agricultural service that will be first class in all respects. A common agricultural service could help all the countries of the region, with Burma, for example, specializing in rice, Malaya in rubber, Java in sugar, and so on. That is only one illustration of a possible functional co-operation promoting greater unity while recognizing diversity. Already in the various conferences that have been held in connection with such matters one can see the beginning of co-operation along these lines. Perhaps the most urgent problem is that of military co-operation for the preservation of internal order. There is a need for an international police force. It should not try to direct internal political development, as, for example, by acting against communism. But it could insure that any change in the direction of either communism or capitalism should be effected peacefully and not by force. One of the most acute difficulties of these countries lies in the maintenance of internal order that was formerly maintained by foreign troops. They distrust outside help, and no outside power is likely to do much for them. But it *might* be possible to build up an international police force incorporating military units from each state that would provide a pool on which they could all draw at need without derogating from their national prestige. This, of course, is only a crude suggestion of a possible line of action. I fear it is impracticable, but I see no alternative if we are to avoid a relapse of the whole region into anarchy.

One thing is certain: that, if we cannot build up regional co-operation, we shall have to face regional competition. The rice millers of Rangoon for the last seventy years have pleaded inability to promote welfare among their coolies because of competition in the world market with Bangkok and Saigon. That did not matter much, except to the coolies. But what is going to happen when Burma, Siam, and Indochina will be competing in the market as national units with strong national interests at stake? Already there are complaints that Siam is making a better bargain for its rice than Burma is. Burma has tried to obtain the co-operation of Siam to present a common front against the buyers, but so far without success. If we cannot have co-operation, we shall have competition, leading to isolation and economic and cultural decline.

THE ECONOMIC DEMOGRAPHY OF INDIA AND PAKISTAN

By KINGSLEY DAVIS[1]

N O ONE can read the recent literature from India and Pakistan without appreciating its buoyancy and hopefulness. National independence has come to these two nations after a long struggle. Its culmination was marked by the dramatic juxtaposition of unexampled good will and unanticipated tragedy (the tactful emancipation of an empire by Lord Mountbatten, on the one hand, and the bloody uprooting of millions of people, on the other); it represented a triumph of the Asiatic against the seemingly invincible European; and it came at a time when new economic and social changes, already in ferment, were pressing for expression. The Indians and Pakistanis now find the future promising; they feel released from the past because, as independent nations, they have no past.

Disillusionment, however, seems sure. Actually, the future cannot shake off the past or hope substitute for probability. One source of sober reality lies in the demographic situation not only because population trends are important but also because they are slow and difficult to alter. The following discussion attempts the unwelcome task of describing the major population trends south of the Himalayas and assessing their influence on the future development of Pakistan and the Union of India. Where space allows, reference is also made to the rest of South Asia, because the demography of India has many features in common with the rest of the region.

TERRITORY AND PEOPLE

Including the Netherlands Indies and the Philippines on the east side and Pakistan and India on the west, with everything between, South Asia embraces a land area of approximately

1. Director, Bureau of Applied Social Research, Columbia University.

⟦ 86 ⟧

three and a half million square miles and supports a population at the present moment of about six hundred and thirty million. With only 6.7 per cent of the world's land surface, it has over a fourth (28 per cent) of the world's population. If it were an industrial area, this fact would be of little importance; but, since it is primarily agricultural and extractive, its high average density (184 per square mile, as compared with the world average of 44) raises a serious problem.[2] One of the chronic difficulties of large sections of the region is too many people in relation to developed resources.

In comparison to the rest of the region, Pakistan and India stand out not so much with regard to population density as with regard to their size. The Union of India, with approximately three hundred and fifty-five million inhabitants, is today the second most populous nation in the world. Pakistan, with about seventy-nine million, is sixth, with probably slightly more inhabitants than the Netherlands Indies; it is also the world's largest Moslem nation. Both countries are big in territory as well as in population. Pakistan has slightly less area than Texas and New Mexico combined, or about twice the area of prewar Germany. The Union of India, without Kashmir, has slightly more than a third as much territory as the United States. Kashmir itself, the territory still in dispute, is half again as large as New York State, though it has only four million inhabitants.

2. Among scholars trained in the humanities it is fashionable to ridicule demographic statistics for backward areas. Actually, in the case of South Asia, we are relatively fortunate in both the quantity and the quality of the population data. The colonial powers have considered it necessary to take censuses, so that most parts of the region have been covered by several censuses. This does not mean, of course, that our knowledge of the population is completely accurate. It never is. There are certain areas of South Asia that have either had no censuses or have been very poorly censused, such as Borneo and Indochina. And, since censuses are taken only occasionally and since obviously the whole region has never been censused at any one time, a statement about the population as of a given date must be based on intercensal or postcensal estimates for particular countries, just as would be the case in Europe or in North America. Fortunately, the areas that are most poorly enumerated are generally those that have the fewest people, so that the error which they introduce is not so great as it might at first seem to be. In the case of India a census has been taken every decade, beginning in 1871–72. Using government personnel as enumerators and building up over the years a census tradition, the administration of these enumerations has been excellent, and the results have proved extremely valuable.

But, like most of South Asia, Pakistan and the Indian Union are not so big in territory as they are in people. Embracing together only 3 per cent of the world's land surface, they support almost a fifth of its population. With less than half the land area of South Asia, they have 70 per cent of its people. They are thus disproportionately populous in comparison both to the world

TABLE 1

AREA, POPULATION, AND DENSITY, 1941 AND 1950

	AREA* (ooo's) (SQUARE MILES)	POPULATION (ooo's)		PERSONS PER SQUARE MILE	
		1941†	1950‡	1941	1950
Pakistan..........	361	70,135	79,000	194	219
West Pakistan....	307	28,169	32,000	92	104
East Pakistan.....	54	41,966	47,000	777	870
Union of India......	1,220	318,863	355,000	261	291
Kashmir.........	82	4,022	4,400	49	54
Without Kashmir.	1,138	314,841	351,000	277	308
South Asia.........	3,411	554,187	628,000	162	184
Without India or Pakistan.......	1,830	165,189	194,000	90	106

* For India and Pakistan, adapted from O. H. K. Spate, "The Partition of India and the Prospects of Pakistan," *Geographical Review*, XXXVIII (January, 1948), 17. For South Asia, *Statesman's Year-Book* (1948).

† Figures for India and Pakistan compiled from *Census of India 1941*, I (Summary), 56 ff. and 116 ff.; IV (Bengal), 44–47; VI (Punjab), 58–59; and IX (Assam), 36. In cases where districts were split by the new boundary, it was assumed that all Muslims went to Pakistan, all Hindus and Sikhs went to India, and the others were split according to the proportions of Muslims and Hindu-Sikhs in the district population. Figures for South Asia are taken primarily from census figures and estimates given in secondary sources such as the *Statesman's Year-Book* and brought up to 1950 by rough extrapolation.

‡ Estimated for India and Pakistan by assuming that the average annual growth rate prevailing in a given area between 1921 and 1941 will characterize that area between 1941 and 1950. For the rest of South Asia, the latest census figure for each country (in some cases quite recent figures) were advanced to 1950 by roughly taking account of past growth trends. When there have been many years since the last census, the estimates may be considerably in error—especially the mortality effect of World War II is not fully known.

and to South Asia, but the first disproportion is by far the greater.

As between Pakistan and India, the former is not so densely settled as India, though the difference is not great (Table 1). Pakistan, however, is a bifurcate nation, its two divisions (East and West Pakistan) being separated by more than a thousand miles of foreign territory and distinguished by differences in language, culture, and economy. Whereas West Pakistan is a predominantly dry region, heavily dependent on irrigation, East

Pakistan is an exceedingly wet region. The former grows wheat and cotton primarily, the latter rice and jute. As a consequence of the difference in climate and economy, the population density is extremely different. West Pakistan has six times the territory but only two-thirds the people that East Pakistan has. Indeed, the latter is one of the most densely settled areas of the globe. It is only slightly larger than Java and has almost as many people.[3]

The territory that is now India (excluding Kashmir) exhibited in 1941 a density of 277 per square mile. This may seem low compared to the density at the same date in England and Wales (718) or in Japan (496), but these are small countries. India's average density should be compared only with that of other large areas. For instance, the average density in India is over six times that of the United States; over twice that of China proper; about seventeen times that of prewar European Russia; over eleven times that of South Africa; and more than two and a half times that of Europe.

POPULATION GROWTH AND FUNCTIONAL DENSITY

The high average densities of India and Pakistan mean little in themselves. But, when we realize, as in the case of South Asia as a whole, that both countries are primarily agricultural, the densities take on added significance. Since in the latter case land is the primary instrument of production, a scarcity of it in relation to people spells poverty. Whereas an industrial country can support a dense population at a high level of living, an agricultural country cannot do so. Even among industrial countries, however, those with a smaller ratio of people to resources are proving more prosperous than those with a high ratio; and, although no country with over 50 per cent of its people engaged in agriculture has a high living standard, those having the most good land per capita seem to be the most prosperous—so prosperous, indeed, that they tend to climb out of the agricultural

---

3. Java's population is currently estimated at about fifty-four million, as compared with our estimate of forty-seven million for East Pakistan. Estimated densities would then be 945 for Java and 870 for East Pakistan.

class rapidly.[4] As long as an agricultural country still has a sparse population, it has today a good chance of industrializing rapidly. This can be seen in Brazil, Argentina, Australia, and New Zealand, for example. But relatively few areas in South Asia are so fortunate. Burma, which is often thought to be sparsely settled, has about 70 persons per square mile, which is half again the number in the United States (48).

Since the Indian subcontinent is one of the oldest regions of neolithic culture, its good agricultural areas have virtually all been long since put to the plow. The village type of subsistence agriculture spreads with extreme slowness, and there are still a few parts of India not yet, or only recently, penetrated, but there is evidence that India was already rather fully settled before the Christian Era.[5] Up until 1600 its population hardly grew at all, being held down by famines, warfare, and disease. After the British came, the number of people began to increase sharply. In 1871–72 the census, when corrected for areas not enumerated at the time, shows a population of approximately 255,000,000. By modern standards the growth was still not rapid, however, because mortality remained very high. However, after the influenza epidemic in 1918, the subcontinent was free from major disasters, with the result that the Indian population grew by 32,000,000 (11 per cent) between 1921 and 1931 and by 51,000,000 (13 per cent) between 1931 and 1941. This 83,000,000 increase in two decades gave the country in 1941 a total of 390,000,000, and for 1950 our estimate places the total for Pakistan and the Indian Union combined at 434,000,000, an estimate that should not be in error by more than 6,000,000.

4. An "agricultural country" is here understood to be one whose male labor force is more than 50 per cent engaged in cultivation, forestry, fishing, and herding. By this definition such a country as Denmark, for example, is not agricultural, although it is commonly thought to be. In 1945 over 65 per cent of the Danish population lived in towns, and 23 per cent lived in Copenhagen, a city of nearly a million people. In India in 1941 only 13 per cent of the population was defined as urban. If more than 50 per cent of the population is engaged in agriculture, it is a sign that the per capita yield is very low—i.e., that the standard of living cannot be high. This may be due to poor techniques and low capitalization, but it may also be due to overpopulation with respect both to land and to capital.

5. Pran Nath (*A Study in the Economic Condition of Ancient India* [London: Royal Asiatic Society, 1929], chap. v) estimates the population around 300 B.C. at between one hundred and one hundred and fifty million.

Since much of the subcontinent is dry, the huge population means great concentration in certain areas. The districts having more than the average density virtually all fall in one solid belt that begins on the irrigated plains of West Punjab, descends the Ganges Valley, comes down the eastern coast, goes around the tip of India, and ascends the western coast to the Gulf of Cambay. Here, in an area that is only 32 per cent of all India, are found 69 per cent of the people. In 1941 the Ganges Valley (as large as Germany and four times the size of Java and Madura) had an average density of 686 per square mile. In the Bengal portion it averaged 829. If the districts having a density of 500 or more are grouped together, they included nearly half the population but less than a seventh of the area of India. Those with 700 or more contained nearly a quarter of the population but only one-eighteenth of the area. Such concentration is not due primarily to cities. The results are much the same when the cities are eliminated. The high densities represent the piling-up of agriculturalists on the land. In some almost purely agricultural districts the general density rises above 1,000 per square mile. India is like Java, Egypt, Japan, and China in having large areas of extremely heavy rural concentration.

If density is measured functionally in terms of the number of farm people per square mile of cultivated land (Table 2), it can be seen that the British Indian figure (422 in 1931 and 535 in 1941) was higher than the figures for European countries having a comparable percentage of their population dependent on agriculture but lower than the figures for some other Asiatic countries. India and Pakistan therefore exhibit two basic conditions associated with extreme poverty—first, a preponderance of their people dependent on agriculture and, second, a large number of agriculturalists per square mile of cultivable land. These circumstances explain why, in an area rich in agricultural resources, millions of people are close to starvation.

EFFECTS OF POPULATION PRESSURE IN AGRICULTURE

For a rural economy some of the major consequences of an already excessive and yet increasing agricultural population are as follows: a reduction in the average size of farm unit below the point of optimum efficiency; a consequent inability to save, accumulate capital, and improve the land; a resulting failure to increase productivity per acre; an inability to use efficiently the

TABLE 2

PERSONS DEPENDENT ON AGRICULTURE PER SQUARE MILE
OF CULTIVATED LAND

	Date	Per Cent of Population Dependent on Agriculture*	Persons Dependent on Agriculture per Square Mile of Cultivated Land†
Korea‡...................	1930	79	981
Java and Madura§...........	1930	63	826
Philippine Islands‖..........	1939	70	573
Puerto Rico#................	1930	66	533
British India**...............	1931	68	422
Yugoslavia††................	1931	76	344
Rumania‡‡.................	1930	72	240
Chile§§...................	1940	38	162
Mexico‖‖.................	1930	74	88
United States##............	1930	25	48
Argentina***...............	1930	30	32

* Figures on occupation distribution are hard to standardize. Many of these are estimated in one way or another and are only roughly accurate. In many instances the percentage of all occupied males engaged in agriculture has been used, by means of a regression line, to estimate the population dependent on agriculture.

† "Cultivated land" is defined as that actually sown or lying fallow. It does not include raw pasture, forest, or land that is potentially cultivable. Again, however, standardization is difficult.

‡ *Statesman's Year-Book* (1933), p. 1074; *Résumé statistique de l'Empire du Japon* (45ᵉ année, 1931), p. 4.

§ *Indisch Verslag* (1937), Parts 1–2; *Netherlands Indian Report* (1937), II: *Statistical Abstract for the Year 1936*, pp. 221–23, 229.

‖ *Census of the Philippines* (1939), II, 53, 496, 906.

Fifteenth Census of the United States, 1930, Outlying Territories and Possessions, pp. 183, 207.

** *Census of India* (1931), I, Part II, 3, 206; India, Department of Commercial Intelligence, *Statistical Abstract for British India* (15th No. of new ser. [Delhi, 1927–37]), p. 458.

†† Yugoslavia, *Statistique générale d'état: Annuaire statistique* (1934–35), pp. 74–75; *Statistički Godišn ak* (1937), pp. 18 ff.

‡‡ *Census of Rumania* (1930), X, xcvi–ciii (estimated from number of persons *not* engaged in agriculture); Institut de Statistica Generala, *Buletinul statistic al Romaniei* (1931–32), pp. 60–63.

§§ Chile, Ministerio de Agricultura, *Almanaque* (1940), pp. 17, 310, and Anexo No. 1.

‖‖ International Institute of Agriculture, *The First World Agricultural Census* (1930), IV, 391; Mexico, Dirección General de Estadística, *Quinto censo de población* (1930), Parts 1–9, 11, 14–19, 21–22, 24–27, 29–32, Cuadro I in each part.

International Institute of Agriculture, *op. cit.*, p. 136; United States, *Census of 1930, Population*, Vol. V: *General Report on Occupations*, p. 39.

*** Argentina, Ministerio de Agricultura, *Almanaque* (1940), p. 310. Percentage dependent on agriculture estimated by writer. Total population to which percentage applied is an official estimate.

increasing number of farm people, with the result that there are underemployment and unemployment; and, finally, the development of certain rural problems, such as chronic indebtedness and elaborate subinfeudation, which help to strengthen the circle of poverty, inefficiency, and debility.

In the case of the Indian region it is possible to document certain of these effects. For instance, with respect to size of farm unit, there has been in British India a steady diminution in the number of acres per farm person. The number fell from 2.23 in 1891–92 to 1.90 in 1939–40, a 15 per cent decline. This drop in the amount of farm land per farmer would have little signifi-

TABLE 3

INDICES OF COMPARATIVE YIELDS IN SIX CROPS
VARIOUS COUNTRIES (BRITISH INDIA = 100)

	Rice	Wheat	Barley	Maize	Potatoes	Cotton
British India.......	100	100	100	100	100	100
Siam..............	116*	112*	....	....	....	....
Egypt.............	241†	....	....	....	....	500†
China.............	293†	152†	....	....	....	....
Japan.............	{256* / 277†}	180*	....			
Italy..............	{337* / 361†}	154*	....			
United Kingdom....	....	313‡	257‡	....	276‡	....
Australia..........	292‡	{116‡ / 109†}	106‡	189‡	134‡	....
Canada............	....	{141‡ / 150†}	153‡	241‡	142‡	
United States......	{155‡ / 61* / 181†}	{140‡ / 133* / 131†}	131‡	230‡	146‡	167†

* Figures indicate percentages calculated from D. Ghosh, *Pressure of Population and Economic Efficiency in India* (New Delhi: Indian Council of World Affairs, 1936), p. 29. The data on rice production refer to an average for the years 1931–32 to 1935–36, and those for wheat production to an average for the years 1924–33.

† Figures indicate percentages calculated on the basis of data given in P. C. Malhotra, "Agricultural Possibilities in India," *Indian Journal of Economics*, XXV (April, 1945), 559. Malhotra took his data from a report by W. Burns, *Technological Possibilities of Agricultural Development in India* (Lahore: Superintendent, Government Printing, 1944).

‡ Figures indicate percentages calculated on the basis of data given in Baljit Singh, *Population and Food Planning in India* (Bombay: Hind Kitabs, 1947), p. 59. The data were computed from the *Statistical Year-Book of the League of Nations 1942–44* and refer to the year 1943–44.

cance if agricultural productivity had risen correspondingly, but it did not. The statistics of yield per acre indicate that the average yield has not risen much since the turn of the century. Some of the commercial crops, such as coffee, tea, and sugar, have shown a substantial rise; but the big crops, such as rice, wheat, and cotton, have not improved. A weighted index shows a rise from 1901–2 until 1920–21, and a decline after that.

Not only has there been a failure to improve per acre yields, but it is well known that these yields are below those for most other areas, as suggested by Table 3. India's comparatively low agricultural productivity is *not* due to any natural deficiency in the land itself, for the subcontinent includes great tracts of rich alluvial soil; rather, it is due to the way the land is handled—to the low proportion of capital invested in it.[6]

The deficiency of capital investment in farming is shown in numerous ways—in the primitive techniques utilized, in the nonuse of both natural and artificial fertilizers, and in the failure to improve the breeds of plants and animals. In order to help his land maintain its fertility, the Indian farmer takes the way that requires least immediate capital but which in the long run is wasteful: he lets the land lie fallow. In 1930–31 nearly a fifth of the land under cultivation was current fallow; fields were taking a rest to regain their natural fertility.[7] Even so, there is evidence that the quality of the Indian land is deteriorating under continued use without compensatory investment. Nearly all the subcontinent has a tropical climate with alternating strong sunshine, torrential rains, and wind. This kind of climate is hard on cultivated soil.[8] Pasture land is overgrazed. Few forests are left. What saves the region from disaster is the fact that most of the erosion is taking place in the high Himalaya Mountains, the silt of which is deposited in the heavily peopled river valleys. Yet the soil is in a depleted state: "In spite of the increasing use of improved seeds, the yield per acre does not seem to improve permanently. . . . It has been a common experience that after a few years the yield per acre from improved varieties begins to decline rapidly."[9] Heavier-yielding varieties remove nutrients from the soil at a higher rate. Unless the soil is reinforced somehow, the net result is to reduce its fertility to the point where the new variety no longer yields a greater return than did the old

6. The low average yields may also be due to the inclusion of more marginal land under cultivation than in the case of many other countries, but this again is an expression of India's poverty and the tendency to use land instead of capital.

7. D. Ghosh, *Pressure of Population and Economic Efficiency in India* (New Delhi: Indian Council of World Affairs, 1936), p. 29.

8. See W. Vogt, *Road to Survival* (New York: W. Sloane Associates, 1948), pp. 225–26; and Sir Harold Glover, *Soil Erosion* ("Oxford Pamphlets on Indian Affairs," No. 23 [Bombay: Humphrey Milford, 1944]).

9. Ghosh, *op. cit.*, p. 46.

variety.[10] In short, the productivity of the Indian soil cannot be increased without investing capital in the soil itself.

With per acre productivity in a static condition, Indian agriculture cannot produce enough of a surplus to finance an exodus from agriculture. In countries that have made the fastest economic advance, a shift in the occupational structure has occurred. An increasing proportion of the people have found their living in manufacturing, transportation, merchandising, and professional services. This shift has enabled these countries, even when their exports remained agricultural, to experience a rapid growth of population without increasing the ratio of farm people to farm land. Hence there is today an inverse correlation between the density of agricultural workers on agricultural land and the per capita real income.[11] At the bottom of the scale are countries like India and Pakistan, where, without any change in the occupational structure, the farm population has grown as fast as the general population[12] and where no corresponding expansion in the total supply of cultivated land has occurred. The inevitable result is an oversupply of farmers who are only partly employed, with a consequent tendency for per capita productivity to decline. Between 1920 and 1941 in British India the population grew by 27 per cent, while the net area sown increased by only 8 per cent.[13] Some expansion of agricultural land is still possible in India and Pakistan by opening up remote areas (such as still exist in Assam) and by extending irrigation, but not at a rate that will match the growth of population. Because of deforestation, overgrazing, and waterlogging from irrigation, future losses may almost equal future gains. In the meantime the rural villages have far more farmers than they need for efficient tillage.

The elimination of the surplus agricultural population would increase the per capita product without seriously reducing the

10. Cf. Baljit Singh, *Population and Food Planning in India* (Bombay: Hind Kitabs, 1947), pp. 57–58.

11. Colin Clark, *The Economics of 1960* (London: Macmillan & Co., Ltd., 1944), chap. iv.

12. B. G. Ghate, *Changes in the Occupational Distribution of the Population* (Delhi: Manager of Publications, 1940), p. 21.

13. Much of this increase was at the expense of cultivable waste and fallow, for the total cultivable land increased by only 4 per cent.

total agricultural output. How big the surplus is depends on how much capitalization one assumes. Under present conditions of low capital investment, the surplus can be roughly estimated by assuming the average-size holding to be one conveniently tillable by a farmer and his family, using one bullock team and one plow.[14] Let us say that it is half again as great as the present holding. This would mean a one-third reduction in the population dependent on agriculture—that is, in 1941 a withdrawal of something like ninety-one million people from farms over all India. In the United States in 1940 the average per capita number of farm acres for the farming population was approximately 35, as compared with India's approximate 2. This suggests that the India-Pakistan area might, with a high degree of capitalization, do without some two hundred million of its farm population.

Since the average Indian farmer tills a plot too small to live on, he can accumulate no capital and is forced to borrow. Since his collateral is poor, he must borrow from a moneylender, who, perforce, must charge him high interest rates. The farmer borrows for nonproductive purposes—weddings, funerals, pilgrimages, litigation, and feasts—because, if he is to live socially as well as physically, he must find the money that his farm does not give him.

With a rising agricultural population on a limited area, agricultural land tends to increase in value. This means that proprietary rights become more valuable and that the possessors of these rights can get a return by letting someone else work the land. Everywhere in the Indian region there have been complaints against subinfeudation, or the multiplication of sub-tenancies. It is said that in eastern Bengal "proprietary rights are quite commonly found seven and eight deep and in some cases 12, 15 or 17."[15] In many areas the *ryot*, the "legal peasant," has been transformed into a petty landlord or middleman. In

14. The economic holding for an Indian farm family is discussed in G. B. Jathar and S. G. Beri, *Indian Economics* (5th ed.; London: Oxford University Press, 1937), pp. 217–21.

15. Radhakamal Mukerjee, "Land Tenures and Legislation," in *Economic Problems of Modern India*, I (London: Macmillan & Co., Ltd., 1939), 237–88; cf. C. G. Chevix-Trench, "The Rural Community," in Sir Edward Blunt (ed.), *Social Service in India* (London: His Majesty's Stationery Office, 1938), pp. 93–94.

zamindari areas the powerful landlord class has managed to increase its revenues from the tenants by exacting illegal rent through *nazarana* ("payment in kind"), *begar* ("payment in labor"), fines, fees, etc. It has also encouraged subletting by tenants. In spite of the exactions of the zamindars, the tenants' rights have been of sufficient value that they could sublet the land, and the subtenants could sublet it again. Nothing illustrates so clearly the bottom man's desperate necessity of finding some scrap of land on which to try to make a living.[16]

In short, the general picture in India and Pakistan is that of an oriental agricultural people long settled in its territory and exploiting that territory intensively but inefficiently. The most fertile areas are filled to capacity by peasants, who, despite the soil's richness, barely eke out a livelihood. As the rural population has grown, plots have diminished in size, underemployment has become chronic, indebtedness has gripped the cultivator, and subinfeudation has increased. The poverty of the farmer means undercapitalization, and this, in turn, means low productivity.

INDUSTRIALIZATION AND POPULATION

The agricultural conditions, for which the Indians were not chiefly responsible, represent the bootstrap by which India and Pakistan must now pull themselves out of that situation. Both countries are in much the same boat. Much has been made of Pakistan's normal food surplus, but future population growth can easily absorb any food surplus that may now exist. Eastern Bengal has long been one of India's most impoverished areas, just as the Punjab has long been one of its richest; the balance of the two does not give Pakistan a favorable point of departure. The Union of India has not been greatly changed by partition. Although it has lost part of its breadbasket, it has retained most of the industry and most of the industrial resources. Both nations must now accomplish a belated and herculean task of industrialization. They are feverishly planning for that task, are

16. Theoretically, if landlordism led to the accumulation of capital in the hands of landlords and this, in turn, were expended on agricultural improvement and industrial expansion, subinfeudation would do no economic harm. But in practice it seems to lead to neglect of the land, because the landlord is shortsightedly interested in revenue for consumption purposes and the tenant has no incentive to improve someone else's property.

making some progress, and will surely eventually succeed; but in the meantime the obstacles are many.

A puzzling historical fact about India is that it was "the first of the oriental countries to feel the impact of industrialism"[17] and yet never completed the industrial revolution, whereas another oriental country, Japan, starting later and with fewer resources, did complete it. The reasons seem to lie in the nature of British control and in the character of Indian culture. But, whatever they were, independence now finds both India and

TABLE 4

COMPOSITION OF INDIAN EXPORTS AND IMPORTS (IN PERCENTAGES)*

	BEFORE WORLD WAR I		AFTER WORLD WAR I		1940-41	
	Exports	Imports	Exports	Imports	Exports	Imports
Food, drink, and tobacco...........	29	15	21	20	22	15
Raw materials......	47	7	50	33	33	26
Manufactured articles†............	23	76	27	43	43	57
Miscellaneous.......	1	2	2	4	2	2
Total.........	100	100	100	100	100	100

* General Motors India, *Economic Survey of India* (New York, 1945), p. 115.
† Articles mainly or wholly manufactured.

Pakistan with little industry in comparison to their large populations. This is true despite the fact that, prior to partition, industrialism was gradually moving ahead.

Evidences of past industrial growth are many. Despite foreign-trade setbacks during the depression and World War II, the per capita volume of both imports and exports tended to rise. Also the character of the imports and exports was changing. Manufactured goods played an increasing part in exports, a decreasing part in imports (Table 4). There was a large increase in the importation of machinery and chemicals required by industry.[18] Industrial production itself grew faster than popula-

17. Herbert Heaton, "Industrial Revolution," *Encyclopedia of the Social Sciences* (New York: Macmillan Co., 1932), VIII, 9.
18. John Matthai, *Tariffs and Industry* ("Oxford Pamphlets on Indian Affairs," No. 20 [London: Oxford University Press, 1944]), p. 18.

tion, as did cities and literacy.[19] Between 1920–21 and 1943–44 in India as a whole (excluding Burma) the output, by weight, of cotton piece goods increased 223 per cent and of cotton yarn 152 per cent. Between 1920–21 and 1939–40 the number of textile looms (cotton, jute, and woolen mills combined) increased 66 per cent and the number of spindles 47 per cent. Iron-ore production gained more than 300 per cent after 1921. Almost any other index of economic activity, such as freight-car loadings, postal receipts, urban growth, will show the same upward trend.[20] The impetus behind industrialization is shown by the "remarkable fact that while industrial production in most countries showed a heavy decline during the period of the great depression which started in 1929, the output of the principal industries in India showed a steady and, in some cases, a marked increase.[21]

Despite the transitory character of much Indian labor in the past, there is now growing up a settled working population in manufacturing cities like Jamshedpur, Madras, Nagpur, and Ahmedabad. This new stability has facilitated the growth of skills and a modern type of vertical social mobility.[22] It also appears, though on incomplete evidence, that the habit of industrial investment is growing among the Indian people.

The evidence appears clear that industrialization has moved ahead in India. Yet no one seems satisfied with the *rate* at which it has moved. This feeling arises from three considerations. First, the urgency is great. India and Pakistan need industrialization as badly as any countries in the world, and they need it quickly. Second, the potentialities of this region for industrial development are enormous, so that the actual perform-

19. Kingsley Davis, "Demographic Fact and Policy in India," in *Demographic Studies of Selected Areas of Rapid Growth* (New York: Milbank Memorial Fund, 1944), pp. 52–53.

20. Economic Advisor, Government of India, *Statistical Summary of the Social and Economic Trends in India* (Washington, D.C.: Government of India Information Services, 1945), pp. 15–17; see also Daniel H. Buchanan, *Development of Capitalist Enterprise in India* (New York: Macmillan Co., 1934), esp. chaps. vii–xiii; and P. S. Lokanathan, *Industrialization* ("Oxford Pamphlets on Indian Affairs," No. 10 [3d ed.; Bombay: Oxford University Press, 1946]).

21. Matthai, *op. cit.*, pp. 12–13.

22. Tulsi Ram Sharma, *Location of Industries in India* (Bombay: Hind Kitabs, 1946), pp. 191–93.

ance seems tragically below what could be expected. And, third, comparison with recently industrialized countries—Japan, Russia, Australia, Argentina—suggests that India's rate has been abnormally slow.

If India's population had not grown during her relatively long period of gradual industrial growth, the economic prospects of Pakistan and the Indian Union might now be brighter. Actually, the population grew more slowly than it would have done with rapid industrialization (as comparison with industrial countries shows),[23] but its growth has borne a higher *ratio* to industrial growth than in most countries, and its period of growth has been prolonged. The same factors that retarded industrialization also kept fertility high; yet at least one of these factors— a colonial economy—also helped to reduce the mortality below what the actual industrialization would normally have reduced it to. As a consequence we find that the Union of India and, to a lesser degree, Pakistan are at the threshold of huge potential industrialization with a population possibly more crowded than that of any country of the past which subsequently achieved the industrial revolution.[24] This fact means not only that complete industrialization will be more difficult to achieve than it otherwise would have been but also that, when industrialization is achieved, it will not raise the standard of living so much as it did in the Western industrial nations.[25] How does population pressure obstruct industrialization? The question is not an easy one, but the following points seem relevant.

1. Population pressure tends to focus economic effort on consumption goods rather than in production goods. The swollen masses are so deprived of immediate necessities that sheer maintenance becomes the dominant aim. As bare necessities are met, the population continues to grow and to require more necessi-

23. Davis, "Demographic Fact and Policy in India," pp. 37–39.

24. Japan is the only possible exception. At the beginning of its industrial expansion (say 1870) Japan, with approximately thirty-five million, had a density of about 235 per square mile. This is less than that in the Indian Union today, but the ratio of farm population to agricultural land was probably greater than in the latter country.

25. Again Japan affords an illustration. She started with an initial handicap of high population density and continued to be plagued by population growth. As a consequence, she had to use more ingenuity and control than Western countries had used in bringing about industrialization, and her people got less out of it.

ties. This makes difficult the accumulation of an economic surplus for investment in long-run heavy industries, even though ultimately the heavy industries, if installed, would yield an enormously increased output of consumer goods. One concrete expression of this difficulty, as already noted, is that the ordinary individual is so near the subsistence point that he cannot save but must borrow for consumption purposes. Even when he can save, he often prefers a high liquidity to a modest return through investment. The business firm finds the demand for food and clothing so insistent that there is greater profit in immediately satisfying this demand with inefficient equipment than in making long-run expenditures on basic equipment. Finally, the government feels the same pressure; if democratic, it cannot ignore the sustenance needs of its citizens in order to build a heavy industry for the future.

2. In a primarily agricultural country the means for industrialization have to be paid for by agriculture. An excess population, as we have seen, leads to agricultural inefficiency by producing underemployment, unproductive indebtedness, small holdings, low capitalization, subinfeudation, and low productivity. Being caught in this vicious circle, the crowded farm population is in no condition to furnish the economic surplus for building an industrial system, despite the fact that this system would help the farm situation more than anything else.

3. Rural population pressure means that most of the land is devoted to food crops for sustenance rather than to commercial crops for the accumulation of an investment surplus. The country thus has few exports to pay for the importation of machinery, technicians, and other necessities of heavy industry. Also, it cannot compete successfully in world markets with other agricultural countries where the amount of land, equipment, and developed technique is much greater per worker. The situation reaches its ultimate futility when the food requirements become so great that the agricultural country becomes an importer of agricultural produce—that is, when the total value of agricultural imports exceeds the total value of agricultural exports. This condition cannot be reached except through charity from the rest of the world. The Union of India has by no means

reached this point and Pakistan certainly not, but the Union is an importer of food, which is a danger signal unless industrialization is hastened.

4. In an overpopulated country labor is thought to be cheaper than machinery. "The results for the economy as a whole are poor; the low amount of capital employed per labourer reduces output per head and lowers national income, and the low wage, in its turn, reduces the efficiency of the worker. . . ."[26] Mechanization is apparently fostered when labor is dear—e.g., under frontier conditions, as in the United States, Argentina, and Australia—not when labor is plentiful.

5. A population whose growth is due to high fertility and a high but somewhat lower death rate has several disadvantages. First, it wastes much energy in reproduction, because its women produce millions of babies each year who will die before reaching a productive age. Second, the high mortality of such a population—high, but not high enough to cancel the traditional birth rate—is necessarily associated with excessive morbidity, which tends to reduce the productivity per worker. And, finally, as a result of both the high birth rate and the high death rate, this type of population is characterized by an unusual burden of young-age dependency. Comparing the 1941 age distribution of India (estimated on the basis of returns from certain provinces and states) with that of the United States for 1940, we discover the following fact: Although the total Indian population was three times that of the United States, it had only the same number of people aged sixty-five and over, and approximately six times as many children up to four years of age.[27] The net result was that only 47 per cent of the Indian people were in the most productive period of life (twenty to sixty), whereas 55 per cent of the American people were in it. In the absence of a high living standard, an excessive proportion in the young ages means child labor, poor education, and less economic efficiency.

The preceding five paragraphs summarize what appear to be the main ways in which heavy density combined with poten-

26. Ghosh, *op. cit.*, p. 40.
27. This was true in spite of the fact that there is much more underenumeration of children in India than in the United States.

tially rapid population growth impedes industrialization.[28] Such a situation is not confined to India and Pakistan alone but is characteristic of several other areas as well. Particularly, there is a general drift in this direction in all South Asia, primarily because this area has so long had a colonial economy. Our argument is not intended, however, to claim that population alone impedes industrialization. The demographic aspect is only one variable in a complex equilibrium—it is as much a consequence as a cause—nor is the argument intended to suggest that industrialization in India, Pakistan, or the rest of South Asia is impossible. In the case of India and Pakistan we have already cited evidence that industrialization is on the way. Such industrialization will come, however, not *because* of India's dense and growing population but *in spite* of it. In fact, the question is not so much whether or not India and Pakistan will eventually become industrialized as it is how soon. The more quickly industrialization comes, the greater will be its long-run benefit. Even at highest speed it will probably tend to double the population. At a slower pace, it might triple the population. How fast the process of modernization can be accelerated depends on the role of India and Pakistan in the world economy, on the ruthlessness and effectiveness of the economic controls, and on the absence of political strife. It seems doubtful that the industrial revolution can be accomplished in time to stave off a population growth that will make the fruits of industrialism less beneficial than would otherwise be the case.

POPULATION POLICY

Any attempt to compensate indefinitely for perpetual population increase by using economic measures alone is bound to fail, because human beings live in a finite world. Unless the eco-

---

28. A redundant and growing population is sometimes alleged to aid industrialization for two reasons: (*a*) it provides an abundance of cheap labor to man new industrial enterprises, and (*b*) it affords a large and expanding internal market that encourages heavy investment and therefore an increasing tempo of economic activity. While there is probably some validity in these contentions, it is nevertheless worth noting with reference to the first argument that a cheap labor supply is usually an inefficient one and, with reference to the second argument, that in a region such as the Indian subcontinent the growth of population is aggravating an already unfavorable situation. It tends to make the business outlook pessimistic rather than optimistic.

nomic measures eventually cause the growth of population to decline—that is, unless they eventually have a demographic effect—they will in the long run prove incapable of raising the level of living.

The question naturally arises as to whether a faster and greater rise in the level of living would be achieved if, along with economic measures, direct demographic policies were also adopted. In other words, should not a program of rapid industrialization be also accompanied by other measures designed to reduce the rate of population growth that normally accompanies industrialization?

In this matter there seem to be only two possibilities, neither of which will be adopted or pushed to the point of effectiveness. One is mass emigration, which is not feasible in the modern world. The other is birth control, which no government has yet found the courage to pursue in an all-out and effective manner. Ideally, in order to maximize real income, these demographic policies would be pursued along with rapid industrialization. Emigration would be encouraged with a view to losing as little as possible in terms of skills and capital and gaining as much as possible in terms of remittances. Birth control would be diffused with the help of films, radio, ambulatory clinics, and free services and materials; aided by research on both techniques of contraception and methods of mass persuasion; and linked clearly to the public health and child-welfare movements.

The skilful and vigorous pursuit of all three major measures— rapid industrialization, strategic emigration, and family limitation—would probably mean that the demographic transition would be accomplished earlier than otherwise and thus make possible a higher standard of living for future generations.

Ironically, the one measure that has the best chance of being pushed is rapid industrialization, but not for demographic reasons. Both Pakistan and India will try hard to improve their economies without encouraging lower fertility or greater emigration. The irony comes from the fact that, although economic change seems more acceptable than birth-control measures because it interferes less with the mores, the truth is that any policy that would rapidly industrialize Pakistan and India would be a far greater shock to the basic social institutions than would any policy that attacked fertility directly. Fast industrialization would sweep both the *ryot* and the *zamindar* from their moorings, transforming them into workers in a collectivized, mechanized agriculture utterly foreign to their habits. The people would not undergo this transformation willingly. Judged by events in Russia, the cost of this transformation and of resistance to it would be tremendous in loss of human lives, livestock, and food production. Also, the existing industrial and business organization, with its vested interests, would have to be completely overhauled. Production schedules, prices, profits, wages, raw materials, location of industries, flow of capital, and mobility of labor would all have to be controlled. How otherwise could a retarded agricultural region be *rapidly* industrialized?

When, therefore, it is said that rapid industrialization is an easier policy than direct birth control, all that is meant is that the *statement of policy* is easier. It cannot mean that the *execution* is easier. In the execution of the policy, a program of forced industrialization would violate far more taboos and arouse more resistance than would the dissemination of birth-control education and propaganda. This suggests that a good bit of the talk about rapid industrialization is just talk. It sounds good and elicits a favorable reaction. But whether enough official action will be taken to speed the industrial process beyond what ordinary capitalistic laissez faire would bring is a moot question.

It seems likely that the two countries will eventually succeed in industrializing; but, because the obstacles are so great (including excessive population), they may not succeed until they have established totalitarian regimes, acquired almost completely planned economies, and experienced sharp temporary rises in mortality. After the economic revolution, be it fast or slow, the conditions of life for the individual should, as in Europe, North America, Australia, and Japan, be of such type as to give a powerful personal incentive for limiting births. A modern demographic balance should then be achieved. The ultimate population will likely be much larger than it would have been had a full-scale population policy been carried out in the first place.

Thus the effect of a full population policy would be not to prevent perpetual population growth (such growth is impossible anyway) but to balance the demographic books at an earlier time. Industrialization does not everywhere yield the same standard of living. The contrast between Japan and Europe, between Europe and America, suggests that real income in industrial countries is strongly influenced by the point at which demographic growth is stabilized with reference to resources. Even if the whole world becomes industrial, the countries with excessive numbers will still be penalized.

In short, if we look candidly at the probable future, we must admit that the demographic situation in Pakistan and India will get worse before it gets better. The current discrepancy between births and deaths which is causing the rapid population growth is artificial. Eventually, the birth rate must drop or the death rate rise. Strife, famine, and epidemic disease are an ever present threat in the Indian peninsula. They are capable of sending mortality suddenly back to its premodern level. With a high density in relation to developed resources and with the virtual impossibility of solving the problem quickly by sheer economic measures or by emigration, the two countries can achieve the maximum standard of living and national strength which their situation allows only if they control fertility by a specific program in that direction. The fact that they probably will not do this does not detract from its advisability. Their unwillingness will not necessarily result in perpetual poverty for their citizens or in absolute catastrophe; but it will result in greater poverty than would otherwise be the case.

What is said here about Pakistan and India applies substantially to the rest of South Asia, but with one important qualification. Omitting Java, the rest of the area has not yet reached the degree of population pressure that the Indian subcontinent is under. The poverty of these other areas is due primarily to other causes. It follows that, if extremely effective economic measures are undertaken soon enough, the population factor may be controlled before it becomes a formidable cause of stagnation in its own right. India, Pakistan, and Java should serve as warnings of what is in store for the rest of the region if a policy of drifting agriculturalism is pursued. Fortunately, the end of colonialism in the region may speed a change from such drifting agriculturalism, but perhaps not without political and economic disturbances of shocking dimensions.

THE RESOURCE PATTERN OF SOUTHEAST ASIA

By KARL J. PELZER[1]

SOUTHEAST ASIA has a predominantly agricultural economy. Industrialization is still in its infancy, and mining industries are not important enough to alter the agricultural character of the region, even in countries like Malaya, Indonesia, and the Philippines. Before World War II, Southeast Asia produced almost all the world's rubber, abaca, kapok, pepper, teak, and cinchona; at least three-fourths the tapioca and coconut products; over half the palm oil; one-third the sisal, plus a substantial share of cane sugar, tobacco, tea, spices, natural resins, gums, essential oils; and such minerals as tin, iron ore, chrome, manganese, and petroleum.

Despite the fact that Southeast Asia is one of the key economic regions of the tropics and serves as a source of both agricultural and mineral raw materials, greatly in demand in the highly industrialized countries of the mid-latitudes, the decisive characteristic and the most pressing problem of the region is poverty. This characteristic Southeast Asia shares with many underdeveloped areas in the world. It is poverty which is largely responsible for the tension and unrest that we observe in Southeast Asia today, in both independent and dependent countries. Poverty manifests itself in a great many ways, such as extremely low average income, widespread tenancy, large-scale rural indebtedness, and low nutritional standards, which cause poor health and low resistance to disease.

An analysis of the resource pattern and the agrarian structure of Southeast Asia will throw light on the causes of this poverty. It is not the fault of one particular racial or social group or of a single political or economic institution. A great many cultural, economic, and environmental factors play their part.

1. Associate professor of geography, Yale University.

Whereas during the sixteenth, seventeenth, and eighteenth centuries the various European nations active in Southeast Asia had, on the whole, limited themselves to trading and the acquisition of high-priced nonbulky commodities, such as spices, the economic policy of the nineteenth century called for large quantities of bulky goods, such as sugar, fibers, oil seeds, coffee, and copra. Since the peasantry of Southeast Asia, almost without exception, raised only subsistence crops and had only limited surpluses, it became necessary for the colonial powers to increase agricultural production. This was done in two ways: (*a*) through the application of pressure on the peasantry to produce for export and (*b*) through the development of large-scale plantation agriculture.

From 1830 to 1870 the peasants of Java were forced to cultivate crops and turn them over to the government in order to meet their tax obligations. In other areas the introduction of taxation to be paid in money forced the peasantry to raise crops for sale. In one way or another the political and economic penetration of Southeast Asia during the nineteenth and twentieth centuries replaced the traditional subsistence and barter economy by a money economy. This was, of course, a slow process that began in different places at different times. But as various regions became linked with the outside world, people gave up the old pattern of raising crops only for family consumption and began to cultivate export crops. In some instances this meant that they increased the production of traditional food crops, for example, rice or coconuts; in other instances they began to cultivate crops that had been introduced by the Europeans. However, the basic pattern of production remained the same as before: little or nothing was done to evolve new and improved types of agricultural implements suited for small holdings; the size of the agricultural units was not increased; nor did the yields increase generally. On the contrary, in the densely populated regions the farm units tended to shrink in size and the fertility to decline. The change from a subsistence to a money economy found the peasantry unprepared to make the necessary technical and psychological adjustments to cope with the new situation or to benefit from it. It is true that in Indonesia and

Malaya in particular the peasantry was engaged in the cultivation of new crops for export; but, since their landholdings were so small, they could often do this only by reducing the area allocated to subsistence crops and by using the proceeds from the sale of export crops for the purchase of food that had to be imported. This proved at times to be extremely profitable, but it also exposed the peasants to the great price fluctuations that characterize world trade. On the whole, however, we can say that one of the chief reasons for the backwardness of the native agricultural economy of Southeast Asia is that it still has the tools, cultivation practices, and small farm units of the days of the closed subsistence economy. Where would we in the mid-latitudes be if we tried to carry on the type of agriculture that was practiced in the sixteenth and seventeenth centuries?

The transition from a subsistence to a money economy brought into the affected areas a new group of people, the traders. Almost without exception the retail traders and middlemen of Southeast Asia are either Chinese or Indians. The Indians dominate Burma, while the Chinese control the rural trade in Malaya, Siam, Indonesia, and the Philippines. Almost invariably the Indian or Chinese traders act also as moneylenders. During the agricultural year they make loans to peasants at extremely high interest rates, which may run to as much as 50 or 60 per cent, and then collect the debt plus interest by buying the crop at harvest time. It is to the advantage of the trader to extend unreasonable credits—preferably not for productive purposes but for the purchase of nonessential goods—in order to tie the peasant so that he has no bargaining power at harvest time. A slump in prices, a bad harvest, or some other event over which the peasant has no control causes hopeless indebtedness and loss of the land which had been pledged as security, and it reduces the peasant-owner to a tenant.

Even when a peasant wishes to obtain credit for productive purposes, he is forced in most countries to turn to a usurer because of the lack of rural credit institutions. No city bank will give him a loan because he is too poor a risk, his productive capacity is too small, and often he has no title to his land. He is caught in a vicious circle—he who needs aid most urgently in the form of credit at reasonable rates of interest, say 8–10 per cent, has to pay the excessive rates that he cannot afford, and he gets hopelessly in debt to a person who is of a different racial stock and may not speak his language. No wonder that there exists so much tension between the rural masses of Southeast Asia and the foreign middlemen from either India or China. The spread of a money economy, brought about by the economic demands of the metropolitan powers without the development of adequate credit institutions and usually without legal restrictions to curtail the predatory activities of the middlemen, caused untold harm and suffering throughout Southeast Asia, bringing in its wake widespread liquidation of peasant holdings and creating the tenancy problem, which has become extremely serious in many parts of our area.

I am, of course, aware of the fact that such practices as the pledging of land as security, followed by the loss of land and the necessity of working as a sharecropper, were recognized by the customary law of pre-European days, but such arrangements were the exception rather than the rule. A peasant who has lost his land and has to eke out a living as a sharecropper is more easily exploited than one who still owns the land that he tills.

The Philippines is one of the few areas of Southeast Asia where tenancy on a large scale preceded the growth of a money economy and did not result from foreclosure proceedings against a heavily indebted peasantry but from the Spanish agrarian policy of creating large landed estates.

It is frequently overlooked that the average agricultural yields of Southeast Asia are very low compared with the yields of other countries. During the period from 1934 to 1938, 62 quintals of paddy, or rough rice, per hectare were harvested in Spain, 53 quintals in Italy, and 36 quintals in Japan, compared with only 15 quintals in Java, 14 in Siam and Burma, 12 in Indochina, and 11 in the Philippines. These striking differences are due primarily to the intensive use of fertilizer and of improved varieties of rice in Spain, Italy, and Japan. The peasantry of Southeast Asia uses insufficient quantities of animal and green manure and almost no commercial fertilizer and usually plants a poor quality of seed. Still more striking would be the differences were we to compare the production of rice per man-hour in Italy, Spain, or the United States, on the one hand, with that of the Southeast Asian countries, on the other. The small holdings so characteristic of Southeast Asia—split up into tiny parcels, tilled by hand or at the most with simple tools pulled by draft animals—require a great deal of human labor and produce such low yields that any other result than poverty should surprise us.

Such practices as transplanting rice and harvesting rice by hand with a sickle or even with a small knife and cutting one stalk at a time demand large quantities of labor during brief periods, while most of the time only a small part of the population is actually usefully employed. Where double cropping is feasible, underemployment is not so pronounced as in areas where only one crop is raised each year.

The demand for a large labor force during harvest time is strongly felt in countries where we have service industries or factories and mines, since a large percentage of the laborers will leave their jobs and return to the rural districts to help their relatives with the harvest and to participate in the festive period that follows. This pattern presents quite a problem for the management of industry.

The creation of large-scale plantation agriculture was the second method used by Westerners to increase the production of tropical crops in Southeast Asia. Indonesia, Malaya, and, on a much smaller scale, Indochina proved attractive to Western and other foreign capital. As a result, at the outbreak of the war Malaya, Indonesia, and Indochina had large plantation industries which employed hundreds of thousands of wage laborers, most of whom were recruited at some considerable distance from the plantation areas and could be sent back to the native villages whenever their services were no longer needed. The structure of the haciendas in the Philippines, on the other hand, differs from that of the plantations found in Malaya, Indonesia, and Indochina because of a different historical background. The haciendas created by the Spaniards consist of conglomerations of small tenant-farm units worked by the descendants of the original owners of the land. The American administration prevented the growth of the plantation system in the Philippines by placing severe restrictions on the amount of public land which could be acquired by individuals or companies. The lack of a sizable rubber industry in the Philippines, for example, is to be attributed to legal restrictions. Firestone, U.S. Rubber, and Goodyear could not obtain the amount of land they wanted for their plantations, so they had to turn from Mindanao to Liberia, Malaya, and Indonesia.[2]

Many features of the plantation industry in Indonesia can be explained only as results of the agrarian legislation that was developed in the second half of the nineteenth century. This legislation made it impossible for non-Indonesians to acquire land for agricultural purposes except under lease arrangements. No plantation owns the land that it is working. Wet-rice land owned by Indonesians could be leased only for brief periods by foreign planters. The additional rule that the planter could not cultivate more than one-third of the land leased from a village and, furthermore, was not permitted to use the same land twice in succession forced the sugar plantations to intensify their operations to such a degree that Java surpassed all other cane-sugar-producing areas of the world in yield per acre. The planters were forced to band together to finance experiment stations in order to breed better cane varieties, since the law forbade them to raise ratoon cane. The necessity of planting sugar cane anew every year increased their costs of production, and for this the planters of Java were able to compensate by higher yields. Here again we have an example of the effectiveness of legal restrictions on agriculture. It would be completely misleading to attribute the high yields of cane sugar only, or even primarily, to the fertility of Java's soil or to the climate of the island. The political climate can be more decisive for an agricultural industry than the physical environment.[3]

The lack of a large plantation industry in Siam is due mainly

2. In 1928 Goodyear did, however, acquire the amount of public land permitted by the Philippine land laws and used this small plantation primarily as a repository for high-yielding clones outside the jurisdiction of the Dutch and British colonial governments—a piece of foresight which proved extremely valuable in the 1930's, when the exportation of rubber clones from countries participating in the International Rubber Restriction scheme became unlawful.

3. A future Indonesian-dominated government of the United States of Indonesia has the legal possibility of either reducing or evicting the plantation industry, should this seem desirable, by not renewing the leases.

to Siam's independent political status rather than to geographical factors. Foreign capital preferred the political climate of Malaya and Indonesia to that of Siam, where the government seemed less stable and predictable.

In 1940 Indonesia, the largest and physically most varied country of Southeast Asia, had the most diversified and efficient plantation industry of Southeast Asia or of the tropics as a whole. This industry, almost entirely owned and controlled by non-Indonesian entrepreneurs, shared with the Indonesian peasants in the production of the large quantities of export crops. A comparison of the two—the plantation industry and peasant export agriculture—is revealing and gives clues as to the direction in which economic development may move in the future. The plantation industry was responsible for the total production of centrifugal sugar, sisal, and palm oil in Indonesia, whereas such commodities as pepper and copra are practically exclusively raised on small peasant farms. Capital requirements for the processing and preparation of the product prior to export is the key to the understanding of this division. The processing of sugar cane into unrefined or refined white sugar, for example, is such a complex process and requires such an expensive industrial plant that centrifugal sugar will never be processed by small peasants. The processing of coconut into copra is so simple and requires so little capital that this industry is perfectly suited to peasant communities. In between these two extremes lies a number of crops which can be raised and processed either by plantations on a large scale or by individual peasants on a small scale because the processing techniques are simple and do not involve costly equipment and the supervision of a staff of technicians and scientists. Rubber offers the best illustration. The industry got its start in Southeast Asia as a plantation industry, but in the 1920's and 1930's the cumulative effect of the rubber production of literally hundreds of thousands of small Asian rubber growers presented the planters with a serious problem. Had it not been for the International Rubber Restriction Agreement of 1934, there can be little doubt that Asian peasant producers would have further increased their share of the world's output of natural rubber at the cost of the plantation industry. P. T. Bauer has presented a large body of evidence showing that the restriction scheme favored the planters and was definitely unfavorable to Asiatic peasants, with the result that the trend toward natural rubber's becoming more and more a peasant crop was stopped.[4]

The tea industry of Java proves that the Western entrepreneur and the Asian peasant can work together and divide the industry so that the peasant raises the crop and the Western entrepreneur then processes it in his factory. The pineapple industry provides another example, this time from the Western Hemisphere. The Hawaiian Pineapple Company recently erected a cannery near Vera Cruz, Mexico. The company does not raise the pineapples because the agrarian laws of Mexico prevent it from owning land; instead, the company buys the pineapples from the Mexican growers.

A general introduction of such a division of labor wherever possible may do a great deal to reduce the tension in Southeast Asia and to assure its peasants a greater income. It would be in the interest of the factories to aid the growers by supplying them with technical guidance and credit for the purchase of fertilizer.

In its one hundred and fifty million people Southeast Asia possesses a very large potential resource. At present the efficiency of these people is low. But that no inherent factors are involved in this inefficiency is brought out by the performance of Indonesians, Filipinos, and members of other ethnic groups of the area who have received adequate education and technical training. The efficiency is so low because the people are poorly educated, poorly nourished, and often weakened by chronic disease. Their tools, production techniques, and farm units may have been perfectly adequate for a subsistence economy, but they are entirely inadequate for a modern economy. Instead of benefiting from the commercialization of agriculture, the people are too often the victims of exploitation by middlemen, who profit more from the export of agricultural commodities than do the producers.

The strength of Southeast Asia lies mainly in its agricultural

4. *The Rubber Industry: A Study in Competition and Monopoly* (Cambridge: Harvard University Press, 1948), and *Report on a Visit to the Rubber Growing Small-holdings of Malaya* ("Colonial Research Publications," No. 1 [London, 1948]).

resources, which, however, are at present only partly utilized. Extensive areas which are arable are still awaiting the pioneer. The productivity of the cultivated land can be greatly increased through the application of the results of scientific agricultural research in the form of improved and disease-resistant seeds and in the form of proper fertilization and improved cultivation. Such an intensification of agriculture leading to greater production per unit of land and unit of manpower would be far more profitable than an attempt to raise production by a further increase in the number of man-hours devoted to the tillage of each unit of land.

The history of commercial agriculture in the tropics shows that this industry is unstable and subject to sudden declines and shifts which may be brought about either by natural causes, such as plant disease, or cultural forces, such as political changes, competition from other parts of the tropics, or the development of a synthetic product. At this moment the agricultural economy of Southeast Asia is about to suffer a severe setback through the loss of its practical monopoly on natural rubber.

Tree crops like rubber are of great value in tropical areas of high rainfall and relatively low soil fertility and have many advantages over annual crops, because trees protect the soil against excessive heat, heavy rains, and accelerated erosion, provided that they are not planted too far apart and provided that the spaces between the trees are covered with eguminous or other cover crops. The decay of fallen leaves prevents an exhaustion of the humus content in the topsoil. Thus, from an ecological point of view, tree crops are far better than annual crops, since the latter require repeated cultivation.

The decline of the market for natural rubber will therefore be a serious blow to Southeast Asia, but such a development could be offset by the creation of an integrated forest industry[5] that would make full use of the cellulose and lignin, which are produced by trees of the tropics at a faster rate than, for example, by the southern pine forests of the United States. Timber, wood

5. "Integration of Forest Industries," *Unasylva*, II, No. 3 (May–June, 1948), 120–21.

pulp, cellulose, plastics, and all the other materials that can be extracted by a modern integrated forest industry can offer a more diversified economic basis than can rubber. It would be possible to create pure stands of commercially valuable, fast-growing trees. After all, the extensive rubber forests grew up in areas once covered by the tropical rain forest with its hundreds of different species—a nightmare to the forester and until now a stumbling block to the wood chemist, who has not yet devised a means of feeding many different kinds of trees into the pulp mill at the same time.

Fortunately, Southeast Asia on the whole does not have the population problem that confronts India. Certain parts of Southeast Asia, such as Java, Tonkin, central Luzon, and Cebu, suffer from high population pressure; but Indonesia, Viet-Nam, and the Philippines possess a considerable acreage of unutilized arable land, and there is room for expansion and for the creation of new farming communities on the pioneer fringe.

Agricultural colonization alone, however, is not enough. What Southeast Asia needs is a multiple attack on the enemy, poverty, through fuller utilization of natural and human resources and through the introduction of such measures as agrarian reforms where required. Only if agricultural colonization goes hand in hand with agrarian reform, agricultural intensification, and industrialization can we expect a real improvement. There is no single solution. Agrarian reform by itself is not enough, since it cannot add new land or reduce population pressure. Even if the Philippine government were to make every tenant in central Luzon an owner of the land he now tills as a share-cropper, poverty would not be eliminated, since the population density of the central plains of Luzon is too high to make the farms large enough. Furthermore, unless the laws of inheritance should be changed within one or two generations, the farms will be subdivided and will shrink to a size to which a *haciendero* would never reduce the tenant farms. But if an agrarian reform should go hand in hand with agricultural pioneering and industrialization to drain off the surplus rural population, then the farm units could be increased in size so as to permit full utilization of the remaining rural manpower and the application of more efficient production methods. Elspeth Huxley has said that the African woman wielding the hoe must give way to the African man cultivating the land with tractor-drawn machinery, in order to increase the productivity of the African tropics. Similar changes are needed in Southeast Asia. They will not come overnight and will not come without aid from the outside—aid in the form of technical guidance and assistance of the type that President Truman called for in his Inaugural Address in January, 1949.

Only a "bold new program" will bring about a diversification and intensification of the economy and a better utilization of the human and natural resources for the benefit of the peoples of Southeast Asia. Only a "bold new program" will end poverty and create the economic and political atmosphere in which communism cannot flourish.

THE POSTWAR PATTERN OF TRADE

By Henry Brodie[1]

THE extensive war damages, postwar economic maladjustments, and internal political disturbances that afflict most countries of South Asia in varying degrees have brought about significant changes in the levels and direction of the foreign trade of the area as compared with that before the war. The usual pattern of South Asia's foreign commerce has been affected further by Japan's reduced economic position in the Far East and to a lesser extent by the civil war in China. An additional element making for change has been the impaired economic capacity of Continental Europe, which has cut South Asia off from traditional and important sources of imports. This paper attempts to examine statistically the over-all effects of these factors on South Asia's foreign trade.

For the purposes of this analysis South Asia's foreign trade is compared for 1947 and 1936, in value terms. Reasonably accurate statistics for 1948 are as yet available for only a few South Asian countries. Even the 1947 official trade returns for some countries are incomplete, and the gaps had to be filled in by estimates. Accordingly, certain of the 1947 statistics presented in this study are only approximately correct. The year 1936 was selected as a fairly representative prewar year. By that time South Asia's trade had achieved a considerable measure of recovery from the depression lows and had more or less adjusted itself to the widespread currency depreciation of the 1930's, as well as to the various systems of empire preferences that were introduced during the first half of the decade.

MAGNITUDE OF SOUTH ASIA'S FOREIGN TRADE

As a result of inflated prices, South Asia's total foreign trade in 1947 of $6.5 billion was more than twice the 1936 figure[2] (see

1. Special assistant to the chief, Division of Research for Far East, Department of State.

2. The difference between the 1947 and 1936 values is magnified by the fact that in 1936 India and Burma were treated as a single trading unit.

Table 4). Imports of $3.6 billion in 1947 represented almost three times the value of imports in 1936, while exports of $2.9 billion were one and one-half times the prewar figure. India, to an even greater degree than before the war, dominated the trade of the region, accounting for more than 40 per cent of the total. Malaya, the Philippines, and Ceylon followed India in that order of importance. Indonesia, which before the war had only slightly less trade than Malaya, ranked below Ceylon in 1947.

TABLE 1

EXPORTS AND IMPORTS OF SOUTH ASIA, 1947 AND 1936

COUNTRY	EXPORTS*		IMPORTS†	
	Value (in $1,000,000 U.S.)	Percentage of 1936 Exports	Value (in $1,000,000 U.S.)	Percentage of 1936 Imports
Philippines........	79	54	169	167
Indonesia.........	93	29	96	52
India............	349 }	51	483 }	116
Burma...........	34 }		54 }	
Ceylon...........	115	122	96	119
Malaya...........	340	92	213	72
Siam............	42	50	23	46
Indochina........	26	25	46	73
Total........	1,096	....	1,180	....

* Derived by deflating 1947 export values by a unit-value index of export prices computed for each country, except India, and designed to measure the relative price changes of its principal exports from 1936 to 1947. For India the official index of the unit value of exports was used. Individual price relatives used in computing the indices were weighted by 1947 quantities. Accordingly, to the extent that the composition of exports of some South Asian countries in 1947 differs from what it was in 1936, the indices do not accurately measure over-all changes in the value of their exports.

† Derived by deflating 1947 import values for each country by the increase in India's unit-value index of import prices between 1936 and 1947. India is the only South Asian country that computes a unit-value import index, and it is believed that the index is reasonably representative for other countries of the area. Although food, which has had a relatively greater increase in price than most other imports except textiles, represented a greater proportion of India's imports in 1947 than of Burma's, Siam's, or Indochina's, this distortion is probably offset by the fact that the latter three countries had a larger proportion of textile imports than India. Textiles experienced roughly the same relative price rises as those of foodstuffs between 1947 and 1936.

In real terms, however, South Asia's foreign trade in 1947 was substantially less than before the war. As a rough approximation, it is estimated that the value of the area's 1947 trade expressed in 1936 prices was 70 per cent of the 1936 figure. Exports were off more sharply than imports, equaling 58 per cent of the prewar amount when expressed in 1936 prices. Imports in 1936 prices were 95 per cent of the prewar figure. Estimated exports and imports of individual countries in 1947, expressed in 1936 prices, and the percentages that these estimates represent of the prewar amounts are presented in Table 1.

From the figures in Table 1 it is apparent that, with the exception of Ceylon and Malaya, all South Asian countries had considerably smaller quantities of exports in 1947 than in 1936. In the case of imports, only the Philippines, India (including Burma), and Ceylon showed larger volumes in 1947 than in 1936.

In 1947 South Asia had an over-all trade deficit of $675,000,-000, in contrast to an export surplus of roughly the same amount in 1936. Much of the deficit was with the United States. Only Siam showed a positive balance of trade. Before the war all South Asian countries traditionally exported more than they imported. Their trade surpluses provided the means whereby they financed their invisible obligations to the metropolitan powers. In 1947 the Philippines financed its trade deficit out of United States aid and other payments, while the other South Asian countries met their deficits by drawing on foreign-exchange holdings or by means of contributions from the western European metropolitan countries.

GEOGRAPHIC DISTRIBUTION OF TRADE

The geographic pattern of South Asia's foreign trade in 1947 shows marked differences from the prewar pattern. These differences are reflected primarily in South Asia's trade with other areas rather than in trade among South Asian countries themselves. As before the war, trade within South Asia represented only a small percentage of the total trade of the region: 16 per cent in 1947, as against 17.5 per cent in 1936. In 1947, 18 per cent of South Asia's exports and 15 per cent of its imports were intra-regional, as compared with 13 and 25 per cent, respectively, in 1936. Even these percentages exaggerate the importance of trade among South Asian countries because they include considerable entrepôt trade, particularly in rubber and tin through Malaya. It is apparent, therefore, that South Asia is not an integrated economic region in the same sense as the European Recovery Program countries, which before the war conducted 44 per cent of their foreign trade among themselves.

The percentages of their total trade that the individual countries conducted with other countries of South Asia in 1947 and in 1936 are exhibited in Table 2.

The percentages that exports with South Asia constituted of total exports for individual countries in 1947 ranged from a low of 5 per cent in the case of Ceylon to a high of 77 per cent for Burma. Countries with high ratios either were large rice exporters, such as Burma or Siam, or else had substantial re-exports through Malaya, like Indonesia. The percentages that imports within South Asia constituted of total imports for in-

TABLE 2

TRADE OF SOUTH ASIAN COUNTRIES WITH ONE ANOTHER

1947 AND 1936

COUNTRY	EXPORTS TO OTHER COUNTRIES OF SOUTH ASIA AS A PERCENTAGE OF TOTAL EXPORTS		IMPORTS FROM OTHER COUNTRIES OF SOUTH ASIA AS A PERCENTAGE OF TOTAL IMPORTS	
	1947	1936	1947	1936
Philippines........	6	1	2	6
Indonesia........	47	16	12	16
India............	9 }	8	7 }	6
Burma..........	77 }		37 }	
Ceylon..........	5	6	21	47
Malaya..........	19	15	38	62
Siam............	51	63	18	30
Indochina........	17	11	4	14

dividual countries in 1947 varied from a low of 2 per cent for the Philippines to 38 per cent for Malaya. The high ratio for Malaya reflected large imports for re-export. The percentages for Burma and Ceylon were primarily a result of the fairly considerable imports of these countries from India.

The relatively limited amount of intra-regional trade results from the fact that exports of all countries in the area consist predominantly of raw materials and foodstuffs. Since South Asia has little industrial development, most of its raw-material exports go to markets outside the area. Exclusive of re-export traffic, trade within South Asia consists principally of rice shipments from the surplus areas of Burma, Siam, and Indochina to the rice- and cereal-deficit countries of Malaya, India, Cey lon, and Indonesia. The limited intra-regional trade in indigenous finished manufactures was represented mainly by India's exports of jute products and textile fabrics and manufactures.

One of the most marked changes in South Asia's postwar trade pattern has been the reduced role of Japan both as a market for exports and as a supplier of imports. In 1947 Japan took less than 1 per cent of South Asia's exports, as compared with almost 10 per cent in 1936. This decline reflected, in part, Japan's diminished need for South Asia's raw materials because of the low level of its industrial output and, in part, the inability of South Asia to supply Japan with needed foodstuffs and raw cotton on anything like the prewar scale. On the import side, South Asia obtained only slightly more than 1 per cent of the value of its imports from Japan in 1947, as compared with almost 15 per cent in 1936. The decline in South Asia's imports from Japan was particularly marked in the case of textiles and to a lesser extent in capital and consumers' goods.

No less significant than the reduced importance of Japan in the foreign trade of South Asia since the war has been the increased importance of the United States. In 1947, 28 per cent of South Asia's total trade was with the United States, as against 18 per cent in 1936. All this increase was accounted for by greater imports from the United States. In 1947 the United States supplied South Asia with more than 30 per cent of its imports, as against less than 10 per cent in 1936. South Asia's imports from the United States would have been even larger than they were had not import controls been imposed to conserve dollar exchange. United States inroads into South Asian markets were particularly marked in textiles and capital equipment, two major categories of imports for the area.

The relative importance of South Asia's trade with the United Kingdom in 1947 remained roughly the same as before the war, accounting for about one-fifth of the total. South Asia's trade with the Netherlands and France was somewhat less important than before the war, although Indonesia and Indochina traded with the metropolitan powers at roughly the prewar proportions.

TERMS OF TRADE

In 1947 South Asia's terms of trade were less favorable than in 1936. As a rough approximation, it is estimated that the index of the terms of trade (ratio of the average unit-value index of export prices to the average unit-value index of import prices) for South Asia as a whole in 1947 was 87 (1936 = 100). In short, every dollar of exports from South Asia purchased 13 per cent less imports in 1947 than in 1936. The terms of trade of individual countries differed widely from the average, as indicated by the estimates in Table 3.

TABLE 3

TERMS OF TRADE OF SOUTH ASIAN COUNTRIES, 1947 AND 1936
(1936 = 100)

Country	Index of Export Prices* (1)	Index of Import Prices† (2)	Col. 1 as a Percentage of Col. 2 (3)
Philippines............	335	303	110
Indonesia.............	210	303	69
India................	365	310	118
Burma...............	420	303	139
Ceylon..............	227	303	75
Malaya..............	180	303	59
Siam................	288	303	95
Indochina............	260	303	86

* See n. * to Table 4.

† See n. † to Table 4. The figure 303 is the arithmetic average of India's monthly import index of unit values for the calendar year 1947; the figure 310 is the same average for the period from April 1, 1947, to March 31, 1948. The latter index is used for India because its trade statistics are for the fiscal year 1948.

The terms of trade were most adverse for such areas as Malaya, Indonesia, and Indochina, the exports of which in 1947 consisted largely of rubber and/or tin, and for Ceylon, which exported principally tea and rubber. The average export price of rubber in 1947 was only 113 per cent of the 1936 price; of tin, 162 per cent of the 1936 price; and of tea, 227 per cent of the 1936 price. Prices of such major imports as textiles and grains, however, were roughly 400 and 425 per cent higher in 1947 than in 1936. The favorable terms of trade of the Philippines reflected the high world-market prices for copra and abaca; of

TABLE 4

VALUE AND DIRECTION OF SOUTH ASIA'S TRADE, 1947 AND 1936*

(In $1,000,000 U.S.)

COUNTRY OF ORIGIN OR DESTINATION

COUNTRY	TOTAL 1947 Value	TOTAL 1936 Value	Southern Asia 1947 Value	Southern Asia 1936 Value	Other Far East 1947 Value	Other Far East 1936 Value	Japan 1947 Value	Japan 1936 Value	United States 1947 Value	United States 1936 Value	United Kingdom 1947 Value	United Kingdom 1936 Value	Other Countries 1947 Value	Other Countries 1936 Value
Philippines:														
Exports...	265.3	147.7	14.9	1.1	6.2	10.0	2.1	8.4	150.5	118.7	8.4	4.2	85.3	13.7
Imports...	511.3	101.1	11.9	6.4	14.8	17.0	1.0	13.3	426.0	61.5	1.3	2.5	57.3	13.7
Net......	−246.0	46.6	3.0	−5.3	−8.6	−7.0	1.1	−4.9	−275.5	57.2	7.1	1.7	28.0	0.0
Indonesia:														
Exports...	194.4†	346.7	91.3	56.6	4.7	36.1	1.7	19.4	23.9	61.5	3.3	17.6	71.2	174.9
Imports...	290.9	181.7	34.8	28.6	45.1	56.1	22.8	48.4	116.8	14.0	22.9	14.3	71.3	68.7
Net......	−96.5	165.0	56.5	28.0	−40.4	−20.0	−21.1	−29.0	−92.9	47.5	−19.6	3.3	−0.1	106.2
India:‡														
Exports...	1,275.0	748.8	115.5	59.8	49.5	119.7	8.0	112.2	255.0	70.9	330.0	246.1	525.0	252.3
Imports...	1,500.0	403.4	104.2	28.8	25.8	86.0	9.4	78.7	435.0	30.2	400.0	177.8	535.0	140.6
Net......	−225.0	285.4	11.3	31.0	23.7	33.7	−1.4	33.5	−180.0	40.7	−70.0	68.3	−10.0	111.7
Burma:														
Exports...	140.8	......	108.2	......	22.3	......	......	......	0.4	......	6.5	......	3.4	......
Imports...	162.6	......	59.9	......	3.2	......	6.1	......	4.4	......	75.2	......	19.9	......
Net......	−21.8	......	48.3	......	19.1	......	−6.1	......	−4.0	......	−68.7	......	−16.5	......

* The figures shown in this table for 1947 are based only partly on the official trade returns of individual countries. Because of certain obvious gaps in the official returns—i.e., India's food imports and Indonesia's rubber exports—numerous adjustments in the official data were made, largely on the basis of more reliable second-country figures. Since these adjustments involved some element of guesswork, the figures in the table should be considered only approximate. All exports are on an f.o.b. basis, and all imports except those of the Philippines are on a c.i.f. basis. Exports include re-exports. Bullion and specie transactions have been excluded as far as possible. Data are on a calendar-year basis except for India and Burma. Indian statistics for 1936 cover the fiscal year ending March 31, 1937, and for 1947 the fiscal year ending March 31, 1948; Burma data are for the period from October 1, 1946, to September 30, 1947. Except in the case of Siam, official rates of exchange were used in converting local currencies to U.S. dollars.

† Includes estimated value of rubber shipped from non-Dutch-controlled territories to Malaya, which is not shown in official Indonesian export returns but is given in official Malayan import returns.

‡ Indian statistics for 1936 include Burma. Imports for 1947 have been adjusted to take account of cereal imports not shown in official statistics.

TABLE 4—Continued

COUNTRY OF ORIGIN OR DESTINATION

COUNTRY	TOTAL		Southern Asia		Other Far East		Japan		United States		United Kingdom		Other Countries	
	1947 Value	1936 Value	1947 Value	1936 Value	1947 Value	1936 Value	1947 Value	1936 Value	1947 Value	1936 Value	1947 Value	1936 Value	1947 Value	1936 Value
Ceylon:														
Exports...	259.6	94.0	12.5	5.8	33.4	2.0	0.1	0.7	36.3	14.9	93.2	45.2	84.1	26.2
Imports...	290.4	80.4	60.4	38.0	44.8	9.3	1.9	5.2	34.0	1.8	51.0	17.0	100.2	14.3
Net.....	−30.8	13.6	−47.9	−32.2	−11.4	−7.3	−1.8	−4.5	2.3	13.1	42.2	28.1	−16.0	11.9
Malaya:														
Exports...	612.5	364.1	115.2	54.0	34.9	30.3	6.4	27.0	207.6	171.4	98.5	31.3	156.3	77.1
Imports...	646.8	294.7	243.5	181.5	98.3	35.5	3.2	18.9	65.6	5.4	131.7	44.7	107.7	27.6
Net.....	−34.3	69.4	−128.3	−127.5	−63.4	−5.2	3.2	8.1	142.0	166.0	−33.2	−13.4	48.6	49.5
Siam:§														
Exports...	120.0	83.7	61.8	53.2	27.4	15.0	......	2.3	22.7	0.3	2.1	1.8	6.0	13.4
Imports...	70.0	50.0	12.7	15.2	31.3	21.8	7.0	12.8	15.2	1.8	7.4	5.1	3.4	6.1
Net.....	50.0	33.7	49.1	38.0	−3.9	−6.8	−7.0	−10.5	7.5	−1.5	−5.3	−3.3	2.6	7.3
Indochina:														
Exports...	68.1	105.9	11.4	11.2	16.9	16.9	......	4.7	5.4	6.4	0.1	0.9	34.3	71.4
Imports...	139.1	62.9	6.2	8.5	13.5	10.6	......	2.1	26.7	1.4	4.0	1.4	88.7	41.0
Net.....	−71.0	43.0	5.2	2.7	3.4	5.4	......	2.6	−21.3	5.0	−3.9	−0.5	−54.4	30.4
Totals:														
Exports...	2,935.7	1,890.9	530.8	241.7	195.3	229.1	18.3	174.7	701.8	444.1	542.1	347.0	965.7	629.0
Imports...	3,011.1	1,234.2	533.6	307.0	276.8	236.3	51.4	179.4	1,123.7	116.1	693.5	262.8	983.5	312.0
Net.....	−675.4	656.7	−2.8	−65.3	−81.5	−7.2	−33.1	−4.7	−421.9	328.0	−151.4	84.2	−17.8	317.0

§ Adjusted for discrepancy between free-market and official rates of exchange for baht, which resulted in overvaluation of imports and undervaluation of exports, and also because official statistics excluded known large shipments of rubber and tin.

Burma, the high export prices for rice; and of India, inflated prices for jute.

A comparison of South Asia's exports in 1947 and 1936 (see Table 5) shows only moderate changes in the relative importance of the principal categories of exports for the two years. In 1947, as in 1936, foodstuffs (including tobacco) and raw materials accounted for approximately 35 and 30 per cent, respectively, of the value of all exports. Textiles (chiefly raw cotton and industrial fibers and products), which represented roughly one-quarter the value of all exports in 1947, were slightly more important than before the war. In 1947, South Asia's exports showed even greater concentration on a relatively few commodities than before the war. Rice, tea, copra, rubber, ores and metals (chiefly tin), raw cotton, and industrial fiber and fiber products accounted for 70 per cent of the total value of exports, as compared with 65 per cent in 1936. For most South Asian countries this dependence on a relatively few export products was greater than the over-all figures for the area indicate. In 1947 copra and abaca accounted for 84 per cent of the value of Philippine exports; rice for 78 per cent of the value of Burma's exports; tea and rubber, 96 per cent of the value of Ceylon's exports; rice, rubber, and tin, 58 per cent of the value of Siam's exports; and tea, hides and skins, raw cotton, and jute and jute manufactures, 64 per cent of the value of India's exports.

1. *Foodstuffs.*—A major change in the foodstuffs category in 1947 was the reduced relative importance of rice and cereal exports. Rice and cereals represented less than one-fifth of all exports of foodstuffs, as compared with more than one-quarter in 1936. This decline resulted primarily from the fact that, because of reduced production and increased domestic requirements, Burma, Siam, and Indochina—the rice-surplus areas of South Asia—exported only about 1.3 million metric tons of rice (rice and paddy in terms of milled rice) in 1947, as compared with approximately 6 million metric tons before the war. The negligible value of sugar exports in 1947 as compared with 1936

TABLE 5

SOUTH ASIA'S EXPORTS, IMPORTS, AND NET TRADE POSITION
BY PRINCIPAL COMMODITIES, 1947 AND 1936
(In $1,000,000 U.S.)

COMMODITY	EXPORTS		IMPORTS		NET SURPLUS OR DEFICIT	
	1947	1936	1947	1936	1947	1936
Foodstuffs and tobacco ...	1,017.5	703.7	1,079.2	267.1	− 61.7	436.6
Rice, flours, and cereals .	188.8	184.0	545.7	75.1	−356.9	108.9
Pulses, oilseeds.........	28.3	57.1	22.1	10.2	6.2	46.9
Vegetable and fish oils ..	58.3	42.7	19.1	7.4	39.2	35.3
Sugar.................	6.3	85.4	36.9	10.3	− 30.6	75.1
Vegetables and fruits....	23.7	9.5	65.2	20.7	− 41.5	− 11.2
Tobacco..............	35.1	35.1	84.7	23.6	− 49.6	11.5
Alcoholic beverages.....	2.3	0.9	45.9	18.9	− 43.6	− 18.0
Tea..................	341.3	160.3	8.0	2.6	333.3	157.7
Copra................	233.4	66.6	8.0	6.3	225.4	60.3
Miscellaneous..........	100.0	62.1	243.6	92.0	−143.6	− 29.9
Raw materials...........	850.4	604.2	304.8	177.6	545.6	426.6
Ores and metals........	111.7	178.2	26.5	36.6	85.2	141.6
Chemicals.............	9.9	5.1	119.9	41.9	−110.0	− 36.8
Rubber...............	544.3	280.5	87.3	56.9	457.0	223.6
Wood, lumber, pulp.....	20.6	20.1	17.1	7.0	3.5	13.1
Hides and skins........	70.5	58.8	11.1	3.5	59.4	55.3
Fertilizers.............	2.7	13.5	24.3	11.5	− 21.6	2.0
Miscellaneous..........	90.7	48.0	18.6	20.2	72.1	27.8
Capital goods...........	35.5	9.2	688.3	224.4	−652.8	215.2
Steel-mill products......	6.2	0.6	87.4	49.0	− 81.2	− 48.4
Other metal manufactures...............	1.9	2.0	67.6	18.3	− 65.7	− 16.3
Transport equipment....	16.7	3.3	209.8	64.1	−193.1	− 60.8
Machinery and motors..	7.3	1.3	303.9	84.4	−296.6	− 83.1
Building materials......	3.4	2.0	19.6	8.6	− 16.2	− 6.6
Fuels...................	43.3	94.0	210.1	96.8	−166.8	− 2.8
Petroleum and products.	37.7	87.9	198.1	89.4	−160.4	− 1.5
Coal.................	5.6	6.1	12.0	7.4	− 6.4	− 1.3
Consumers' goods.........	17.4	13.6	283.9	112.2	−266.5	− 98.6
Metalware.............	3.2	1.3	37.4	10.1	− 34.2	− 8.8
Soaps, cosmetics, drugs..	10.8	9.7	88.6	27.6	− 77.8	− 17.9
Machines (clocks, radios, etc.).................	0.2	1.2	44.7	32.8	− 44.5	− 31.6
Paper................	2.0	1.1	84.3	27.7	− 82.3	− 26.6
Glass and pottery......	1.2	0.3	28.9	14.0	− 27.7	− 13.7
Textiles.................	769.9	414.7	724.7	272.5	45.2	142.2
Raw cotton and waste...	119.7	167.5	100.2	24.0	19.5	143.5
Raw silk..............	0.3	0.2	4.8	4.0	− 4.5	− 3.8
Raw wool.............	9.6	12.0	9.6	2.2	....	9.8
Industrial fibers........	129.6	88.8	4.0	6.9	125.6	81.9
Industrial-fiber products.	404.4	111.2	30.3	10.9	374.1	100.3
Clothing yarn..........	1.1	2.4	67.5	26.8	− 66.4	− 24.4
Fabrics and manufactures	105.2	32.6	508.3	197.7	−403.1	−165.1
Miscellaneous...........	201.7	51.5	320.1	83.6	−118.4	− 32.1
Totals...............	2,935.7	1,890.9	3,611.1	1,234.2	−675.4	656.7

resulted primarily from the sharp reduction of combined Philippine and Indonesian exports to about 10 per cent of the 1936 amount. Tea exports in 1947 increased to one-third the value of all exports of foodstuffs, largely as a result of the increased supplies available from Ceylon and India rather than from favorable prices. The substantial relative and absolute increase in the value of copra exports in 1947 reflected in part the very favorable export prices ($3\frac{1}{4}$ times 1936) and in part increased physical exports (10 per cent above 1936).

2. *Raw materials.*—Raw-material exports in 1947 were distinguished chiefly by the substantial increase in the relative importance of rubber. The value of rubber exports in 1947 represented 64 per cent of the value of all raw-material exports, as compared with 46 per cent in 1936. A 40 per cent rise in the physical volume of exports of rubber largely accounted for its increased relative importance. Ores and metals, the next most important raw-material exports, were much less important both absolutely and relatively in 1947 than in 1936, largely because of lower Indonesian and Malayan tin exports and reduced Philippine gold exports.

3. *Textiles.*—The substantial reduction in the absolute and relative importance of raw-cotton exports was a major change in the 1947 textile export picture. The decline in raw cotton to 16 per cent of the value of all textile exports in 1947, as compared with 40 per cent in 1936, reflected the drop in Indian cotton exports. In 1947 India exported less than one-third the 1936 amount of 3.3 million bales. Part of this reduction in exports was a result of increased consumption by Indian cotton mills, but even more important was the reduction in plantings of cotton for purposes of increasing food production. Industrial fibers and industrial fiber products (mostly Indian jute) accounted for 70 per cent of all textile exports for 1947, as against less than 50 per cent in 1936. The improved relative position of fiber exports reflected both very favorable export prices and relatively favorable export volume for jute.

4. *Other exports.*—The postwar decline in the absolute and relative importance of fuel exports was due largely to the limited recovery of the Indonesian petroleum industry. Exports of pe-

troleum products from Indonesia in 1947 aggregated less than 800,000 metric tons, as against more than 5.5 million metric tons in 1936.

b) IMPORTS

In 1947, as before the war, foodstuffs, capital goods, and textiles accounted for the bulk of South Asia's imports (see Table 5). Approximately 70 per cent of the total value of imports fell into these three main categories in 1947, as compared with 62 per cent in 1936. The most significant change in the over-all South Asian import picture was the increase in the relative importance of imports of foodstuffs. Foodstuffs represented 30 per cent of the value of all imports in 1947, as against 22 per cent in 1936. As in the case of exports, numerous changes occurred in the relative importance of individual imports within the principal commodity groups.

1. *Foodstuffs.*—The increased relative importance of foodstuff imports in 1947, as compared with before the war, was accounted for almost entirely by the expansion of rice, flour, and cereal imports. India, with net rice and cereal imports of more than 2.5 million metric tons in 1947, as compared with 1.3 million tons before the war, was responsible for most of this increase. The increased relative importance of imports of rice and cereals was reflected principally in a large increase in imports from outside South Asia. In 1947 South Asia derived 70 per cent of its imports of rice, flour, and cereals from sources outside South Asia, as compared with only 15 per cent in 1936. Reduced production in the principal cereal-growing countries of South Asia and population increases accounted for this rise. Rice and cereal production of South Asia in 1947 was roughly 5 per cent below the 1936–39 average, while the population had grown by about 10 per cent. South Asia's increased dependence on outside sources for foodstuffs in 1947 was reflected in a large expansion of imports from the United States. In 1947 South Asia derived 25 per cent of the value of its food imports from the United States, as against 6 per cent in 1936.

2. *Capital goods.*—Capital-goods imports in 1947, as in 1936, accounted for roughly one-fifth the total value of imports. As before the war, the United Kingdom was the principal source of

South Asia's capital-goods imports, supplying half the total. The United States filled in most of the gap that resulted from the inability of Japan and western Europe to supply capital equipment to their former markets in the area. In 1947 South Asia obtained 36 per cent of its capital-goods imports from the United States, as compared with 17 per cent in 1936.

3. *Textiles.*—Textile imports represented about one-fifth the total value of imports in 1947, as before the war. No significant changes occurred in the distribution of imports as between different types of textile products. Most important were the shifts in the sources of imports. In 1947 South Asia derived less than one-tenth the value of its imports of textile fibers and manufactures from Japan, as against 50 per cent in 1936. The reduced importance of Japan as a supplier of textiles was accompanied by a sharp increase in the importance of the United States. In 1947 South Asia obtained 40 per cent of the value of its imports of textile manufactures from the United States, as compared with only 4 per cent in 1936.

4. *Other imports.*—Imports of fuels, principally petroleum products, representing 6 per cent of the value of all imports in 1947, were somewhat less important relatively than in 1936. However, South Asia was much more dependent on other regions for its fuel in 1947 than in 1936. In 1947 more than 80 per cent of South Asia's imports of fuel came from outside the area, as compared with only 40 per cent in 1936. The reduced role of Japan as a source of South Asia's imports is significantly marked in the case of other consumers' goods as well as textiles. In 1947 South Asia obtained only a negligible share of such consumers' goods from Japan, in contrast with 20 per cent in 1936.

COMMODITY SURPLUSES AND DEFICITS

The most significant postwar change in South Asia's net trade position has been the area's shift from a food-surplus to a food-deficit area. Before the war South Asia not only was self-sufficient in the production of all essential foodstuffs but also had substantial export surpluses of rice and cereals, pulses, fats and oils, and sugar. In contrast, in 1947 it had a large rice and cereal deficit, a sugar deficit, and only a small pulse and oilseed surplus. The rice and cereal deficit alone accounted for more than half the total trade deficit of the area. Only in the case of copra, tea, and vegetable and fish oils were South Asia's food surpluses equal to or greater in value than in 1936.

Whereas before the war South Asia's fuel exports and imports roughly balanced, in 1947 the area had a large fuel deficit. As in 1936, large export surpluses were shown for raw materials and a moderate over-all surplus for textiles, despite the usual large deficit for textile fabrics and manufactures. South Asia was a large deficit area for all types of consumers' and capital goods in 1947 as in 1936.

FUTURE TRADE PATTERNS

It is not the intention of this paper to give careful consideration to the question of future South Asian trade patterns. Nonetheless, certain broad generalizations can reasonably be made regarding the outlook for the area's trade, at least over the next few years.

The physical volume of South Asia's trade can be expected to show continued limited expansion above present levels. However, recovery of trade, particularly exports, to even prewar quantities will not be possible as long as civil disorders inhibit production over much of the area. The indications are that South Asia will remain a rice- and cereal-deficit area unless major efforts are made to step up output to compensate for population growth.

Certain significant postwar changes in the geographic distribution of South Asia's trade are likely to be of fairly long-run duration. While a gradual growth in South Asia's trade with Japan from the present low levels is to be expected, trade on the prewar scale appears unlikely for some time in the future. As long as South Asia is limited in its ability to supply Japan with needed foodstuffs, raw cotton, and petroleum products, the possibilities of expanding trade between the two areas necessarily are limited. South Asia's trade with the United States, particularly its imports, has already declined in relative importance from the postwar highs of 1947 and is likely to decline still further as Japan and other prewar suppliers expand their trade.

However, it is reasonable to expect that the United States will retain a substantial share of its postwar gains in South Asian markets. Factors supporting these gains are the changes in the colonial and debtor status of much of South Asia and the competitive advantages that accrued to the United States as a result of its being able to exploit the markets of the area ahead of other sellers immediately after the war. The prospects are that trade within South Asia will remain at existing relatively low levels until greater economic complementariness among the individual countries is achieved by increased industrialization in the area.

AGRICULTURAL AND INDUSTRIAL PLANNING IN SOUTH ASIA

By B. M. PIPLANI[1]

I AM an officer of the government of India, loaned for the present to the Food and Agriculture Organization of the United Nations. The following analysis of agricultural and industrial plans in South Asia and the views expressed on their problems are my own and do not in any way represent the ideas or policy of my government or my present employers.

In spite of considerable differences in social institutions, economic conditions, and political developments of the countries in this region, it is quite possible to analyze their development plans and discuss the major problems in an integrated manner. We must start with the basic prewar features of the economy of these countries.

Malaya, Indochina, Siam, Indonesia, and the Philippines had a highly specialized foreign trade—tin, rubber, rice, tea, petroleum, and sugar. They had an aggregate adverse balance of trade with Europe, offset by an export surplus to the United States.

India, Pakistan, Burma, and Ceylon constituted a large free-trade area, exporting chiefly jute, rice, oilseeds, tea, rubber, manganese ore, and hides and skins. Over one-fourth of its trade was with Europe with which, as with the United States, it had export surpluses.

Japanese trade—imports of raw materials and exports of consumer goods and small-scale capital equipment—was an important element in the economic well-being of these countries and provided the basic balance in regional economy.

Except in India, Pakistan, and Ceylon, war operations destroyed a good deal of production equipment in agriculture, industry, and transport. But nearly everywhere equipment was

1. Deputy secretary, Ministry of Agriculture, Government of India.

overworked, replacements had to be deferred, and import of production materials severely restricted. The conduct of the war also brought inflation all around. This has retarded recovery of production everywhere. The regional production indices of food, textiles, and forest products for 1947–48 were 95, 71, and 68, respectively. The index of export trade is still lower—for India it is about 66. Imports generally exceed exports in the whole of the region, and, excluding the Philippines and Pakistan —the former because of special United States grants—the region has a current annual deficit of about $250,000,000 in the balance of payments, of which about half is against United States transactions. Only for maintaining life and avoiding starvation deaths, at a cost of $500,000,000, the region imported in 1947–48 about two million tons of cereals over and above its rice exports. This compares with the phenomenon that 40 per cent of first-year Marshall aid to Europe was used in foodstuffs and fertilizers.

The reconstruction and development plans of the South Asian countries have to be examined against this background, first, with regard to the scope and nature of the specific projects. In agriculture these countries have schemes for increasing the production of rice and cereals, oilseeds, fruits, and vegetables. Some, although few, schemes cover tobacco, tea, silk, and rubber. The specific projects concern irrigation, including minor works in flow irrigation; ground-water projects and drainage; land reclamation; fertilizer distribution and the development of indigenous manures; improvement of seed varieties and of tools and implements; control of crop and livestock diseases; improved transport; processing; and storage.

A number of important points arise from the nature and scope of such agricultural projects. First, the agricultural plans relate almost exclusively to food production and ignore raw materials for the international market. Food production and distribution have been, in view of large imports and the consequent effects on the balance of payments and the national economy, the most important question since the end of the war in India, Ceylon, Malaya, and the Philippines. In the rice-exporting countries of Siam, Burma, Indochina, and, to some extent, Pakistan rice production offers the most lucrative field because of high prevailing prices. Further, with dwindling markets for raw materials like rubber and copra and the uncertainty about their future, countries like Ceylon and Malaya prefer, in spite of higher ultimate real costs, to increase local food production.

Second, even in food production the plans are inadequate. In one of the publications of the FAO it was calculated that, on the basis of a maximum energy value in calories per person per day, an increase of 40 per cent in per capita food supplies was necessary in underdeveloped countries. This is without taking into account the needs of the increasing population (at a minimum rate of 1 per cent per annum). With about eighty-five million tons of rice and cereal production in the area, the present plans, even if fully carried out, will not raise the basic food-grain production by more than 10 per cent. Moreover, the deficiency in milk and meats, tuber crops, and fruits and vegetables will continue to be as large as it is today.

Finally, there is the question of the effects of the above-mentioned increase in food production on the rural and industrial sectors of the national economies. The per capita national income of countries in this region varies between $60.00 and $90.00 per annum. A 10 per cent increase in food production, even with the existing low standards of nutrition, can be absorbed only if real incomes in the area rise by about $12\frac{1}{2}$ per cent. This underlines the urgency of developing industries and agriculture simultaneously. In the absence of large amounts of capital equipment, industrial development cannot be carried out unless a large labor force is freed from the land by the use of improved agricultural techniques. From the point of view of some economic stability and of guaranteeing provision of the basic industrial commodities of common use, diversification of economic life, however limited in scope, is the only safeguard against failure through international arrangements to insure the disposal of the staples of world commerce. Judged on the basis of real costs, this may be considered as a backward step. But, unless common problems are resolved on an international basis, it is difficult to envision any other alternative. Moreover, these developments are obviously of a transitory nature, necessitated

by structural adjustments, and the benefits of international ex-
changes on an expanded basis should accrue in due course under
different settings.

The industrial projects now envisaged by the countries of
South Asia cover both the replacement of worn-out plant and
equipment and the setting-up of new production units. They include transportation, electric power, textile production, fertilizer
manufacture, iron and steel, coal, and other minerals. The
smaller industries for which replacement or expansion plans
have been drawn embrace sugar, glass, cement, paper, chemicals, tanneries, rubber goods, and others. The latest plans in
India also include some advanced manufactures, e.g., machine
tool, telephone manufacture, shipbuilding, manufacture of
electrical machinery, prefabricated houses, and production of
penicillin and sulpha drugs.

It is necessary to consider, next, the magnitude of the finances
required to accomplish the projects that have been put forward.
As to agricultural plans, available information forecasts that
total expenditures during the next three and a half years will
reach $750 million to $1 billion. Most of this will be incurred on
local materials and resources. I estimate the extent of foreign
equipment at one-third the total. As to industrial plans, an
estimate of costs was made last year by the Industrial Development Working Party of the Economic Commission for Asia and
the Far East. Expenditure for industrial reconstruction and development for the next five years is predicted at some $7 billion,
and, of this amount, foreign-exchange requirements may be
$3.8 billion. These figures do not include costs of industrial
plans in Siam and Pakistan. Making a rough allowance for
them, the total cost of agricultural and industrial plans in the
South Asian area for the next five years can be taken at some
$8.5 billion, with less than half the total being in terms of for-
eign currencies. This latter will be shared among dollar, sterling,
guilder, and the franc.

In judging the feasibility of the plans to which I have referred,
three separate sets of problems have to be considered: (1) the
basic conditions of political stability and the soundness of socio-

economic institutions; (2) the supply of technical and managerial ability; and (3) the supply of capital.

Establishment of peace and the continuance of law and order under strong governments is the most urgent need in Indonesia, Indochina, Burma, and Malaya. In the remaining countries the basic condition of political stability has been established. Beyond that, however, it is necessary to create a climate that will provide local and foreign enterprise with sufficient incentive for new industrial ventures. In this connection recent socio-economic policy needs examination.

In some countries there was a tendency for a time to modify by legislation the ownership rights in land and some industries. On the whole, however, there has recently been a more realistic appreciation of economic needs. In industry and in central banking organization the form, pace, and limits of state ownership or regulation have been clarified or are in the process of clear definition. Policy regarding abolition of landlordism, though accepted, is being followed gradually because of the need to insure payment of adequate compensation.

Heavy taxation imposed during the war through supertaxes, excess-profits and capital-gains taxes, and the limitation of dividends have affected the growth of industry and trade during the last couple of years. The latest budgets in India, Pakistan, Ceylon, and Siam seem to appreciate this fact, and due concessions have been made to private enterprise.

For a variety of reasons the labor force has been rather restive since the war. The wise and firm regulation of labor-management relationships so far in most of the countries provides good ground for future optimism in this connection.

Most of the South Asian countries have been battling against inflation. Through food-distribution subsidies, general economic controls, and import restrictions, prices in some areas have been prevented from rising further. But the urgent need is to increase agricultural and industrial production.

To conclude, socio-economic policy during the last eighteen months has attempted, on the whole, to provide the essential conditions of confidence for private enterprise.

Regarding technical ability, standards in agriculture, industry, and transport are poor in comparison with Europe and with the United States. But there has been considerable improvement since the war; and, with extensive arrangements for technical training abroad, chiefly under government scholarship schemes, further progress in raising general standards of technical efficiency can be envisioned in the near future. The problem of highly experienced technical experts at the top in different lines must be solved by direct government employment or by negotiations with interested foreign firms. There has been a certain amount of confusion of thought in this country regarding the proposed application of President Truman's "Point Four" program. Some technical advice is already being furnished by the United Nations specialized agencies. A hundred times more, however, is being furnished concurrently by experts invited by governments to report or advise on specific projects. High-level technical aid and development of projects under conditions satisfactory both to the aided country and to foreign enterprise are two facets of the same thing. This point has only recently been clarified for the first time by Mr. Maffry of the United States Council of the International Chamber of Commerce. Managerial ability is not much of a problem at this stage of economic development, to my mind, in most of these countries.

Finally, the total requirements of capital to be supplied during the next five years are listed at $8.5 billion, with more than half expected to come from internal resources. The projects—which are mostly government schemes—represent the basic minimum needed to prevent current standards of living from deteriorating. Available data on internal savings shows that, throughout the area, capital formation and investments during the last couple of years have been most inadequate. For one thing, during the last fifteen years—but particularly since the end of the war—large savings have been used for taking over foreign industrial assets (some $4–$5 billion). Moreover, some $8 billion of national savings have been immobilized in sterling balances. Further, most of the countries in this region have worked with very unfavorable terms of trade since the war, though somewhat less so recently. For example, one ton of food grains imported in India in 1938–39 was paid for by the export of one quarter-ton of jute manufactures or 100 pounds of tea. Today it is necessary to export for it one-third ton of jute manufactures or about 300 pounds of tea. These among other reasons explain the present state of internal savings. In spite of incentives recently offered and the efforts that are being made to encourage local capital formation and to canalize savings for developmental purposes, local savings will be inadequate to serve the amounts mentioned above, without even considering the financial requirements of an accelerated rate of development.

The position, though serious, is capable of solution. Whereas the prewar flow of investments from Britain, France, and Holland ceased some ten years ago—and, in fact, large funds moved in the reverse direction—there is now some evidence of reflow of foreign investments into Ceylon, Pakistan, India, Malaya, Siam, and the Philippines. But it is chiefly the extent to which their sterling credits are made available during the next two or three years that will determine the pace of economic advance in these countries. Since the war the sterling balances, which represent their hard-earned savings during an inflationary period, have been available for developmental and reconstruction needs only at the rate of 1 per cent per annum. With rapid progress in British recovery, larger supplies of capital equipment have become available since mid-1948. Under the Sterling Group Agreement, Japanese industry is also making its contribution, though its scope is limited by the supply of raw materials. For certain projects of urgent nature, however, perhaps up to $2.5 billion, physical equipment can be obtained only from the United States. The problem thus narrows down to whether some arrangements can be made immediately among Britain, the United States, India, Pakistan, and Ceylon whereby equivalent dollar funds could be made available against sterling balances, for financing the required capital equipment. It might be agreed that sterling balances transferred to the United States in payment of supplies would not be convertible for, say, a five-year period and that some of the necessary goods could be supplied through the Japanese industry, thus somewhat reducing SCAP's expenditure. Unless arrangements of this character are made quickly, there is real danger that the temporary trade measures which are undertaken to meet difficulties in dollar balance of payments may develop into permanently detrimental economic alignments all around. To take an example, India has recently entered into bilateral trade agreements with Argentina, Belgium, France, the Allied Zone of Germany, Russia, Poland, Hungary, Czechoslovakia, Finland, Egypt, Siam, and others. Now most of the import equipment negotiated is to overcome dollar-payment difficulties. But, since manufacturing costs are generally higher in those countries, the terms of trade have moved further against India. What is the solution under these conditions when the choice for a country is either to reduce the pace of development or to pay a higher price in terms of real effort to attain some progress?

My analysis has been confined to minimum governmental projects. The rate of development of this area will be much quicker and the whole picture will be different if a flow of investment on private account begins on the basis of straight assurances given by the more progressive of the younger nations regarding adequate arrangements for earning and transferring of profits as the normal reward of risks and regarding orderly repatriation of capital if necessary at a later stage. Since the war, total world investments in foreign countries have been of the order of $10 billion, four-fifths of the amount being from the United States. With the end of the sellers' market, fields for internal investment to maintain the current high levels of production are going to be restricted in the years to come. There is also the likely re-emergence of countries like Belgium, Switzerland, and Britain once again as creditor countries. It is to be hoped that, in the interest of general economic expansion and international peace, the next few years will see the resumption of the nineteenth-century free international flow of capital.

RAPPORTEUR'S REPORT OF ROUND-TABLE DISCUSSIONS ON ECONOMIC FORCES

By Daniel Thorner[1]

FIRST, a word on the ground that I shall attempt to cover in this brief report. Our discussions showed rather broad agreement on the way in which the older societies of South Asia were transformed under Western influence. No one denied the resulting existence of formidable economic problems today. These phases of the discussions are sketched only in their barest outlines.

The question of what should be done about these problems called forth several sets of proposals. In the case of each set, however, the further question of what was likely to be done (or what actually was being done) received almost uniformly the same answer; much less than should or could be done. This gap and some of the reasons offered to explain it occupy the central part of my report. An appraisal of the economic discussion brings the statement to an end.

TRANSFORMATION OF OLDER SOCIETIES

The economic problems of South Asia in the middle of the twentieth century are the product, it was generally agreed, of the extension of Western influence in the area. They are a legacy of imperialism, not so much of the older mercantile expansion of the sixteenth to eighteenth centuries as of the more systematic economic opening-up of the chief countries by modern steam transport (railways and steamship lines) roughly since the middle or latter half of the nineteenth century. This made possible the extension of commercial agriculture and facilitated the growth of industrial crops, the extraction of minerals, and the import of Western manufactured goods. The economies of the

---

1. Research assistant professor of economic history, Department of South Asia Regional Studies, University of Pennsylvania.

colonial countries became subordinate, dependent parts of the metropolitan capitalistic economies of the ruling powers— favorite spheres for the profitable investment of new capital or reinvestment of profits from earlier operations. In the process the older societies were drastically transformed. Formerly they had been self-sufficient economies—"backward" economies— some noteworthy for what may be called "friendly backwardness." The economic foundations of these older societies were dissolved over the years, without the foundations for a new or modern type of life being provided to replace them. They lost their old world without gaining a new one. The present economic position of the peasantry throughout South Asia is very black: stark poverty, heavy indebtedness, loss of land resulting in tenancy, and (particularly in India) a formidable growth of landless laborers, a low level of nutrition leading to poor health, and low resistance to disease.

Urbanization in the area has proceeded slowly. The cities have generally served only as commercial centers. There is little industry. Even in India, actual factory workers number only 1 per cent of the total population; and the strength of the Indian middle class should not be exaggerated. Capital accumulation in the area is slow, and the prospects for rapid industrialization on the basis of domestic economic strength were rated as slight. Analysis of recent trade patterns offered little encouragement. In a word, those countries which have gained independence or a new status *politically* have remained dependent *economically*. The population problem attracted much attention. The growth of India's population, in particular, was seen as likely to swallow up increases in food production. Similarly, the demand of India's multiplying millions for barest consumer goods might divert attention from the underlying need to expand India's heavy industry and prevent that development of heavy industry which alone, in time, could lead to an adequate supply of consumer goods.

WHAT SHOULD BE DONE?

To meet these grave, depressing problems, several sets of proposals were put forward. The plan of campaign which attracted the most support called for heroic, if not revolutionary, measures of a socialistic sort. The peoples of South Asia, it was said, had not a moment to waste in the fight for economic survival. Their position was likened to that of a man already up to his neck in water and threatened by a rising tide. Rapid large-scale industrialization under public auspices and broad governmental control was essential; presumably, it was to be carried through at the expense of the peasantry. Yet agricultural development was stressed heavily, too. It was to proceed parallel with the growth of industry as rapidly as possible. In the agricultural field, stress was placed on sweeping agrarian reform coupled with a series of techniques and measures designed to increase crop yields per unit of land, without requiring expensive capital equipment. To execute such a program, a strong-handed, perhaps ruthless, government, in some views, appeared essential. Along with industrialization would go a broad campaign for birth control. In short, South Asians were called upon to pull in their belts (Indians particularly to tighten their *dhoties*), produce less children to play with at home, and expect repressive measures if they resisted. It is relevant to note that most supporters of this rather radical program hoped to obtain from the United States part of the funds to finance it. To this we shall revert later.

Throughout the discussion of industrialization the case of India naturally received the lion's share of attention. Several speakers observed that, in its relatively large indigenous middle class, India was quite different from Southeast Asia. In fact, the capitalistic elements in India were stated to be the real power in that country. Under their leadership, in the view of some, a capitalistic industrial revolution of India along nineteenth-century lines was under way. It was frankly stated that the capital to nourish this process was likely to be squeezed out of India's underfed population in a fashion similar to the Hungry Forties of early Victorian Britain.

In another view, both the wisdom and the actuality of such a course of capitalistic-style revolution at the expense of the masses were doubted; strong opposition was simultaneously expressed by this speaker toward anything smacking of socialism. Instead, his emphasis was placed on the need for the fostering of conditions necessary to provide local and foreign enterprise with sufficient incentive for new industrial ventures. Hence unduly dramatic steps were to be avoided, while law and order, stability, and gradualism were recommended; thereby, in time, the free international flow of capital in nineteenth-century style might start up again and could be tapped for a fairly broad program of development.

As opposed to all three positions just stated, a fourth view was that it was not easy to improve matters, that industrialization should be gradual, that the main thing was the improvement of agriculture, and that the mere technical improvement of agriculture was very difficult. Alongside this sector of opinion were heard voices which frankly despaired of any progress at all, while still another view was that none of the proposals put forward was markedly different from things advocated by enlightened colonial regimes a decade or so back. As contrasted to these counsels of despair, a voice or two spoke up hopefully for vast new sources of power, perhaps solar energy. One lone voice staunchly insisted that the way out was for the countries of South Asia determinedly to shun industrialization, to block the growth of a spirit of acquisitiveness, and to cling to their traditional cultures. As against this, the point was made that the people of the area did not desire to serve as a set of permanent museum pieces, living relics of a long-forgotten age and society.

During the presentation of the various positions, the merits of diversification versus specialization in economic development were debated inconclusively. On the other hand, there seemed fairly general agreement that the area as a whole did not present the features of an economic "region," however defined. Such foundation as existed in the area for regionalism had to be sought in spheres other than the economic.

WHAT IS BEING DONE, AND WHAT IS LIKELY TO BE DONE?
AND WHY THE LARGE GAP BETWEEN THESE AND
WHAT OUGHT TO BE DONE?

The chief reasons why so much less is expected to be done than should be done lie at first sight in the realm of politics, particularly the conflict between nationalism and colonialism. Here, though, we doubtless will remember that politics is the sphere where many kinds of issues, including economic issues, are fought and decided. Colonialism, both as a heritage and as a live fact, hangs like a heavy thundercloud over the entire area, obscuring the future of Indochina, Indonesia, and, in a somewhat different way, Malaya. Little can be expected of the latter countries without a prior satisfactory settlement of the colonial issue. India, Pakistan, and Burma are plagued by internal issues partly traceable to social and ethnic differences, differences compounded and in part acute because of the way in which they were inflamed during the period of imperial political hegemony.

Outstanding in the current scene is the spectacle of both India and Pakistan spending at least half their current budgets on military preparations, apparently each against the other. Such national jealousies in the area, in part manipulated by vested interests, severely hamper economic plans and activity. In referring to this in the course of the discussion, the ominous-sounding suggestion was made that perhaps an externally created "co-prosperity sphere" or economic *Grossraum* was needed for economic efficiency.

Turning to more strictly economic reasons for the disturbing gap between necessity and actuality, one speaker remarked that the task being set for these countries might be beyond the strength of any government that had ever existed or was likely ever to exist in the area. If India, for example, starting from its present position, were to try to do what the Soviet Union had done, it would pass through the greatest ordeal ever faced by a nation. In a word, there was no royal road to industrialization. If the most rapid economic progress was the goal, several speakers observed, then communism seemed to promise the most and bid fair to take over the area.

To the regret of many, the United States appeared to sit up and take notice only when communism was the question. Ardent appeals from the area for help from the United States in meeting pressing economic problems seemed to be judged largely in such a context; decisions in the past had been, and probably decisions in the future would be, affected by the fact that the area as a whole is not termed "vital" to United States (military) security and that the chief country in the region, India, is not considered by the State Department a "sensitive" zone in the cold war. Whatever the possibilities may be for United States technical assistance and advice, substantial capital funds for the area from the United States government or government-influenced agencies—and other bodies on their periphery, I might add—do not seem likely in the immediate future.

The attitude of United States private investors is still less favorable. Historically, they have been interested in investment in Asia in terms of individual projects, say, for mineral or petroleum extraction or for assembly abroad of goods manufactured in America. There is not much common ground between them and foreign governments seeking aid for heavy industry, especially if that industry is to be more or less under governmental control or supervision. The unsympathetic attitude of American spokesmen for American investors was shown by their cool reception of Nehru's statement in January, 1949, that foreign firms would be permitted to operate and invest in India on a plane equal to that of indigenous firms. The magnitude of Nehru's concession, when considered in the light of the debate some years ago over the Government of India Act of 1935, in which one of the largest groups of clauses was the protection of British firms against discrimination by any Indian government, should not be underestimated. In the eyes of some American bankers, however, India by this statement of Nehru's was simply trying to make little of the fact that considerable powers had already been established, or were about to be established, over the operations of indigenous Indian as well as foreign firms. For their part the Indians took this as indicating that the United States was in the fantastic position of trying to get better conditions in India for American houses than Indian houses themselves had. In short, to conclude this brief sketch of the economic phase of the proceedings, it would appear as though these countries for some time to come would have to promote their own economic development primarily from their own resources, a prospect which, as we have seen earlier, does not at first sight seem very promising.

SOUTH ASIA IN THE WORLD TODAY

APPRAISAL

Reflection upon the position of the United States as brought out in our proceedings indicates several angles from which that analysis perhaps may be supplemented. The extent of United States commitments in western Europe under the Marshall Plan and related developments appears to have been brought out insufficiently. Further, in view of our discussions about the difficulties of industrialization, it is of significance that western Europe, the area which is the subject of the keenest dispute between the United States and the U.S.S.R., happens to be one of the most industrialized parts of the world. From this angle at least, neither power turns out to be so foolish as it is sometimes said to be. The United States, as has been widely observed, is now virtually the sole strong supporter for capitalistic or partly capitalistic economies; does the United States have the economic strength to take on simultaneously the problems of the South Asian world and other underdeveloped regions? In this connection, is it not expected that at the "end" of the Marshall Plan in 1952, the countries of western Europe will again have rather serious problems in securing adequate supplies of dollar exchange?

Perhaps these considerations help to explain the comparative reluctance of large American private investors and governmental agencies to extend capital to South Asia. So far as the Point Four program is concerned, one warning may be recorded about recent demands for state underwriting of Point Four loans against risk by private investors. There is nothing new about such loans in South Asia. The Indian railways, Asia's largest system, were founded under such risk-free debentures a century ago, in 1849. Once the government of India guaranteed these debentures, incentive to economy was lost, and both wild extravagance and shoddy construction occurred. For the entire second half of the nineteenth century practically no dividends were earned by any of these lines, with one important exception. The state therefore had to put up the money to enable the railways to pay 5 per cent dividends; the losses on this score proved a crippling burden on India's finances. It would be folly indeed for the United States to tread the same path a century later.

Review of the discussion about the capital needs of the South Asian countries indicates much vagueness, almost casualness, about their plans for economic development. It would almost appear as though a few ounces of fresh data rigorously analyzed were worth tons of nineteenth-century Royal Commission Reports and twentieth-century all-embracing brochures on planning. The fact is that there is *no* census of industrial capital in India, no solid, up-to-date study of national income, and only the vaguest estimate of capital formation. How, then, does India know whether it needs the $90 billion of capital over a 15-year period as estimated under the Bombay Plan of 1944, or the $8 billion for a $3\frac{1}{2}$–5-year period as mentioned here? Certainly, there is no really comprehensive over-all plan for India, on the basis of which the pattern or timing of industrial development is to be guided. Such over-all planning as did exist in India has now given way to a dis-co-ordinated series of specific projects sponsored by influential groups who find it difficult to obtain capital goods or technical know-how in their own immediate industry or business. There has been no thorough searching analysis of the extent to which domestic resources can be tapped for raising the necessary capital, and it may be that there is something to be said for the view expressed here in the last few days that domestic mobilization would yield, in time, results of rather surprising dimensions. If this is the statistical picture for India, what must be the case for the rest of South Asia, particularly if we put Indonesia aside in a category of its own, not necessarily higher than India?

These remarks about the deficienies of our statistical data for the whole region—involving, as they do, rather serious consequences for our capacity to measure its needs and requirements—could be protracted greatly. I have no intention of doing so. My purpose in raising the subject was not to suggest that, before forming any useful judgments about the area, we needed all the data suitable for the most refined studies of the National Bureau of Economic Research. I did wish to indicate that our knowledge of the area is quite uneven and that in some sectors of high importance for our discussions we are virtually without any solid data whatsoever. Relatively speaking, the area has not been important to the United States, and only a limited number of Americans have studied the area seriously.

Seen in this context, it is scarcely surprising that our initial discussions of economic affairs seemed somewhat unsure. Had we been more precise than we were, we would probably have been running ahead of our data. Among its valuable services the 1949 Harris Institute has revealed to us more clearly than before that our economic knowledge of the area requires strengthening.

To sum up in a few words. Economic analysis of South Asia has shown that the region is passing through a period of profound economic change, perhaps the most thoroughgoing change in its history. The indications are that a time of troubles is ahead. That should not necessarily incline us toward long-term pessimism. The character, the pattern, and the outcome of these changes are uncertain and carry us over into the realm of politics, which is the subject of another report.

PART IV

POLITICAL FORCES IN SOUTH ASIA

NATIONALISM, COMMUNISM, AND REGIONALISM

By Carlos P. Romulo[1]

ASIA today is a study in contradictions. Amid the conflicts that divide it, we find at work a powerful impulse toward integration and unity. With no military power to speak of, it is gradually assuming the role of a third force interposed between the two great powers, the United States and the Soviet Union. Ruined by the war, betrayed after the victory, disillusioned by its friends, menaced by new enemies, Asia has emerged from her travail as the most dynamic region in the world today. Strong winds are blowing across the ravaged face of Asia, sowing seeds of great social and political changes that may alter the course of history and transform the very texture of our society for a long time to come. It is a historical misfortune that the renascence of Asia should coincide with the ruthless struggle among the great powers for the mastery of the world. In an era of real peace and a just order among nations the immense creative energy generated by Asia's awakening might have been channeled into constructive enterprises, to the lasting benefit of mankind. There are three main drives behind the revolutionary changes sweeping across Asia. They are nationalism, communism, and regionalism. Of these, nationalism is the oldest and still the most powerful.

The history of the Philippines provides the pattern of developing nationalism throughout the region. During the three centuries under Spanish rule, the Philippines had won the distinction of having the oldest and most agressive nationalist movement in Asia. The oppressive character of Spanish rule had produced uprisings and rebellions once every three years on the average. Hand in hand with the desire for liberty, this oppressive rule had developed a sense of common nationality

1. Philippines representative to the United Nations.

among a people speaking different languages and divided from one another by strong sectional loyalties. This growing sense of nationalism and desire for liberty together culminated in the Philippine revolution of 1896 and, but for the intervention of the American occupation during the next four decades, would have created a new independent state in Asia at the turn of the last century—the prototype of a simple and straightforward freedom movement from colonial status, untainted either by the racialist and regionalist appeal of Japanese anti-Western propaganda or by the ideological appeal of communism.

On the eve of Pearl Harbor, as a newspaper editor and publisher, I visited all the countries of Southeast Asia, including China, Burma, India, Siam, Indochina, Malaya, and Indonesia. In a series of articles written for my newspapers and for worldwide distribution in the course of my travels, I warned the Western powers that the regional, anti-Western appeal of Japanese propaganda had made serious inroads in the region, and I predicted that the peoples there, unlike the people of the Philippines, would either be indifferent to a Japanese invasion or welcome it with open arms. Events quickly showed how close to the truth my estimate was; for I found that nationalism was the dominant force among the peoples of Indochina, Malaya, Burma, and Indonesia, as it was in China and India, and as it had been in the Philippines throughout the three centuries of Spanish rule and, in a somewhat less violent form, throughout the four decades of the American occupation. I found little or no tinge of communism in the libertarian movements in those countries. They were essentially nationalist struggles for independence and were recognized as such by the metropolitan powers, even while they opposed them with all the power at their command. The Communist rising in China was still in the embryo stage and was not yet a serious threat to the Nationalist government.

It was only after the war that some of the nationalist movements in Asia began to be suffused with Communist influence and to be described to the Western world as Communist-inspired. To be sure, these nationalist movements developed strong leftist strains, reflecting the universal trend. In Indochina, the leadership fell into Communist hands, not so much on account of the intrinsic appeal of communism as because the Communist party was identified with the nationalist struggle, first against the Japanese and later against the French, who made the grievous miscalculation of trying to reinstate their prewar control of the country through violent means.

In the Asiatic countries where the metropolitan powers bowed to the historical imperative and recognized the native peoples' right to a free and sovereign life of their own—as in the Philippines, India, Pakistan, and Ceylon—the nationalist movements were saved from perversion and found healthy expression in new democratic states functioning in the Western tradition. Even hapless Indonesia, all but abandoned by the Western powers to the mercies of the Dutch "police actions," mustered sufficient will and energy to put down the Communist rising within the nationalist movement. In Burma the strength of the socialist leadership is in direct proportion to the faithfulness with which it represents the popular will for social and economic reform. In China, where the Communists are winning their greatest victories today, they owe their success as much to the bankruptcy of the Nationalist leadership as to any positive appeal which communism may have for the Chinese masses.

I have no intention of minimizing the importance and the probable consequences of the Communist triumph in China. Whatever its cause, it stands forth as the most decisive development in Asia since the defeat of Japan. It is bound to affect the balance of power not only in Asia but throughout the world. It has already caused the partial retreat of America from Asia. It undermines the security of the free states of Asia and strengthens the Communist movements within their gates. It opens up the grim prospect of Communist ascendancy over the entire region. Those are facts that we must face—bitter and unpalatable though they may be.

There was a fateful moment after the war when America could have made all of Asia safe for freedom and democracy. Asia hoped for a new life after the war. Without exception the peoples of Asia looked forward to a new dispensation based on the Four Freedoms and the promise of the Atlantic Charter. That promise was never fulfilled except in the Philippines. Elsewhere America returned to Asia as a liberator and remained— in Asiatic eyes—as one of the protectors and preservers of the colonial system. American guns helped restore French rule in Indochina against the wishes of the inhabitants. American tanks and planes enabled the Dutch forces to carry out their infamous "police actions." And when the United Nations intervened in the dispute, American sympathy for the Indonesian cause was too lukewarm and equivocal to impress Asia as anything more than a pious protestation of an intention already discarded in practice.

What a difference it might have made to the situation in Asia today if America had stood uncompromisingly for the freedom of Asia! That would have electrified all of Asia's peoples. The consequent disillusionment has had a profound and far-reaching effect in Asia. In lieu of peace, the peoples of Asia found themselves involved in new conflicts. The new life of freedom under justice for which they had fought did not materialize; instead, they were subjected to fresh attempts at domination. They found their interests subordinated as in the years before the war to the interests of Europe; their wishes disregarded when these ran counter to the demands of power politics; little account taken of their fate as they were forced to revert to their age-old role of pawns in the new struggle for the mastery of the world. Even their modest hopes for the reconstruction of devastated areas and a measure of relief from the crushing burden of poverty imposed by the destruction caused by the war and the limitations of their own feudal economy were destined to disappointment, as the recovery and security of western Europe took prior claim on the funds and resources that might have been their salvation. As with economic assistance, so with security from attack or subversion. Coincident with the grand sweep of the Communist armies to the Yangtze, a Europe-first policy went into effect. American forces in Asia were reduced, heightening the feeling of abandonment among those who had looked to them as tokens, if nothing else, of their own security.

The crowning touch was the reversal of American policy on

Japan, which has confronted Asia, barely four years after the war and before a peace treaty has even been signed, with the specter of a revived and strengthened Japan. This reversal of policy springs from the same primordial weakness. This weakness, in turn, springs from the constant temptation to adopt piecemeal remedies and makeshift solutions for every problem as it arises, instead of adhering to a set course essentially based on inflexible principles of right and justice and embracing the world as a whole.

Japan, in the opinion of a certain group of influential Americans, must be rebuilt speedily as a bastion against the encroachment of Soviet power. Japanese industries must, therefore, be revived, Japanese commerce must be stimulated, the Zaibatsu must be re-established, right-wing political groups must be encouraged, and reparations must be stopped. Whatever the objections of China, the Philippines, Australia, New Zealand, and India, the Japanese economy must be revived and Japan developed as a potential ally. Little or no account is taken of the legitimate fears of the wartime allies of America and the West in Asia, and there is a tendency not to inquire too deeply into the question of whether or not we should make certain that it is a peaceful and democratic Japan that we are helping to revive and strengthen. We seem to feel that it does not matter, although it does matter greatly, even decisively, as the story of Greece and Korea and China so plainly shows.

The upshot of all this has been to deepen the Asiatic peoples' awareness of their common needs and problems, and to heighten their sense of common danger and common destiny. Out of the crucible of Asia's travail is now emerging a strong feeling of regional kinship and unity. The dream of Asiatic unity is an old one. I was one of its advocates in the Philippines, years before the war. In 1945, at the San Francisco conference, I pointed up the role that a free and united Asia could play as one of the stoutest pillars of peace. The formation of a regional association of Asiatic states working in equal partnership with like-minded groups of nations to safeguard human liberty and foster its growth under a regime of enforcible world law has always been one of the major objectives of our foreign policy.

It was not until 1947, however, when the Asian Relations Conference was held in New Delhi, that the ideal of Asiatic unity began to take definite shape. At this conference the peoples of Asia through their spokesmen recalled their ancient heritage of wisdom, dignity, and freedom and defined Asia's role in world affairs as an exponent of the moral factor, a mediator between embattled ideologies, a firm and consistent advocate of peace in a world divided into hostile camps. These precepts were applied faithfully in the first practical test of Asiatic collective action. The New Delhi Conference on Indonesia in January, 1949, acting strictly within the framework of the United Nations, brought moral pressure to bear on the just and speedy solution of the Indonesian problem. The conferees followed this up by putting the question on the agenda of the recently concluded General Assembly session and by keeping it on the agenda of the forthcoming session, pending the outcome of the negotiations between the Netherlands government and the Republic of Indonesia.

The New Delhi Conference envisaged an association of Asiatic states dedicated to peace and pledged to use their combined influence in support of freedom and justice. This would make the Asian Union conceived in New Delhi the first born within the United Nations to operate strictly in accordance with the principles and purposes of the Charter, without benefit of military pressure but only with the force of embattled conscience. The over-all objective is to throw the collective weight of Asia behind the United Nations effort to establish a workable system of international co-operation and security.

With regard to the problems of communism and colonialism in Asia, it is our hope that the projected Asian Union may develop into an effective counterpoise against the menace of a renascent imperialism, on the one hand, and of an aggressive totalitarianism, on the other. This would also be its role in the struggle between the great powers for world supremacy. I consider it significant that no Communist delegate took part in the New Delhi deliberations. The evolving Asian Union would be non-Communist rather than anti-Communist, democratic according to the new pattern of a free society, the better to enable it to perform the all-important work of synthesis in a divided world.

It remains to be seen how long and how effectively it can play this role under increasing Communist pressure, on the one hand, and waning or indifferent Western support, on the other. It would seem to be the wisest course for the Western powers, particularly the United States, to give every encouragement to the non-Communist states in Asia who are willing to stand for their freedom in the face of the Communist advance. In keeping with her own history and traditions, America should seek to befriend, influence, and guide the forces of freedom and social progress in Asia along democratic channels instead of trying to contain and stifle them within the arbitrary mold of a negative anti-Communist policy.

The battle for Asia is not yet over; it has just entered the crucial stage. Even if all China should fall under Communist control, it does not necessarily follow that the rest of Asia will go Communist. China itself is too vast and populous a land, too massive and unwieldy, too heavily overgrown with the mellow traditions of individualism and tolerance, to be recast in the iron mold of a doctrinaire ideology. There will be a time—a long time, it is almost certain—of internal reorganization and adjustment, of agrarian reforms and reforms in government, but the basic characteristics of the Chinese people will reshape, instead of being shaped by, the mold of imported systems. In the meantime, the free, non-Communist peoples outside China and the non-Communist elements within China itself can still be rallied under the banner of a strong, positive, uncompromising policy. The tides of change in Asia have not yet congealed into set patterns; everything is fluid; and no possibility should be ruled out, including the maintenance of a union of free Asiatic states strong enough to withstand the Communist pressure.

There is a mighty race for the still fluid and indeterminate loyalties of Asia. Those loyalties have today only one thing in common: nationalist sentiment and the desire for freedom. The regional spirit which has but recently sprung up among the Asiatic peoples is an extension of that sentiment and desire. The methods and principles of Western democracy have a special appeal to countries like the Philippines that have had some experience of democracy. But the methods and principles of communism have an appeal no less to those peoples who, from their condition of colonial bondage, may be led to believe that they have nothing to lose from aligning themselves with communism, which promises plenty for all and loudly professes its irreconcilable antagonism to the colonial system. Asia can still be saved for freedom and democracy; it would be folly indeed to write it off or to let it go by default to communism.

PROBLEMS OF NATIONALISM

By HAROLD R. ISAACS[1]

WE ARE confronted in South Asia with a vast political
transition, comparable, I think, to the transitions that
took place in Western society at the emergence of the
capitalist social order. We are witnessing the breakdown of the
system created by Western capitalism in Asia and the beginning
of a long and tortuous process of change. I think we can begin
to understand these problems only in this context.

When I was in Java recently, a Dutchman said to me: "Now
really, don't you agree that all this has come much too early?"
and I said: "No, I am afraid it has come much too late." He
looked at me rather blankly, and I am afraid I did not make
much progress in explaining to him what I meant. To a Dutchman engaged in the rather desperate effort to retain some degree of control in a rich former colony that reply was, I suppose,
a rather unexpected way of putting the problem. But neither is
it a simple matter for the nationalists themselves to measure
what they are or to understand where they are going.

Triumphant or emergent nationalism in South Asia is caught
in a cruel paradox. It is coming to its triumph when nationalism
as such is bankrupt. These countries are gaining their opportunity to create their own national states only now, when the
era of the nation-state is obviously coming to an end. They are
receiving only now the opportunity to begin to build national
political economies, when it seems fairly plain that the national
political economy is a diseased and dying thing in our world.
This fact obviously is not readily evident to the people engrossed
in these nationalist movements, stubbornly fighting against
their immediate enemies to achieve immediate objectives.

Thanks to the declining power of the old empires and the
blows struck by Japan, the nationalist movements in the former

1. Associate editor, *Newsweek Magazine*.

colonies of South Asia have been able to throw off or are in the process of throwing off Western rule. They can achieve and are achieving now the elementary victory of political independence. They can restore to this extent the self-respect which subjection denied them. They can put an end to dependency and to the kind of exploitation designed to serve foreign investors rather than the well-being of their own people. This is still a goal that commands immense force and can marshal great masses of people under the nationalist banner. It is a goal that must be sought, and, as the French and Dutch have shown in Indochina and Indonesia, it involves bitter struggles that cannot be avoided.

But to the wide and crowded realm of new problems that lies beyond the victory over the Western ruler, simple nationalism brings very little that is useful or promising for the future. It is late in the sense that national sovereignty in the nineteenth-century connotation is no longer capable of giving people the means of solving their most urgent problems of production, livelihood, health, education, and security. Each of these countries can quickly assume the external trappings of national independence, complete with diplomatic missions, armies, and seemingly autonomous economic policies. But they enter a world that is inhospitable to individual nations, especially weak and backward nations. They enter a world in which the nation is no longer the effective unit of political and economic life but is, on the contrary, an anachronistic form of social organization which is retarding, almost more than any other single factor, the forward progress of peoples everywhere.

It is not necessary to labor the point that we are living in the era of decline and disappearance of the nation-state. Every major event in world history in the last forty years has shown, convulsively as a rule, that the world has outgrown the national form of organization. Out of two world wars and a major depression we learned that the old system no longer functioned fruitfully. We have witnessed the gradual whittling-down of the number of contending nations in the shrunken sphere of world economy, and we have discovered that the prime problem of our time is the reorganization of our society into units larger than the nation, into a unit, indeed, as large as the world itself. Hitler's attempt to conquer Europe, Japan's attempts to mold Asia into a single sphere under its control, the creation of the United Nations, the emergence of huge spheres controlled by the two surviving contenders for world power, have all been, in their various ways, attempts to come to grips with this demand of our time.

By now all the great empires that rose in the epoch of the nation-state have fallen or else have declined to dependent status. In world politics it is no longer a matter, as it was before 1914, of a mad scramble among rival groups for pieces of the world's territory and wealth. It is an issue now between the two emerging titans of world power, the United States and Russia, of organizing the world itself. In this struggle there are combined both the elements of a struggle between national powers, on this enormously enlarged scale, and a profound conflict between contending sets of politico-economic institutions. Today every lesser country in the world is subject to the conditions created by this world power conflict. None is independent. None enjoys national sovereignty in the older sense of that term. Even Russia and the United States themselves cannot any longer insure their internal progress and their external security as self-contained national entities. They are forced to try to erect new systems of supra-national dimensions into which every smaller country is drawn.

No new nation can in these circumstances hope to emerge and grow by the old means previously open to independent nationalities. Even the simplest kind of national economic development is now subject to world conditions. The world power struggle and the conditions inherited from the war determine all the principal limits of international political life and the terms of internal economic change, industrialization, and participation in the world market. Virtually every country is in some degree a dependent, a pensioner, or a victim of the larger power sphere into which it falls, either on the basis of subsidy, as in the case of the nations participating in the Marshall Plan, or in the form of satellites feeding a planned central economy, as in the case of the Russian sphere. Older European lands like Italy or Czechoslovakia, France or Poland, illustrate this fact in different ways. A tiny new nation-state like Israel can make its way only on foreign subsidies. New nations like India or Burma or the Philippines face the staggering problems of internal transformation without any immediate prospect of fitting into a world system that will allow them to begin to thrive. China, the buffeted victim of a hundred years of imperialist rivalries and depredations, emerges in the Russian totalitarian sphere and cannot hope to repeat even the limited achievement of nationalist Russia in the sphere of industrialization. National sovereignty is a myth, and those in South Asia who emerge with it as the prize of victory find themselves facing the future almost empty-handed.

Such is the real political context in which we now have to place the countries of South Asia. It perhaps can be said that India has the size and the potential strength to go farther along the road of developing as a nation than any of the others. This may be debatable; but the Southeast Asian nations are, without exception, immediately and mortally subject to these new world conditions. Burma, Siam, and Indochina, all bordering South China, are in a state of uncrystallized conflict. They are confronted with the early possibility of having on their northern frontiers a very dynamic force indeed in China. Chinese influence in those countries will be decisive, both in its effect on the development of Communist movements within those countries and/or in the sense of direct Chinese intervention in their affairs. Their prospects of prolonged independence as nineteenth-century-type sovereign states are very dim.

Malaya is a separate case. It has even less of the makings of a nation with any chance of prolonged survival than any of the others. This is partly the result of the historic circumstance of its plural population, more or less evenly divided between Malays and Chinese. In Malaya you find a rather pathetic attempt going on to *create* a Malayan nationality, to which the Malays are a little allergic and to which the Chinese are certainly indifferent. You find in Malaya soberer people thinking of the future of the country much more in terms of the ultimate extent of the direct Chinese influence from the north on the one hand, and the possible effect of the Indonesian influence from the south, on the other. A great many people foresee the possibility of a division of the country between those two spheres. The nature of the relationship between them will be determined, I suppose, by whether or not the Indonesian federation by that time is in a hostile, or in a co-operative, relation to China. Either is possible.

All these countries have to solve staggering internal problems. They have to increase their food production. They have to rebuild and build transportation systems. They have to begin to industrialize on a noncolonial basis, that is, they have to begin to reorganize their economies in a way that will provide them with a more balanced system of production instead of leaving them wholly dependent on one or two major raw materials supplied to foreign processors.

These tasks obviously cannot be accomplished in this day and age by each individual country, acting for and by itself. The alternative goes right to the heart of our world-wide problem. These new countries, wisely and necessarily winning their political independence and putting an end to colonial rule, must find the way of breaking out almost at once from the confining barriers of obsolete nationalism. They can thrive only if there is a new world order into which they can fit. They can begin to solve these problems only if they can function within some larger framework providing opportunities for common planning, common work, pooling of capital resources and of needs. In the absence of such an order—and there is no sign of it as yet—they are doomed to stifle, each within its own boundaries, or to seek lesser expedients in the hope of getting along somehow until broader opportunities offer themselves.

Since 1945 there has been a growing awareness of the need to break out of the purely national arena. In 1945, when these struggles were just beginning in the wake of the Japanese surrender, there was very little consciousness among the nationalist leaders in South Asia of this aspect of their problem. I remember what must have been one of the very first moves made in this direction when Ho Chi-minh of Viet-Nam sent a message to President Soekarno in Batavia asking him, first, to join with him in a common declaration of purpose in their common struggle and, second, to form a preparatory commission looking forward to future co-operation among all the countries of Southeast Asia. The Indonesian republican leaders rather scorned that proposition; they laid it aside and would not have anything to do with it. They believed that they were going to achieve their national independence without great difficulty and did not want to admit any new complications. Within a comparatively short time, by 1947 in fact, when Soetan Sjahrir came to Lake Success to plead the Indonesian case in the situation created by the first Dutch police action, this attitude had greatly changed. By then Sjahrir was greatly interested in the possibility of co-operation or joint action in some form with the other countries of South Asia. Obviously, this change was the result of direct and rather bitter experience.

Some other developments reflecting the impulse to find a broader framework have been mentioned in this discussion. One was the Asian Relations Conference in 1947. It was designed more as a demonstration than as a political act and had no direct political consequences. The Southeast Asia League that was formed in Bangkok later in 1947 was an abortive affair which was put together largely under the auspices of certain Siamese, especially Nai Pridi, who was at that time prime minister. He saw in it, in the first place, the opportunity to aid his own effort to get the neighboring territory of Cambodia out of French control; and, second, being a politician of some imagination, he saw a great deal in the possibility of organizing the beginnings of a federation in Southeast Asia. If he had not been thrown out of power by a coup d'état the following November, he probably would have made Bangkok an important center for this effort. With the downfall of Pridi and the coming to power of Marshal Phibun, the whole idea was abruptly abandoned. There was even an attempt to depict the league as a Communist conspiracy, which it was not, although several Viet-Namese Communists participated in it.

The next major development along this line was, I believe, the Delhi Conference on Indonesia in January, 1949. The headlines at the time spoke of the creation at New Delhi of an "Asian bloc." Obviously, no such bloc was formed there, although even as a diplomatic myth the very idea of such a bloc stirred and startled the chancelleries in London and Washington. The truth of the matter, however, was a good deal less substantial than the appearance. The conference was the first joint political move by a group of Asian states. But it was a very halting first step indeed. It produced no permanent results.

The conference was called by Pandit Nehru, the prime minister of India, two weeks after the Dutch army perpetrated its second "police action" in Java. Nehru had long seen the possibility and the desirability of solidarizing India with the Indonesian nationalist movement. India, almost alone, extended material aid to the Indonesian republicans during the long and tortuous struggle against the Dutch after 1945. It seemed to Nehru that the Dutch were enjoying the tacit support of the Western bloc in the United Nations, and his first impulse, after the Dutch attack, was to open a full-blown diplomatic offensive which would compel a Western retreat.

Nehru is a man of great attainments, who is not really at home in the hugger-mugger of politics. He is still moved by a broadly socialist outlook. He is still suspicious of the Western imperialism he fought all his life. As a leader in the Indian freedom movement, his inspirational and emotional qualities outweighed his indecisiveness in specific political issues. Now, as a leader in power, he is forced to make constant compromises both in domestic and in international politics and to trust less than ever to his instincts and impulses. This happened very clearly in connection with the conference on Indonesia.

When the invitations to the conference had already gone out and before any replies had been received, Nehru made a speech, on January 2, at Ahmedabad. He lashed out at the Western powers, charging them with sacrificing the struggle of the Indonesian nationalists to the European concerns of the Western bloc. It was a bitter and outspoken attack which appalled not only the British and American embassies but also the group of professional diplomats and former civil servants surrounding Nehru in the Indian Ministry of Foreign Affairs. Between January 2 and January 22, when the conference convened, a very considerable change took place. This change was not unrelated to skilful pressure applied by both the British and the Americans on Nehru and on his principal foreign affairs adviser, Sir Girja Shankar Bajpai.

The result was that the conference was watered down and turned out to be a rather tame and docile affair. The Western powers were relieved. But people in India and in other South Asian countries were disappointed. There had been a swift electric response to the conference call among most South Asian nationalists. They came to Delhi with great expectations. They left quite empty-handed.

In the first place, the chances for South Asian organization at this conference were dimmed by Nehru's invitations to the Arab nations. He wanted obviously to stage the broadest possible demonstration of UN members. He also doubtless wanted to impress upon Pakistan and on the Moslem minority in India that his government was closely aligned with the Moslem nations. But the net result was to limit the agenda of the conference and to silence all those who wanted to take advantage of the opportunity to go beyond the single issue of Indonesia. The Arab delegates were anxious for a chance to talk about Palestine as well as about Indonesia. But, while many of the other delegations present had other topics they would have liked to introduce, few were willing to be drawn into the Palestine issue, which was at that time before the UN. The result was that the agenda were strictly confined to the single item of Indonesia. On that single item the caution dictated by the Indian leaders, assisted by Australia, eliminated all proposals for direct aid to Indonesia by the conference states. Instead, the program was reduced simply to the drafting of a resolution for submission to the UN Security Council. Even the proposal, made and strongly seconded by some delegations, to set up permanent machinery for future consultation was watered down. It emerged as a vague resolution calling for future discussions without any implementing machinery. It was not meant to have any concrete result, and, indeed, as the sequel showed, nothing came of it.

One consequence of the limitation of the agenda was the fact that, amid all the to-do over the Dutch war in Indonesia, nothing—literally nothing—was said about the French war in Indochina. There was a delegate present from Viet-Nam. He had not been invited. He was politely received, given a visitor's badge, and permitted to attend the public sessions. But the Viet-Nam issue was carefully kept out of the speeches and deliberations of the conference, except for a single oblique reference by the representative of Burma. Aside from the desire to avoid the touchy Palestine issue, which would have been admissible if Viet-Nam had been discussed, and aside from the desire to keep the conference within strict limits, Nehru and his advisers also showed signs of being afraid of the Communist coloration of the Viet-Nam nationalist leadership. They were anxious to impress upon the Western powers the total respectability of the conference. They managed only to disappoint several delegations which were anxious for a broader discussion of Southeast Asian affairs. They also disappointed the Indonesians, who had hoped for a much more aggressive show of solidarity and were asked to be content with the draft of a resolution for the UN. The Philippines delegate, Carlos Romulo, said at the closing session: "We have effectively championed the cause of Indonesian independence without offending or antagonizing anybody." This, if true, was the most notable achievement of the conference.

Another significant regional development affecting South Asia has been taking place within the context of the British Commonwealth, or more correctly now, the Commonwealth. Great Britain has been trying, ever since its withdrawal from India and Burma, to work out some new form for maintaining its position in Asia. It has begun to shape up with the devising of the new formula which kept India within the Commonwealth as a republic. The ultimate object would be to create a new band of participating nations linked to Britain, including India, Pakistan, Australia, New Zealand, Ceylon, and possibly even Burma, although Nehru's attempt to organize "assistance" to Burma under Commonwealth auspices in February, 1949, backfired rather badly. Part of this project is a somewhat more distant dream of creating a new dominion out of Malaya, including Singapore and the other Straits Settlements, British Borneo, and perhaps even Hongkong if it can be kept out of Chinese Communist hands. This British design moves slowly and against great obstacles but is by no means to be ignored in sizing up the regional possibilities.

The other arena in which an attempt is being made to deal with South Asia as a whole lies in the UN Economic Commission for Asia and the Far East, known as "ECAFE." This commission has held several uniformly unproductive conferences. For one thing, it includes Russia and the United States, and every question that comes before it is affected by the cold war. For another, it is dominated by the Western powers. Until last year the Dutch spoke in its councils for Indonesia, although after a bitter struggle the Indonesians were finally admitted as associate members. The French still speak for Indochina, the British for Malaya. The other Asian delegations defensively act as purely national units, each with its own plans and its own hope of securing dollar credits. The organization as a whole has, up to now, served as little more than an agency for gathering statistics, frequently of dubious value, and a clearing-house for information which is often quite irrelevant.

At the ECAFE conference held in Bangkok in March, 1949, all these weaknesses were painfully apparent. Each delegation came armed with only the narrowest kind of nationalist thinking. Only the Indian delegate gave a flicker of a broader spirit when he informally indicated that India might be willing to share with some of the other countries its own limited and badly needed supply of steel.

But the most remarkable and most paradoxical thing at the conference was the prescription offered by the Soviet delegate. He characteristically pandered to all the narrowest nationalist conceptions and managed to sound remarkably like an American of the McKinley high-tariff era. Each new Asian country, he said, had to concentrate solely on developing its own resources. How did they think, he argued, the United States had achieved its industrial power? Once it broke from England, he said, it began to develop its own economy, set up high tariffs, and by the end of the nineteenth century had established its economic as well as its political independence. Interestingly enough, he stressed this American example much more heavily than that of the Soviet Union itself, which achieved its own relative degree of industrialization by throwing up barriers against the rest of the world and proceeding to exploit its own labor force ruthlessly, converting a very considerable portion of it into plain slave labor for the purpose. But there were gaping mouths around that conference table as the Russian spoke. He made the British and even the American delegate sound radical by comparison.

In any case, all the forces operating at the conference, all the currents of thinking, uniformly tended to press these Asian groups back into their own narrow nationalist confines. The result was total futility. There was not a single serious impulse to shift ground from the national to the regional scope and from the regional scope to the world scope. Until that impulse develops, South Asia will continue to suffer from economic, as well as political, incoherence.

None of this can be regarded separately from the internal social problems in each of these countries. I think enough has been said about the magnitude of the problems of South Asia to make it quite plain that these problems are never going to be solved by old ideas or old solutions. This will be true whether you speak of individual nations or a region or two regions, i.e., India-Pakistan-Ceylon and Southeast Asia. None of the so-called "normal," old-fashioned, traditional, or conventional methods makes any sense. On the contrary, only the most heroic kind of drives and the boldest kind of new thinking are going to result in any effective growth. The crucial questions therefore are: Are the nationalist leaderships in South Asia capable of producing such drives or of generating new ideas? Do they represent the kind of social forces capable of assuming leadership over the whole people and of carrying out the drastic programs that are obviously called for? Have these nationalist leaderships any effective alternative to the Communist totalitarian method of coping with the problems of backwardness? The crux of the political problem in South Asia lies right here.

Each of these nationalist groupings represents in some degree the upper classes. These upper classes vary in character. Only in India do you have a very well-developed capitalist and middle class. In the other countries they emerge from the landed class, the landed aristocracy, the intellectual aristocracy. They are usually tied to existing archaic land relations. Very few of them have any real impulse to revolutionize land relations, which would be the beginning of an approach to the agrarian problem. Although most of them call themselves socialists of some kind, many still suffer very heavily from narrow nationalism and economic conservatism. That kind of outlook is not able to face up to the problems that demand solution. Sooner or later such leaders are going to give way to other forces which are going to offer some other, more dynamic, answers.

I think it a great mistake to regard, as is often done, the people of the backward countries as inert masses to which things simply happen. They are also in motion, and it is not a question of whether they want what anybody thinks they ought to want; they obviously want something different from what they have, or we would not have the convulsions which lie at the center of the present political turmoil in these countries. It is not a matter of free choice and free movement of small groups of leaders. These leaders are responding to reacting to profound impulses that come from very deep in the mass of the people, and if they are unable to come forward with a program that can begin to solve the people's problems, then somebody else is going to.

The Communist movement in Southeast Asia is already a significant political factor. The fact that China is moving swiftly into the totalitarian sphere, with all that that portends, means that the pressure on all these countries is going to be enormous. If there is any alternative to the organization of Asia along totalitarian lines, it will have to emerge soon. We are left with little time. Somebody here said, speaking of the population problem, that these countries are "up to their necks in water" and that there is no space or time in which to move around. It is no less true to apply that figure of speech to the political picture.

It is not going to be possible to repeat in South Asia the nineteenth-century pattern of developing national sovereignties and national economies. The real issue is whether the West and the new leaderships in Asia can develop a twentieth-century program of coherence in which these backward countries can fruitfully find their place.

PROBLEMS OF NATIONALISM

The so-called "chaos" in Asia is largely of the West's own making. We fought our wars there. We left the continent with a legacy of ravage, backwardness, poverty, and ignorance, preserved through one, two, and three centuries while the West enriched itself at Asia's expense. Today the emerging ex-colonies face gigantic tasks of reconstruction and construction. The real question is whether there *is* an alternative to the totalitarian methods, which were first exemplified in Russia and which we shall see unfold in China. These methods call for creation of a police state and putting great masses of the people to work as virtual slaves. These methods are not so fundamentally different, after all, from the essential framework of imperialist exploitation in Asia, only they would now be applied for major internal developments rather than for the benefit of overseas investors and would be applied on an infinitely larger and more brutal scale. Have we an alternative to offer the people of Asia, a way of building a new life on the basis of expanding freedom and through the construction of a new world economic system? That is the question that lies before the Western world, and the time given to us to answer is not unlimited.

ECONOMIC ORIGINS OF INDONESIAN NATIONALISM

By JUSTUS M. VAN DER KROEF[1]

THE rise of Indonesian nationalism has in the past few decades—and in particular since the establishment of the republic—been the subject of a number of studies which have regarded the problem primarily from a political or cultural point of view. Much has been written about the restrictions placed by the Dutch on the development of Indonesian political life, about social discrimination, about cultural antagonism and the general aversion of nationalists to the Westernization brought in the wake of Dutch rule.[2] Attempts have been made to link the nationalist movement in the Indies to the general process of emancipation in the Orient indicated by such terms as "the rebirth of Asia" or "the awakening of the East."[3] In these studies little attention has been paid, however, to the specific economic grievances which determined much of the character of the native movement. For example, the conflict between indigenous and Western systems of economy, the rise of trade-unions and their relationship to nationalist parties, the emergence of socialism and communism in Indonesia in terms of a general reaction against the West, the process of edu-

1. Instructor in the history of civilization, Michigan State College. [Mr. van der Kroef did not attend the Twenty-fifth Institute of the Norman Wait Harris Memorial Foundation. His paper was submitted after the end of the Institute, but since it deals with one of the major topics discussed at that Institute, it is felt that its inclusion will add to the general usefulness of this volume.—EDITOR.]

2. Cf. J. Th. Petrus Blumberger, *De nationalistische Beweging in Nederlandsch-Indie* (The Hague, 1931), pp. 17–85; R. M. Noto Suroto, *Van Overheersching tot Zelfbestuur* (The Hague, 1931), pp. 13 ff.; A. C. van den Bijllaardt, *Onstaan en Ontwikkeling der staatkundige Partijen in Nederlandsch-Indie* (Batavia, 1933), pp. 12–27, 43, 56 ff.; J. S. Furnivall, *Netherlands India* (Cambridge, 1944), pp. 238–46; Charles Wolf, *The Indonesia Story* (New York, 1947), chap. i; and David Wehl, *The Birth of Indonesia* (London, 1947).

3. For example, Robert Payne, *The Revolt of Asia* (New York, 1947), pp. 3–12; and Rupert Emerson *et al.*, *Government and Nationalism in South East Asia* (New York, 1948), pp. 3–27, 182 ff.

cational emancipation and the economic difficulties connected with it, and the nature of Dutch economic policy in general— all these lie at the roots of Indonesian nationalism. However, they have seldom been studied very closely, although they are vital to an understanding of many of greater Asia's problems.

Perhaps because of the fact that in later years political issues in Indonesia seemed to assume overriding importance, the above-named problems have not received as much attention as they deserve. And yet the economic condition of Indonesia under Dutch rule never left the nationalist mind. As late as 1946, Soetan Sjahrir, the Indonesian statesman, could write: "The standard of living in Indonesia in 1940 was, as has been claimed, higher than 40 years before, in spite of the depression, and considerably higher than during the period of the Dutch East India Company. One has to look at such statements in their relation to the total increase of production. During the last 50 years increase of production was indeed immense. As a result it was possible to give our nation an outer appearance of a modern ruled country with an organized output of production, pompous and impressive banking buildings, comfortable hotels and good transport-roads. But, at the same time, there was a reverse side of the medal too. While production and exports amounted to an annual value of hundreds of millions of guilders, the Indonesians led a bare existence on a level of about half a penny a day. . . ."[4]

I

When in the middle of the nineteenth century the Dutch abandoned the economy of state monopoly over Indonesia's agrarian riches and a beginning was made in 1854 with the opening-up of Java to individual capitalist enterprise, liberalism in the Netherlands had scored its biggest victory.[5] An unprece-

4. Soetan Sjahrir, "Our Nationalism and Its Substance: Freedom, Social Justice, and Human Dignity," *The Voice of Free Indonesia*, May 4, 1946.

5. On Indonesia's economic condition during this period consult S. van Deventer, *Het landelijk Stelsel op Java* (Zaltbommel, 1865), I, 32–89, II, 320 ff.; H. T. Colenbrander, *Koloniale Geschiedenis* (Amsterdam, 1925), III, 12 ff.; W. B. Bergsma, *Eindresumé van het Onderzoek naar de Rechten van den Inlander op den Grond op Java en Madoera* (Batavia, 1896), III, 52–189; G. Gonggrijp, *Schets eener economische Geschiedenis van Nederlandsch-Indie* (Amsterdam, 1928), pp. 46 ff. For the early nineteenth-century state-monopoly system consult D. C. Steyn Parvé, *Het koloniaal Monopoliestelsel*

dented wave of big entrepreneurs gradually descended upon the islands, attracted by the vast agrarian resources of the region. The new imperialism was, from an economic point of view, primarily the result of a stagnation of the processes of production in most European countries. The export of capital through loans to foreign countries and through direct investment in overseas territories had now become the *deus ex machina* through which (from the point of view of Hobson and Keynes) a part of the accumulated savings which had been withheld from Europe's production machinery was brought back into circulation. Colonial expansion became the substitute for important technological inventions, which, in the past, had ended economic stagnation and depression through the prospect of a cheaper, easier— and more profitable, from the point of view of the investor— production of goods and services. Investments in colonial overseas territories were, of course, primarily attractive because the investments could be politically and juridically supervised by the colonial nation. Other factors were the rich returns and dividends expected from the fruits of colonial agricultural production, for which there was an increasing demand all over the world, and the element of cheap native labor. The profits thus realized in the colonies not only were directed toward a greater world consumption of tropical produce but were, of course, also used for new investments, and hence a large amount of liquid reserves was at all times kept in readiness for such purposes by the larger enterprises. Meanwhile, investments grew: private investments in the Netherlands East Indies around 1900 were estimated at 750 million guilders, in 1915 at 1,500 million. Total capital invested in big enterprise in the East Indies for the year 1929–30 was estimated at 4 billion guilders. By 1939 Dutch and foreign investments in the Indies (government loans not included) amounted to well over 3.5 billion, while the government loans totaled close to 1.4 billion guilders. More than 75 per cent of all private investments in the Indies were of Dutch

---

getoetst aan *Geschiedenis en Staathuishoudkunde* (Zaltbommel, 1851), *passim;* and G. H. van Soest, *Geschiedenis van het Kultuurstelsel* (Rotterdam, 1869–71), III, 45 ff. For the parliamentary history of liberalism in colonial policy see W. J. van Welderen Rengers, *Schets eener parlementaire Geschiedenis van Nederland, 1849–1891* (Amsterdam, 1918), I, 316 ff.

origin by 1939. At the eve of the second World War, total Dutch investments amounted to 4 billion guilders, or 20 per cent of the Netherlands' national wealth.[6]

The result of the existence of these vast nonnative investments was the gradual disappearance of the indigenous entrepreneur from the market or, if he continued to exist, the increasing dependency of the small native producer on foreign capital. Gradually the native cultivator, who in the past had tilled his own soil and disposed of his own products, was no longer able to compete and, moreover, had to put up with all kinds of limitations on his freedom to dispose of his products by a government bound to protect the more weighty interests of the Western enterprises. In all phases of agricultural production (but especially in the cultivation of tobacco and sugar) did the native free farmer remain alone with his capital, trying to copy Western methods, but seldom succeeding, hampered by the lack of technical help and by the overpowering competition of the more efficient foreign trade-associations and estate-owning companies. Western enterprise not only controlled the fruits of its own production but also concerned itself with buying up raw materials, produced by natives, which could be processed and manufactured in the Indies for Western consumption. Individual indigenous producers incapable of delivering their products in great quantities were also faced with the problem of having to transport their produce over vast distances as soon as their products could fill a demand more remote than that expressed by local markets. The farther the market was from the place of cultivation, the more completely the trading became centralized in Western hands. Soon the manufacture of the agrarian product and the trade in it could occur without the participation of the native producer of raw material. This process, as Boeke described it, began with money advances to the native producer by Western enterprise in order to assure delivery and to influence the price. Soon the Western trader began to intervene in the production itself, especially at a time of economic depression, when the demand for the quality rather than the quantity of the

6. J. A. Jonkers, "Economische Aspecten van de Verhouding Oost-West," *Indonesie*, I (1947), 212–16.

product became stronger.[7] Since the native farmer was often un-willing or unable to satisfy this new demand, he gradually lost control over the finishing process of his product and soon was provided only with seed and seed plants. The purchaser began to insist on controlling the production process, often through the purchase of the land under cultivation. The indigenous farmer became, through such methods, little more than a wage-earner of the Western capitalist.

In recent decades, however, the government has made an ef-fort to raise the indigenous entrepreneur from this position. There was, indeed, a decided increase in the share of native ex-ports, while native rubber and coconut cultivation also seemed to be able to hold their own as regards Western competition in the same field. But these factors did not balance the two scales of Indonesian production. To begin with, there was the size of operations. "The Western concerns were without exaggeration some two or more thousand times as extensive as were the corre-sponding native concerns."[8] The Western concerns, furthermore (especially since the crisis of 1885), had rested upon a very firm capital foundation and were thus capable of sustaining heavy losses and of expanding at will. In the latter half of the nine-teenth century the majority of the Dutch trading companies re-constituted themselves as holding companies and corporations, with a vast superstructure of banks, syndicates, unions, experi-ment stations, and laboratories. But the small native industries were largely without capital investment and had little immedi-ate contact with the world markets and almost no improved technological processes at their disposal. And the few modest co-operative societies were, in Boeke's opinion, "like coral reefs in an ocean"; each unit struggled on, relying on its own re-sources, while state intervention, however incisive, came seldom into direct touch with the individual native entrepreneurs be-cause it largely dealt with the collecting groups, the wholesalers, the manufacturers of native raw materials, and the exporters.[9]

7. J. H. Boeke, *The Evolution of the Netherlands Indies Economy* (New York, 1946), pp. 10–11.
8. *Ibid.*, p. 8; cf. also *Verslag Handel en Nijverheid* (Batavia, 1930), pp. 21–34.
9. H. van Helsdingen, *De Inheemsche cooperatieve Beweging* (Batavia, 1935), pp. 56–67.

Without the constant supervision of the Dutch government and the assistance of agricultural agents, credit institutions and experimental stations, native agriculture and industry, except on the basis of a restricted local consumption, would have disappeared long ago. The great gap that existed between European and native production is indicated by the figures given in Table 1.[10] With the possible exception of rubber, every aspect of

TABLE 1

PERCENTAGE OF EUROPEAN AND NATIVE PRODUCTION IN TOTAL VALUE OF CERTAIN AGRICULTURAL EXPORTS IN 1929, 1933, 1938, AND 1940

PRODUCT	1929		1933		1938		1940	
	Eur.	Nat.	Eur.	Nat.	Eur.	Nat.	Eur.	Nat.
Sugar	99	1	99	1	99	1	99	1
Cocoa	87	13	98	2	98	2	94	6
Tea	78	22	84	16	82	18	82	18
Gambier	62	38	61	39	64	36	67	33
Rubber	59	41	60	40	52	48	50	50
Tobacco	55	45	54	46	70	30	95	5
Oils	38	62	38	62	43	57	43	57
Nutmeg	35	65	33	67	20	80	28	72
Coffee	27	73	31	69	42	58	70	30
Coconut*	10	90	5	95	5	95	9	91
Kapok*	4	96	9	91	17	83	25	75
Pepper	1	99	1	99	1	99	3	97

* And by-products.

production on the European estates increased—at the expense of native cultivation. The figures for coffee production alone show in what manner the native producer was driven into a corner by the powerful Western estate-owners.

The political effects of these conditions can well be imagined. A chronic sense of frustration on the part of the small native industrial or agrarian entrepreneur gradually led to nationalist agitation. As early as 1911, Javanese batik (i.e., printed native cloth) traders took measures to protect their interests against unfair competition from other quarters—Dutch, but primarily Chinese. Their association, which took their religion as the unifying element, was called Sarekat Islam, and, after a number of bloody riots against the Chinese, the organization took on a

10. Boeke, *op. cit.*, p. 23.

more definite nationalistic character, condemning indiscrimi-
nately all nonnative economic control (Dutch, Eurasian, Chinese, Arabian) in Indonesia. The government was aware that
the true character of the Sarekat Islam (which by 1923 had over
a million members) was more firmly rooted in specific economic grievances than in political aspirations, and in a report in
1920 it declared: "The essence of the native movement is:
the effort to remove the restrictive competition of non-native
capitalist concerns by endeavouring to end the entire non-native domination, politically, as well as economically. The core of
the nationalist movement is, therefore, the revolt of the increasing productive powers of an early-capitalist native society
against the economic and political domination of 'foreign capital.' "[11]

This resentment against Dutch capitalist control gradually
changed into a fight against all capitalism. In later years the
Sarekat Islam often seemed to be out-and-out socialistic and
the vanguard in countless labor disputes. But, even when its
spokesmen were condemning capitalism, they were careful to
distinguish between "Western" capitalism and "Eastern" capitalism. The latter was permissible; against the former they
waged an incessant fight. In later years native businessmen in
the cities felt this distinction, too. Local chambers of commerce
constantly reverberated with disputes between Dutch and native members, and upon occasion the latter would secede and
form separate groups on the grounds that "their economic interests were wholly incompatible with the viewpoints of Dutch
businessmen."[12]

Agrarian unrest similarly manifested itself. Peasants formed
protective leagues against the buying practices of the Dutch
plantation enterprises, which sought to make the farmer entirely
dependent upon the planting and harvesting conditions stipu-
lated by Dutch interests. As many peasants were unable to compete with European enterprise and since Java had witnessed an
unprecedented increase in population in the previous half-centu-

11. *Mededeelingen der Regeering Omtrent Enkele Onderwerpen van algemeen Belang,
1920* (Batavia, 1920), col. 14.
12. Report in *Bataviasch Nieuwsblad*, July 24, 1935.

ry, an agrarian proletariat was created, often composed of former independent peasants. When labor unions were formed among the native workers on the Western plantations, the stage was set for nationalist agitation. A constant fight was waged by these unions against further lease of farm land to Dutch plantations and for the establishment of a free peasant class, which could maintain itself despite Western competition. As the government, however, was committed to protecting the interests of the Dutch planters, who also had organized themselves into pressure groups, such as the infamous Suikerbond ("Sugar Association"), the demands of such organizations were never realized, and, although the government did exercise the most stringent supervision over the leasing of land by natives to nonnatives, it could not prevent large-scale acquisitions by Westerners. Under the impact of revolutionary socialist leaders, countless uprisings of agrarian workers and small farmers occurred in the present century. All nationalist parties, primarily the Partai Nasional Indonesia, headed by Soekarno, represented themselves as championing the interests of the agrarian proletariat and the peasants.[13]

II

Indonesia, until very recently, remained almost exclusively an agrarian country, where industrialization played an insignificant role in the national economy. Whatever industry came into existence dates chiefly from the turn of the century and, as in the case of agricultural production, was characterized by complete Western control. Either native industry prior to the outbreak of the revolution in 1945 was confined to local consumption (cigarettes, umbrellas), or else its products were bought by middlemen and traders for shipment to the Netherlands for the finishing process (batteries, cottons, pottery). Not one commodity produced by native entrepreneurs was sold directly and for immediate consumption on the international market. With the possible exception of the native cigarette industry, the industrial plant could maintain itself only with a

13. *Mededeelingen der Regeering Omtrent Enkele Onderwerpen van algemeen Belang,* *1920,* p. 12; and Erich H. Jacoby, *Agrarian Unrest in Southeast Asia* (New York, 1949), pp. 254–55.

maximum of government aid, and even then only in the form of isolated workshops with a maximum of ten to fifteen laborers and with the "assistance" of greedy Chinese middlemen. The sense of native enterprise became dulled under such conditions and formed the basis of further agitation.[14]

The economic role which the Indonesian played remained the one of the laborer, the employee, or the coolie. This was in a sense characteristic of the entire position of Indonesian economy; as one authority has remarked: "In many respects the relationship between mother-country (including the laboring classes) and the colony is one, which is similar to that between the bourgeoisie and the proletariat."[15] Much more than in the realm of capital did the modern Indonesian draw his nationalist aspiration from his affiliation with the industrial or agrarian proletariat. The entire nationalist movement in Indonesia was only in part the work of intellectuals; by far the greater agitation was stirred up by the ranks of labor. The strike in Indonesia was not an economic device for the improvement of the standard of living but almost invariably a new nationalist tactic directed not only against management but also against Dutch political control. Strikes occurred repeatedly, overtly for the purpose of wage increases or the establishment of pensions, accident insurance, or retirement plans, but in reality motivated almost exclusively by political reasons. The importance of the role of labor in these years is well illustrated by the fact that all the chief nationalist groups (including the Indonesian Communist party) fought one another to the bitter end for the control of the workers' movement.

The first Indonesian labor union dates from 1908 and was formed among the workers of the various trolley and railroad companies in Java. The statutes of the organization, which included European as well as native employees, carried no overt revolutionary character; no mention of the word "strike" or of "the rights of labor" (characteristic of later Indonesian unions)

14. Boeke, *op. cit.*, chap. i; and J. W. Meyer Ranneft, "The Economic Structure of Java," in B. Schrieke, *The Effect of Western Influence on Native Civilization in the Malay Archipelago* (Batavia, 1929), pp. 83 ff.

15. J. W. Meyer Ranneft, "Drie Stroomingen," *Koloniaal Tijdschrift*, XXV (1939), 119.

was made; the chief emphasis was upon mutual protection, social care, pensions, and medical aid for the affiliates.[16] The true character of the union did not become clear until 1920, when the Indonesian Communist party was formed under Sneevliet, and the organization was completely brought under its control. In that year the bitter struggle began between the Communists and the growing nationalist party, Sarekat Islam (SI). As more unions were being formed rapidly, notably among the employees of the government pawnshops, among the teachers of public schools, and among the workers of the government public works and services, both the SI and the Communists realized that a central federation of all these unions could transform the Indonesian proletariat into a powerful fist. "Then the struggle for freedom from colonial oppression," as one observer has put it, "could be fought on two fronts; the labor movement could become an important factor in the general political structure."[17] As early as 1919, plans for such a federation had been formulated by members of the SI, who even declared that a central direction of the various unions could lead to "independence and the transformation of a capitalist society into a socialist society." But the Communist leader, Semaoen, was able to form the first federation. At a congress in 1920, where representatives of twenty-two unions were present, the first labor union central was formed, completely dominated by the Communists. Semaoen had plans to seek affiliation of his group with the Third International, but at a new congress the next year the unions sympathetic to the SI formally seceded from Semaoen's federation and, with a few older unions, formed a separate federation.[18]

The main reason for this split and the formation of two separate federations was undoubtedly due to the diverging objectives of the nationalists and the Communists. Both wanted an end to Dutch colonial rule, but there further agreement ended. The Communists sought the Marxian state at the end of the struggle, the SI—springing, as has been indicated above, from

16. Cf. *Javasche Courant*, February 19, 1909, No. 14.
17. J. Th. Petrus Blumberger, "Vakbeweging (Inlandsche)," *Encyclopaedie van Nederlandsch-Indie* (The Hague, 1919), VII (Aanvullingen, 1935), 429.
18. *Mededeelingen der Regeering Omtrent Enkele Onderwerpen van algemeen Belang, 1921*, chap. B, *passim*.

the small native entrepreneur class—wished no such thing. The latter took labor to its bosom for tactical reasons; it was willing to champion its rights and pay lip service to socialist precepts, but it remained largely indifferent to Communist economic theory. As the chairman of the SI, Tjokroaminoto, once declared during a congress in 1920: "First of all we must fight for political freedom. We wish to be treated with the same rights as the Europeans. It is not necessary to adhere to certain sets of principles, but it is important to show force. Later on we shall see if we are socialists."[19]

This admonition "to show force" did not fall on deaf ears. In the years 1920–22 the national economy was rent asunder by a series of crippling strikes, many of them unauthorized by either the federation or the executive committee of the union itself. This spontaneous outburst on the part of groups of employees of various unions was the first warning to the Dutch government that the structure of the old-time economy was gradually changing. A dispute on a mid-Java trolley line, where workers demanded an eight-hour day and a 10 per cent wage increase, met with little opposition from the management at first, until the strike spread like wildfire to other trolley and railroad services. The management of the various companies considerably stiffened their attitude, and in some places violence occurred. Ultimately, after "gentle pressure" from the government, the demands of the unions were met. Another strike of considerable importance occurred among the native employees of the sugar refineries and plants, which involved primarily the agrarian element of the population. This strike greatly influenced the future economy of the European plantation companies, since it raised for the first time the problem of the minimum wage and provided a new potent weapon for the entire labor movement. In the case of the sugar strike, the government went so far as to make a special investigation and to "remind the management of the sugar companies of their moral obligation as regards their employees."[20] These reminders were ultimately successful, and the wage demands of the workers were satisfied.

19. *Mededeelingen der Regeering . . . 1922*, col. 5.
20. *Mededeelingen der Regeering . . . 1929*, col. 12.

As a result of this—from the labor point of view—successful start, the next decade was characterized by a huge increase in the membership of most unions. In 1918 there had been 700 members and 5 unions; in 1920, with the establishment of the two federations, the figures were 8,000 and 28, respectively; 31,000 and 57 in 1931; 60,000 and 34 in 1940.[21] Figures for the Japanese occupation and for the period since the outbreak of the revolution fall outside the scope of our study, but this increase and the consolidation of the multiple unions into fewer and larger ones indicated a growing sense of solidarity—political as well as economic—in proletarian ranks. The unions themselves spread to every type of industrial activity, and organized labor became an ever increasing power in the national economy. The Indonesian world seemed especially fond of the sympathy strike, as is shown in the case of the well-known strike of the government pawnshop workers in 1922, when more than 8,000 workers refused to return unless the government met their demands, and in the case of the strike among employees of printing-shops in Soerabaja in the same year. The last strike spread to government employees, teachers of public schools, stevedores, etc., and reached such proportions that the government was forced to intervene. But most of the demands of the strikers were met. Each victory added strength to the budding native movement, and, as the Indonesian gradually awoke intellectually and began to aspire to a new sense of human dignity, his affiliation with some labor union often became the most potent weapon he could wield in his fight for social and political equality. This aspect of the workers' movement is well illustrated by the above-named pawnshop strike. In an effort to supervise the native's irregular financial dealings and to prevent extortion by moneylenders, the government had established a system of pawnshops which served the average Indonesian's perennial financial needs. The employees of these shops were largely natives, and a union among them had been in existence since 1916. The great strike of 1922 occurred not for economic reasons or because of political agitation but solely because at a pawnshop in Djokjakarta one employee refused to carry pawned objects from a storeroom to

21. *Statistisch Abstract van Nederlandsch-Indie* (Batavia, 1940), pp. 12–13.

the auction hall as he had been accustomed to do. The reason for this refusal, as the government, after a careful investigation, explained, was because the employee in question had come to regard this carrying of the pawns as manual labor, suitable only for a coolie—"it was contrary to his dignity and standing in his community." Hundreds of fellow-employees concurred—and were likewise fired as the strike spread all over Java. At first the government did not relent; ultimately the workers returned, and no more "coolie labor" was required of them![22]

All during the twenties Communist agitation was rife in the Indies, and the young labor movement was often the center of the turmoil. Constant work stoppages (especially on the railroads), mass meetings, enlivened by incendiary propaganda, open declarations advocating the overthrow of the government and the establishment of the dictatorship of the proletariat, characterized the activities of a new and powerful Communist labor federation, the SKBI, founded in 1928. At the same time, nationalist agitation reached the high-water mark. The Sarekat Islam and the Partai Nasional Indonesia, also bidding for the favors of the proletarian world, kept the country in a constant state of unrest. At no time was the true character of the labor movement in the Indies so well illustrated as in this period; strikes broke out merely for political reasons, and the effect of this proletarian unrest would even have been greater had there been a measure of unity among the nationalist parties and the Communists themselves. The Dutch government, since the turn of the century committed to a progressive colonial policy, was more than embarrassed. At first it tried to calm the excitement, but when this proved to be useless, it ruthlessly crushed the Communist party and its labor organizations—which meanwhile had affiliated themselves with the "League against Colonial Oppression" (an agency of the Third International)—and exiled many labor leaders in the interests of "the general quiet and order." The result was, at first, the almost complete demise of the labor movement and then the rapid reorganization of unions on a—seemingly—nonpolitical basis. The government

22. J. Th. Petrus Blumberger, "Vakbeweging (Inlandsche)," p. 432.

indicated that it welcomed organized labor but would not permit the use of labor for purposes of political agitation.[23]

Even though the overt violence did indeed diminish, the workers' movement retained much of its political character. After the expulsion of the Communists the struggle for complete control over the Indonesian unions continued between the Sarekat Islam and the religiously neutral Partai Nasional Indonesia. Neither organization attained any victory, primarily because the very necessity of control by one single organization proved purposeless. Beginning in 1934 the various Indonesian nationalist parties exhibited the same type of consolidation as the unions: factional differences lost their meaning. With the realization that, without unity, nothing could be attained, nationalist parties, together with important labor unions, formed large federations such as the "Gapi" and the "Frani."[24] Labor and nationalism, though both shirking the open violence of the twenties, which had proved to be so useless, were one by the outbreak of the second World War. Not a single nationalist party, not a single labor union, could be found in 1940 which differed in its major objectives from its fellow-organizations. Although the Indonesian workers' movement could not boast of the organizational structure and the multiple devices of labor pressure that characterize the unions of Europe and America, no single economic factor contributed so much to the rise of a modern Indonesia as did the native labor federations.

III

One of the outstanding characteristics of a modern colonial economy is the sharp division that exists between the industrial (skilled or unskilled) labor market and the intellectual (including white-collar) labor market. The former is never flooded, for industrialization has not occurred so intensively in the colonies that an unemployed segment of the industrial proletariat has been created. The latter, especially since the turn of the century, is always crowded, and semieducated native elements, for whom

23. *Ibid.*, p. 433, and *Handelingen van de Volksraad* (Batavia, 1919 ff.), 3rde gew. zitting, 15 Maart, 1929, pp. 145 ff.
24. *Bataviasch Nieuwsblad*, May 4, 1938; October 14, 1939.

a little learning has, as often as not, proved to be a dangerous thing, have constituted, since its inception, much of the rank and file of the nationalist movement. Education has been the Trojan horse which the Dutch have allowed to enter within the secure walls of their island empire, primarily because the native regarded education not as a thing worth having in itself but always from the point of view of economic self-improvement. More than one Dutch authority has warned that education of the native should not occur too rapidly for "it might force up the wage-demands."[25]

The Dutch system of education in Indonesia dates largely from the second half of the nineteenth century, but no broad opportunity was given the native to avail himself of any type of school until well into the present century.[26] Despite attempts to reach as far as possible into the uneducated layers with the establishment of village schools, the percentage of native illiterates was, as late as 1930, still about 95.[27] That meant that the literates were very much in a class by themselves. Those natives who had obtained Western primary or secondary education (about 2 per cent of the literates) had got this far often at the cost of considerable sacrifice of the parents, for whom education was equivalent to a greater income. These natives usually obtained the smaller administrative positions in business or government service; but, inasmuch as opportunity in this respect remained fairly limited, the supply exceeded the demand, and requirements for the most insignificant posts increased almost yearly as a result. It is no exaggeration to say that in the decade before the outbreak of the second World War there existed in the chief cities of Indonesia a restless, partially employed, native white-collar class, which, because of its limited education and restricted economic opportunity, provided a major source of political discontent. Although the number of Indonesians in the various types of positions in government service increased, this growth was by no means sufficient to absorb the total in-

25. A. D. A. de Kat Angelino, *Staatkundig Beleid en Bestuurszorg in Nederlandsch-Indie* (The Hague, 1930), III, 220.

26. I. Brugmans, *Geschiedenis van het Onderwijs in Nederlandsch-Indie* (Batavia, 1934), chaps. i–ii.

27. *Statistisch Abstract van Nederlandsch-Indie* (1931), p. 22.

crease in the number of trained, native white-collar workers, technicians, and intellectuals (see Table 2).[28]

Inasmuch as the government remained the biggest employer, as well as the formulator of a policy of emancipation, the partici-

TABLE 2

PERCENTAGES OF THE THREE CLASSES OF POPULATION WITH RESPECT TO
TYPES OF POSITIONS HELD IN GOVERNMENT SERVICE
FOR 1928 AND 1938*

TYPE OF POSITION	1928			1938		
	Eur.	Nat.	For. O.	Eur.	Nat.	For. O.
Technical and maintenance	84.77	14.83	0.85	77.14	20.12	2.74
Administrative, technical..	77.06	22.28	0.66	55.81	41.98	2.21
Financial...............	80.45	18.8	0.75	67.08	30.46	2.46
Administrative, clerical....	93.66	5.1	1.24	65.18	32.16	2.66
Supervisory..............	92.46	7.33	0.21	83.97	15.68	0.35

* These three divisions of the population were the ones employed under the Dutch East Indies law code. Each group had its own jurisprudence and legal provisions and type of citizenship. Transfer from one group to the other was possible and did frequently occur. Under "Foreign Orientals" (here "For. O.") were classified all nonnative Asiatic inhabitants of Indonesia, except the Japanese; they constituted less than 2 per cent of the total population.

TABLE 3

DISTRIBUTION OF POPULATION GROUPS AMONG FOUR CATEGORIES OF
GOVERNMENT POSITIONS IN 1940 (IN PERCENTAGES)

Population Group	Lower Personnel	Lower Intermediate	Intermediate	Higher
Europeans...............	0.6	33.3	57.6	92.2
Indonesians..............	98.9	60.6	38.0	6.4
Assimilated Indonesians*...	0.2	3.4	2.0	0.5
Chinese..................	0.3	2.7	2.3	0.8
Other foreign orientals.....				

* This group included persons of mixed European, native, or Chinese blood.

pation of all classes of population in the administration was something of an index to colonial economy and to the sincerity with which the Dutch conducted their "ethical" colonial mission. Table 3 shows that the increasing number of Indonesians

28. *Verslag van de Commissie tot Bestudeering van Staatsrechtelijke Hervormingen, ingesteld bij Gouvernementsbesluit van 14 September, 1940*, No. IX/KAB (Batavia, 1941), I, 56. This report will hereafter be referred to as "*Rapport Visman*," after the name of the chairman of the investigating committee which wrote it.

who had obtained college or professional training held only a small percentage of the higher and intermediate positions in the government.[29]

Since during recent decades hundreds of Indonesians have obtained higher education—a condition fostered by the establishment of a number of professional colleges in Indonesia itself —the flood of qualified graduates could not be absorbed by colonial society. The inevitable result was the rapid growth of another class of unemployed, this time that of the highly trained native intellectual, who refused on the basis of his education to be satisfied with a minor position. Again it should be pointed out that the frustration which the educated native thus felt had primarily an economic background; the factor of prestige, though important in terms of nationalism, remained secondary. The failure of the Dutch government to absorb within its economic framework the educated Indonesian, regardless of his rank and family background, constituted a major cause of the revolution. This fact should have been known to the government, after the report of a special investigating committee in 1940: "A matter of ever recurring grievance, is the small number of Indonesians who are considered for the higher positions. The Government should have more confidence in the capacities of Indonesian intellectuals. Even though the choice might be limited, the Government would do well to take an occasional risk, even if things were less capably run according to Dutch standards. What would be lost in quality would be gained in appreciation and confidence."[30]

Nowhere is the basic dilemma of modern colonial policy so well illustrated as in this statement. Two opposing trends of administration collide here. The first represents the colonial status quo and the philosophy that a colony exists—when all is said and done—for the benefit of the colonial power. To the Dutch it was unthinkable that every Indonesian with the proper qualifications should be given the opportunity to compete with full-blooded Dutchmen in all, especially leading, positions in government and business. Yearly the Netherlands witnessed the emigration of a goodly crop of its own intelligentsia to Indo-

29. *Ibid.*, I, 56.   30. *Ibid.*, II, 23.

nesia, since the mother-country failed to provide sufficiently rewarding opportunities; the Indies constituted an important safety valve to Dutch intellectuals. On the other hand, Dutch policy had declared itself to be "ethical" and progressive; rapid emancipaton was the avowed goal of colonial administrators. Indonesians could not help learning to distrust this supposed emancipation, and the revolution was in many respects nothing but a desperate attempt to obtain a measure of economic and social standing on the part of those natives, whom one authority accurately described as "burning with an unbridled desire to govern,"[31] a desire which at no time was even partially satisfied.

Since the leadership of the nationalist parties was recruited from this educated portion of the native world, which throughout felt that the education which it had obtained, often at considerable sacrifice ,was bootless economically as well as socially, nationalist demands inevitably took on a socio-economic character. The nationalist wished political liberty but also an end to Dutch colonial capitalism; above all, he wished to take a place in his own land commensurate with his abilities. The inevitable result was the popularity of socialism and communism in nationalist circles. The struggle for economic opportunity also meant a struggle for social equality, and not a single nationalist party in Indonesia can be found today which, since its inception, has not advocated doctrines which smack of leftist ideologies. In analyzing this problem, Soetan Sjahrir wrote: "Freedom doesn't mean anything if we fail to give it a social content. Looking back at the history of western countries, we observe how by neglecting this very fact the political freedom of the individual after the French Revolution turned into its reverse when the industrial revolution came to an end. Freedom under a liberalistic capitalistic system was misused by mighty economic groups for a freedom of unlimited exploitation. The social structure of colonial countries is one of economic servility of the ruled to foreign powers amongst which the capitalistic system is rampant."[32]

Schooled in the same academic tradition as the Dutchman, the native intellectual saw in a more just distribution of the

31. F. M. baron van Asbeck, "Indonesie in Azie," *Indonesie*, I (1947), 15.
32. Soetan Sjahrir, *op. cit.*

social product the only road to a true emancipation of his fellow-Indonesians, unhampered by the economic interests of the larger Dutch enterprises; for with the establishment of these enterprises the entire indigenous economy had been upset. Suddenly the native found that in his land there existed, side by side, two different types of economic activity: his own, geared to local consumption and almost unfamiliar with the use of money, and that of the Dutch, a late capitalism, sensitive to world demand and exceedingly fluid in its organization and operation.[33] As the administration penetrated into the remotest areas of the Indies and as, through the government's taxation program, the native had an unfamiliar money economy thrust upon him, he was often forced to supplement his simple earnings from the sale of his farm products or craftsmanship with work on plantation or factory. And over it all loomed the problem of increasing overpopulation, with the result that, in so far as government figures can be relied upon, growing numbers became unemployed or held only irregular and part-time work. In the decade before the outbreak of the second World War there was a steady migration from the country to the cities, where the struggle for economic survival had already reached a very high pitch. The emigration-colonization attempts of the government, whereby peasants from densely populated Java were transported to the outer provinces and given free land and implements, did not seem to affect this situation in the slightest. The native population of the five major cities of Indonesia increased by 30 per cent in less than a decade.[34]

Native nationalists did not fail to notice these conditions and to make them the basis of much of their agitation. The Soerabajasche Studie Club (a group of moderately nationalist intellectuals) took the lead, early in the thirties, in organizing the "intellectual proletariat" for purposes of exerting pressure on the government in its demand that specific percentages of academic positions in the civil service be given to qualified natives. At the same time the Studie Club agitated for an overhaul of the

33. J. H. Boeke, "De economische Theorie der dualistische Samenleving," *De Economist*, XXV (1935), 773 ff.
34. *Statistisch Abstract van Nederlandsch-Indie* (1938), p. 6.

existing agrarian economy, demanding that native peasants be given a better chance to compete with Western enterprise. To fulfil the native's perennial monetary needs, a Bank of Indonesia was established by the Studie Club, only to collapse after a few months because of lack of funds. The government refused to grant the necessary subsidies. At the same time the Pendidikan Nasional Indonesia, which by 1935 had become the largest single nationalist organization, with more than half a million members, sponsored a drive among native white-collar workers and succeeded in uniting most of the clerical and lower technical personnel in government service. After repeated pressure, new positions formerly held by Europeans were opened to natives, but the government followed so halfhearted a policy in this respect that the reforms were practically useless and the flames of a militant nationalism among the semi-intellectual natives were fanned ever higher. In the native press constant demands were made that "the sons of this country be given a full chance to develop the nation" and that the "era of white intellectual supremacy must come to an immediate end." Finally, mention should be made of the native co-operatives sponsored by the Sarekat Islam and the Studie Club, where scores of native craftsmen and peasants not only found a new lease on their economic lives but at the same time were fully indoctrinated with the idea that the end of "foreign" capitalism was the only solution to the ills besetting their growing country.[35]

IV

Apart from these factors, the general economic policy of the Dutch government in Indonesia was one which could not fail to arouse deep resentment, again especially in the native world. The tremendous gulf that separated the average native from the average European economically became a major source of irritation as the emancipation of the Indonesian world continued. In a country where approximately 75 per cent of the native population lived from the fruits of agricultural production, the gov-

35. Cf. *Soeara Oemoem*, April 3, 1935; *Indonesia Ra'ja!*, May 14, 1936, and August 3, 1938; and J. Th. Petrus Blumberger, "Nationalistische Beweging, Indonesisch," *Encyclopaedie van Nederlandsch-Indie*, III, 34 ff.; V (Aanvullingen), 116 ff.

ernment noted in an official report in 1940 that the average native's income was about 20 guilders per year in the rural areas, which were inhabited by some 85 per cent of the total population of Indonesia. Yet natives (97 per cent of the total population), at the level of this average income, paid almost as much in taxes in the decade before the second World War as did the other—and infinitely wealthier—groups of Europeans and Chinese combined (see Table 4).[36]

TABLE 4

TAX YIELD ACCORDING TO POPULATION GROUPS
(IN MILLIONS OF GUILDERS)

Year	European and Foreign Oriental	Native
1913...............	47.6	55.3
1923...............	191.9	110.6
1930...............	184.1	128.6
1933...............	113.9	112.8
1936...............	114.9	110.2
1939...............	135.6	143.8

This distribution might even be considered rather fair until one is reminded of the figures with reference to the income tax, which began with annual earnings of 900 guilders and up. In 1939 the government revealed that approximately 50 per cent of the total European group earned between 3,000 and 8,000 guilders a year, but only 1/200 of 1 per cent of all Indonesians fell in this category. Taxes were, furthermore, so distributed that the mass of native landowners paid about 10 per cent of their meager enough income in taxes, which was exactly as much as upper-class Europeans paid on incomes ranging between 8,000 and 9,000 guilders a year.[37] Nationalist attempts to increase the corporations tax on the larger estate-owning enterprises in order that the tax burden on the small native cultivator might be alleviated were in vain, thanks to the efficient pressure of planters' organizations.[38]

It would not be inaccurate to say that about half the sums

36. *Rapport Visman*, I, 17 and 44.
37. *Ibid.*, pp. 44-45.
38. Cf. *Handelingen van den Volksraad*, Ond. 3, st. 4, April 17, 1936.

spent by the government for purposes of emancipation was paid by native Indonesians themselves. The irony of this fact lies primarily in the native's inability to obtain the full benefits of the money he had paid for this purpose. He would pay for the upkeep and expansion of the educational system, but, once his children had attended the schools, the barrier of colonial conservatism prevented them from reaping the immediately tangible benefits of the system. The government might establish

TABLE 5

ORDINARY GOVERNMENT EXPENDITURE ON
EMANCIPATION PROJECTS (IN MIL-
LIONS OF GUILDERS)

Year	Total Spent	Percentage of Total Ordinary Government Expenditure
1919..............	93.7	24.5
1921..............	128.4	25.0
1924..............	76.6	19.0
1930..............	119.2	22.5
1936..............	52.4	15.0
1939..............	63.2	14.8

agrarian institutes to help the peasant in a more scientific form of production, but it could not curtail the growth of Western enterprise so that the native cultivator would at last come into his own. Native industry might receive subsidies and thus maintain a precarious existence, but any type of government aid that could conceivably be harmful to European industry was out of the question. And so it went with every economic aspect of the emancipation program which colonial policy-makers were busily creating. To native nationalists, who were sufficiently distrustful of the emancipation program as it was, it became clear, furthermore, that the sums spent by the government for national and popular development were steadily decreasing and that, in view of the unparalleled profits made in the sugar industry alone, a much higher corporations tax would be a gesture of good faith. But emancipation sums decreased, and the tax on Western enterprise was never raised (see Table 5).[39]

39. *Rapport Visman*, I, 41.

Nor did the suspicion—prevalent in nonnative circles as well —that the government had not broken completely with the old policy of exploitation for the benefit of the mother-country disappear. This was borne out by the fact that, although the Netherlands allowed its currency to devaluate in the midthirties, no such arrangement was effected in Indonesia, which, despite a storm of protests, was rigidly kept on the gold standard. Inasmuch as Indonesia depended for its economic stability entirely on its exports and since the Netherlands levied high import duties on its own colonial imports, the results, in the words of Meyer Ranneft, were that "Indonesia's finances became worse than those of any other country in its surroundings."[40] The high tariff duties which the colony had to pay became all the more odious in view of the special trade agreements effected between Holland and Indonesia, whereby certain quotas of colonial exports had to be shipped to the home country, and other preferential status was given the Dutch commodities. When the Dutch government, especially since the depression, made a determined effort to halt the flood of cheap Japanese goods into the Indies, it seemed not to realize that Japanese commodities were the only ones within the average native's budget and that a curtailment of these imports would cause genuine hardship, since neither the Netherlands nor any other country could provide equally cheap and durable substitutes. Economically speaking, there was not the slightest reason in the world why Japanese imports should be curtailed, since Dutch commodities had always been sufficiently expensive to keep them out of the purchasing range of the average native. But since Dutch industry—especially textile production—needed a boost, the Indonesian market was flooded at periodic intervals with commodities from the home country, which in the far greater majority of cases were bought only by nonnatives. This dumping process met with increasing opposition in the native world, and under the leadership of the Soerabajasche Studie Club attempts were made to manufacture those goods

40. J. W. Meyer Ranneft, "Holland's Fout in Indie," *De Gids*, II (1936), 319.

formerly of Japanese origin in Indonesia itself by the native co-operative workshops.[41]

On this basis the general economic structure of Indonesia under Dutch rule was exceedingly weak, since it was susceptible to the slightest deterioration of world markets and international production. The national budget through the years reflected this weakness and susceptibility. The brief economic crisis of 1920–21 and the depression of the early thirties offered ample

TABLE 6

INDONESIA'S NATIONAL DEBT
(IN MILLIONS OF GUILDERS)

Year	Floating Debt	Constant Debt	Total
1913	20.6	84.1	104.7
1914	89.0	82.4	171.4
1918	138.3	254.0	392.3
1923	235.8	1,067.9	1,303.7
1928	7.4	1,011.7	1,004.3
1931	186.7	1,139.8	1,326.5
1933	261.4	1,261.0	1,522.4
1937	34.2	1,324.1	1,358.3
1939	122.6	1,250.0	1,372.6

proof in this respect. As producer of agrarian and mineral goods, the national economy was always badly hit by every collapse of the price structure, the more so since the government itself participated in the production process. Given the low income of the native population, taxes could hardly be raised, and, since the core of the ordinary expenses remained constant, the government had recourse increasingly to loans, while it also tried to reduce expenses by eliminating many branches of its services. The last measure, as has been indicated above, adversely affected a growing native class of white-collar workers, technicians, and professional men, with a corresponding rise in nationalist agitation. The former resulted in a steady rise of the national debt to the extent that the money borrowed in recent decades far exceeded the capital investments of the government in various enterprises (see Table 6).[42]

41. Cf. J. van Gelderen, *La Politique de crise des Indes Néerlandaises* (Geneva, 1935), pp. 12 ff.; and *Report of Java Bank, 1933–1934* (Batavia, 1934), pp. 23–55.
42. *Rapport Visman*, I, 49–50; and R. M. Soenario, *Verschulding en economische Toestand op Java's Platteland* (Batavia, 1939), pp. 17–19.

The delicate machinery of modern colonial administration was, furthermore, so constructed that any attempt to curtail expenditures would in the end affect the entire emancipation program, and the situation in 1940 in Indonesia had reached such a state that a government committee admitted that in the past certain aspects of the government's task had been so restricted that "the welfare program has for more than five years been languishing."[43] The costs of the war and the havoc created by the Japanese occupation added to the by no means promising economic picture that the Dutch bequeathed to the new Indonesian federation. This economic heritage could have been an entirely different one had industrialization occurred on any appreciable scale and the populous backbone of the Indies thus been given a more lasting economic stability than the type of Western estate production afforded, had the government completely abandoned an economy designed for the benefit of the foreign investor, and had it in the last analysis made a genuine attempt to strengthen the structure of native economy from the peasant to the craftsman and entrepreneur. Under such conditions Dutch economic policy would have been in harmony with the aspirations of the awakening Indonesian masses. As it was, only the gravest suspicions and the deepest grievances could result from the colonial economic structure. Although, since the end of the first World War, Indonesia had had a representative organ, the Volksraad ("People's Council"), this body had no decisive authority in the formation and approval of the national budget. It could make recommendations, could even veto the budget, but its authority was superseded by that of the governor-general and the legislature in the Netherlands. It is indicative of the economic trend that the records of the People's Council show that yearly a bitter but powerless opposition raised its voice against the distribution of the budgetary appropriations, only to be overridden by the more powerful representatives of government and Western enterprise.[44] Joint opposition to the government's economy as it was presented in the council was a

43. *Bataviasch Nieuwsblad*, October 5, 1940.
44. Cf. *Handelingen van den Volksraad*, 1ste gew. zitting, 1928, Ond. 1, Afd. I: st. 5; 1ste gew. zitting, 1934, Ond. 11, Afd. III: st. 4.

major factor in the growth of solidarity among the few delegates of native nationalist parties. Where formerly nationalists were deeply divided, in later years, when the council had been given a voice in the determination of the budget, they exhibited unity and a willingness to forego factional differences for the sake of making a determined stand against "ethical" exploitation.

V

In the confusing picture of Indonesian nationalism, with its multicolored background, the shape and context of its economic aspects alone emerge clearly. The religious, the social, the political, and the cultural aspects are inextricably interwoven, and the platform and origin of each nationalist party differ in fabric from those of the others. But on the economic issues all saw eye to eye; they were a constant source of strength. The Indonesian revolution resembled other great revolutions in history. In so far as it reflected middle-class intellectual aspirations of greater participation in the government and in so far as it was a reaction to existing economic conditions, it mirrored the French; in so far as it employed Marxian principles, it partook of the Russian; and in its desire for civil liberty and economic security it reflected the English revolution. What gives the Indonesian upheaval its unique quality, however, is the fact that all these factors operated within the framework of a plural economy, i.e., the existence side by side of a late capitalism as exemplified by Western enterprise; of an early (and in some cases pre-) capitalism, typified by native village economy covering 80 per cent of the entire territory of Indonesia; and, third, of a mixture of these two, employing techniques of both and operating, for example, in native quarters in the cities and in the welfare measures undertaken by the government. Since a colonial government, *sui generis*, stands committed to give the greater weight to the first of these types, it follows that, whenever it seeks to "emancipate" or to "lift up" the second type, it must employ measures which will ultimately bring the two into tragic conflict. This conflict precisely constitutes the economic origin of Indonesian nationalism. It is the collision that resulted when precapitalist native society began to acquire the techniques of a full-blown capitalism which it found in its country. In an effort to become the Westerner's equal as soon as possible, these skills and techniques were acquired by the native world, but only with the result that the colonial principle collided headlong with native aspirations. From this conflict much of the character of Indonesian nationalism stems: its predominant leftist ideology, its faith in the possibilities of social engineering, and the type of its leadership.

But at the same time this conflict produced an inner void. Though anxious to outdo the Westerner and to acquire the skills whereby his economic position might be improved, the native remained "indifferent regarding the origin from which that knowledge and technique eventually have sprung, namely the culture and mind of the West."[45] This uncertainty and indifference, as Sjahrir has so ably noted, produced a sense of seclusion together with a realization that Western skills had to be mastered in order that Indonesia might take its place among the nations of the world. Despite this realization, a deep aversion against the West arose; the nationalist needed the Dutch, yet despised them. The techniques were acquired without sympathy for their origin; and, once they were acquired, native intellectuals had in many cases but precious little opportunity to put them into practice. In a sense Dutch colonial policy thus committed a double error: it created a society where its standards were the only ones of real importance, but, even though the native adhered to them, he still remained on the outside—yes, was even given to understand that the Dutch respected his *adat* (custom and usage) and preferred that he stay within their limits. But within a plural society native standards are always in danger of being effaced, for there is no homogeneity in cultural life to sustain the old traditions. Furthermore, because of the colonial framework, the entire community tends "to be organized for production rather than for social life; social demand is sectionalized, and within each section of the community the social demand becomes disorganized and ineffective,"[46] so that

45. Soetan Sjahrir, *op. cit.*, April 27, 1946.
46. J. S. Furnivall, *Netherlands India: A Study of Plural Economy* (New York, 1944), p. 459.

individual members of the colonial community were prevented from obtaining all benefits that a homogeneous society offers. The reaction to these conditions led to a nationalism with a distinct anti-Western character, which—in view of the colony's future development—could not help being detrimental to the native nationalist movement itself. To the Indonesian applies what Pandit Nehru once observed with respect to the Indian movement: "We suffer from the disease of nationalism and that absorbs our attention and it will continue to do so till we get political freedom."[47]

47. *Towards Freedom: The Autobiography of Jawaharlal Nehru* (New York, 1943), p. 383.

COMMUNISM AND REGIONAL
INTEGRATION

By MILTON SACKS[1]

PARALLEL to and connected with nationalism and regionalism has been the emergence of communism as a potent political force in South Asia. Since World War I, Communists in South Asia have built organizations in India, Ceylon, Burma, Siam, Indochina, Malaya, Indonesia, and the Philippines. Some of these organizations have survived years of illegal existence. In providing answers to the problems confronting nationalism, the Communist movement itself has developed dissident wings in India, Ceylon, Burma, Indochina, and Indonesia. The strategy and tactics employed have uniquely contributed to shape and direct the evolution of nationalism in South Asia. In considering the prospects for unity in the area, it is necessary, therefore, to evaluate in some measure the role played by the Communist movement.

Communism and nationalism found a common soil in which to flourish in South Asia in the period following World War I. By that time colonial rule had already altered the character of indigenous social organization, infusing it with new standards and concepts derived from Western civilization. The basic two-class structural division of society remained relatively unchanged, but the native ruling class, as an intermediary through which foreign domination maintained its sway, underwent transformation. From the small re-educated urbanized population, an embryo nationalist leadership emerged. Some of these elements were attracted to the recently formed Communist International, which, deriving its prestige and authority from the Russian revolution of 1917, called for world revolution and the liberation of all colonial peoples. Thus, from the very outset, some of the nationalists were presented with a body of doctrine

1. Foreign affairs analyst, Department of State.

that professed to illuminate the only sure path to national independence. Communists collaborated with other nationalists in the struggle against the metropolitan powers but competed with them for leadership of the awakening dependent peoples.

Early Communist doctrine had little bearing on the question of regional unity. The "Theses on the National and Colonial Question," adopted at the Second World Congress of the Communist International in 1920, did call on Communists "to combat the pan-Islam and pan-Asiatic and similar movements, which are endeavoring to utilize the liberation struggle against European and American imperialism for the purpose of strengthening the power of Turkish and Japanese imperialists, of the nobility, of the large landowners, of the clergy, etc." The Theses further made it incumbent on Communists "to continually expose the deception fostered among the masses of the toilers in all, and especially in the backward countries, by the imperialist powers aided by the privileged classes of the subject countries, in creating under the mask of political independence various government and state institutions which are in reality completely dependent upon them economically, financially and in a military sense."[2] These commandments had little practical meaning in the interwar period but were to re-emerge as basic Communist doctrine following World War II.

The influence of communism as a factor making for regional unity arose out of its international and interracial program. In the period between the two world wars these factors were completely offset by the general political and economic partition of South Asia. Regional unity was largely an academic question, since the essential precondition for voluntary union in a federation is national independence. One of the principal concerns of Britain, France, and the Netherlands was to gain such advantages as would benefit their own home national economies. Consequently, they tried to limit penetration of their private domains by competing powers. Internally, imperial rule attempted to develop local and particularistic political entities

2. Central Executive Committee of the Communist Party of America, *The Theses and Statutes of the Communist International as Adopted at the Second World Congress, July 17 to August 6, 1920, Moscow, Russia* (n.p., n.d.), pp. 65–66.

among the subject peoples. The Communists were forced to adapt their organizational forms to the specific area which they sought to penetrate. Communism was able to develop only in so far as it provided leadership for peasant and nationalist revolts.

This situation is seen clearly in the actual history of growth of the Communist movement in South Asia. The efforts made in the early 1920's to build a "League of Oppressed Peoples" and an "Intercolonial Union" as regional organizations to develop national revolutionary movements in South Asia were failures. These organizations soon broke up into their constituent nationalities. They were succeeded by the "League against Imperialism," which was created in Brussels, Belgium, in 1927 by the indefatigable Willi Münzenberg, builder of Communist front organizations. The league developed into little more than a propaganda and liaison agency for the European and Asiatic Communist parties. It was on national soil alone that Communist and nationalist movements thrived.

The Indonesian Communist party was formed in 1920 as a separate entity. The Indian party was founded in 1924. Communism was introduced into Indochina, Malaya, and Siam through the Chinese Communist party's South Seas Committee, established in 1926, which maintained liaison with the Indonesians in Singapore. By 1927 it had grown sufficiently to take on the title of "South Seas Communist party," but was still under the authority of the Chinese Communists. This organization was dissolved toward the end of 1930, and parties on a coequal basis were established in each of the areas through absorption of indigenous quasi-Communist organizations. During this period other international front organizations operated in the area— e.g., the Red International of Labor Unions and its Pan-Pacific Trade Union Secretariat, the International of Seamen and Harbor Workers, and the International Red Aid. These organizations had little effect on the activities of the Communists within the nationalist movements except in so far as they provided a network for dissemination of Communist International propaganda.

It must be noted that, by the time World War II began, the Communist movement in South Asia had undergone the same evolution that featured the transformation of the Communist International into a disciplined instrument at the disposal of the Soviet Union. The South Asian parties dutifully changed their line at Moscow's beck and call. Those who failed to go along were expelled and provided a nucleus for dissident Communist groupings.

Among those expelled in 1927 was Tan Malakka, a founder of the Indonesian Communist party, who originated a scheme for regional unity which he named "Aslia." He called for the construction of an all-inclusive "South East Asiatic Revolutionary party" whose objective would be the establishment of a federation embracing the entire South Pacific area, including Malaya, Indonesia, and Australia. This ambitious scheme achieved little support. Tan Malakka is today an important dissident Communist leader in Indonesia, heading his own faction within the nationalist movement. Australia's present active interest in the Indonesian problem indicates that he was not so far from the realities of South Asian politics as one might have supposed.

World War II completely changed the power structure in South Asia. Except in India and Ceylon, the British, French, and Dutch rules in the area were smashed by the Japanese. The nationalists and the Communists were quick to profit from the new situation. On the one hand, the Japanese, primarily concerned with conducting the war, needed a native leadership to help provide a stable base in the newly occupied territories. On the other, the Allies were anxious to develop an anti-Japanese movement as an adjunct to their own military struggle. The nationalist movement was the only force that could fulfil the requirements of either side. The individual nationalists made their choice with the same goal in mind—the acquisition of independence. The Communists, who supported the Allied nations out of loyalty to the Soviet Union, were among the chief organizers of the anti-Japanese guerrilla movements. When the war ended with the victory of Allied arms, they were in a strategic position in many areas of South Asia.

In Indochina, Communist Ho Chi-minh was president of the new democratic republic of Viet-Nam. In Malaya the Communists headed the guerrilla movement, which actually governed many of the towns for a brief interim period. In Burma the Communists were an influential component of the Anti-Fascist People's Freedom League, the major nationalist political force. In Indonesia they were part of a coalition supporting the Indonesian republic. Elsewhere, as a result of chaotic conditions attendant upon the defeat of the Japanese, they had unprecedented opportunities to influence the pattern of events.

At this time, international Communist policy attempted to utilize great-power co-operation through the medium of the United Nations Organization to achieve their objectives. Such steps as would alter the world balance of power were subject to negotiation and compromise leading to attempts at collective agreement between the Western powers and the Soviet Union. Similarly, national Communist tactics operated to create coalition regimes in which the Communists would participate. Throughout Southeast Asia the Communists joined with nationalists in demanding that the provisions of the Atlantic Charter and the new United Nations Organization be implemented. In this vein they welcomed the occupying Allied forces and hoped to negotiate agreements that would grant them recognition. From 1945 to 1947, the Stalinist Communists of South Asia generally followed a policy of compromise, even indicating a willingness to establish a new basis for union with the former colonial powers, Britain, France, and the Netherlands.

The Communists further functioned within the framework of the established governments. In Indochina the Communists helped suppress dissident Trotskyist elements. In Indonesia they disavowed Tan Malakka's Indonesian Communist party, established in 1945, and supported the republic against attempts by elements under his control to take over leadership. Under the direction of Alimin, a new Indonesian Communist party was formed in 1946 which upheld the republic and the signing of the Linggadjati Agreement with the Dutch. In Burma the White Flag Communists (Stalinists), as opposed to the Red Flag Communists, generally co-operated with the Burmese government.

During this two-year period the policy of the Communists in South Asia favored regionalism in an effort to maintain the gains of emergent nationalism. As early as 1945, Ho Chi-minh attempted to join with Soekarno in Indonesia to carry on a common struggle for recognition by the United Nations. The Communists also supported movements that aimed at achieving regional Asian solidarity. Communist Tran Van Giau was one of the delegates from the Viet-Nam republic to the Asian Relations Conference in Delhi in 1947. He was also elected vice-president of the Southeast Asia League, a private regional organization formed in Bangkok in September, 1947, to promote an official federation of Southeast Asia that would include the Philippines, Indonesia, Malaya, Burma, Viet-Nam, Cambodia, Laos, and Siam.

When the international situation changed and the international Communist movement embarked on the course formulated in the decisions of the European Cominform, set up in September, 1947, a complete readjustment took place in Communist colonial strategy. An article on the crisis of the colonial system, which appeared in the Soviet periodical *Bolshevik* of December 15, 1947, explicitly detailed the policy changes later adopted by the Indian Communist party at its congress in February, 1948.[3] The article set forth a new platform for South Asian Communists. The former coalition course was abandoned and replaced by a revolutionary program. This policy gravely affected the position of communism as a factor for regional unity in the area. Communists became, in effect, an opposition force; on the basis of international considerations, they fought the activities of their national governments that held promise for regional unity.

The new colonial policy was a restatement of the ideas contained in the 1920 "Theses on the National and Colonial Question." It characterized the developments in India, Burma, Ceylon, and the Philippines as devices of the imperialists designed "with perfect safety and even profit to themselves, to grant formal independence to certain of their colonies." It attacked the imperialists for deceiving the people with the mousy squeakings of corrupt parliamentary parties and with playing with 'freedom of expression' by means of a thoroughly mercenary

3. E. Zhukov, "Obostreniye krizisa koloniyalnoĭ sistemy" ("The Sharpening of the Crisis of the Colonial System"), *Bolshevik*, 1947, No. 23 (December 15, 1947), pp. 51–64.

bourgeois press. This is an attempt at ideological disarmament by means of constitutional-liberal illusions, trade unionism, and other pretty charms of bourgeois 'Civilization.' " Opposition was expressed to "demands for the 'voluntary' entry of the 'free' colonies into the British Commonwealth of Nations, the French Union, of the 'Union' of the Netherlands and Indonesia." The "English and American colonizers" were further attacked for their support of pan-Islamism and pan-Asianism, defined as reactionary ideologies that "serve to block the development of the struggle for national liberation." Clearly, the only kind of unity that would now meet with Communist favor was one that would place South Asian states in the camp of the Soviet Union.

This conception of unity was underscored by an attack on the theory "now fashionable in Europe, of the third power." The article specifies: "According to this theory, the countries of the Orient should maintain strict neutrality in the struggle between the two forces, Communism and Imperialism. It is significant that the theory of the third power has especially wide currency and success among the Indian bourgeoisie. It is needless to point out that the long ears of the Laborites stick out on the authors of this theory. The meaning of this whole theory amounts to this: the imperialists and their helpers seek to calumniate the USSR, and to this end place her on the same level with the American imperialists."[4] This theme has since pervaded Communist declarations concerning South Asia.

The meeting of the World Federation of Democratic Youth, a Communist front organization, in February, 1948, at Calcutta, India, was the occasion for the public unveiling of this line for South Asia. The conference was attended by representatives of youth from eleven countries of Asia—India, Pakistan, Burma, Malaya, Indonesia, Viet-Nam, Ceylon, China, the Philippines, Nepal, and Korea. Far from contributing to regional co-operation by creating a feeling of regional Asian solidarity, the conference made invidious declarations concerning its host, the Indian government, and alleged that imperial powers in Burma, Pakistan, and Ceylon had changed their direct domination to

4. *Ibid.*, p. 63.

indirect domination and "with the unreserved collaboration of the ruling classes, were seeking to create confusion among the popular masses by giving them a hypocritical gift of fake independence." The conference called on the youth of Southeast Asia to "continue their implacable struggle against world imperialism" and warned them against "the danger of being seduced by illusory slogans" that would divert them from the struggle for the "complete defeat of imperialism and its allies." It was following this conference that the Malayan Communists engaged in guerrilla warfare, as did the Burmese Communists in April, 1948. In their turn, the Indonesian Communists moved toward a break with the republican government, accusing it of capitulation to the Dutch, and then embarked on open insurrection in September, 1948.

The most recent activities of the Communists directed against regional unity have been manifest in the intemperate attacks launched against the Indian efforts to organize a bloc of nineteen Asiatic countries to deal with the Indonesian situation. A typical article is that contained in the March, 1949, issue of *Political Affairs*, the American Communist magazine. This article echoed the line taken by Radio Moscow.[5] "The Asian conference questioned the imperialists' tactics regarding Indonesia, but did not offer proposals that would weaken imperialist domination. On the contrary, following the line of proposals by the Indonesian Republic, the conference suggested methods by which Dutch hegemony might be *strengthened* through creation of a United States of Indonesia under Dutch control. . . . The conference concerned itself primarily with the establishment of an Asian bloc aimed against the colonial liberation forces and the anti-imperialist struggles led by democratic China. Its aim was to present the United States with the foundations for an 'Eastern Union' as worthy of Marshall Plan 'aid' as the Western Union. The significance of this conference lay in its efforts to consolidate the present leadership of the Asian countries against the militant demands of the people, particularly the

5. Badji Tembaga, "Indonesia: The Struggle for Independence," *Political Affairs*, XXVIII, No. 3 (March, 1949), 46–57.

workers and peasants, and their consistent anti-imperialist leaders."[6]

It is apparent that Communism in South Asia favors regional co-operation only if such a movement takes place under its leadership and is tied in with the world policy of the Soviet Union in its struggle with the West. Barring a major change in the international situation, there is little reason to believe that the Communists will change their position. They can be expected to oppose any move toward regional co-operation if it is based on existing states or metropolitan powers who have interests in the area.

6. *Ibid.*, p. 54.

EXCERPTS FROM ROUND-TABLE DIS-
CUSSIONS ON COMMUNISM
IN SOUTH ASIA

Mr. William L. Holland: I would like to ask Mr. Sacks whether the new Moscow "international" line since 1947 has been as successfully applied in Indochina as in other parts of Southeast Asia. If not, what are some of the reasons?

Mr. Sacks: Indochina represents somewhat of a deviation from the pattern. Its significance for evaluating the Communist movement within the country is not clear. The statements that Mr. Isaacs has collected from Viet-Nam certainly indicate deviation. On the other hand, aside from Ho Chi-minh, former members of the now dissolved Communist party have certainly been pressing for the application of the international Communist line. That has become apparent through radio broadcasts made recently, the sending of delegates to the World Peace Conference in France, and the fact that Communist spokesmen like Nguyen Van Tao, the minister of labor, are the ones who make these declarations. It is evident that there is some major difficulty involved there. I might underscore this by saying that the Moscow radio has been referring recently to the Communist party in Viet-Nam as the leader of the present struggle, without qualifying the statement in any way. On the other hand, Ho Chi-minh said recently that the Communist party was dissolved in 1945, which it was, in fact, I might say also that the French maintain that the party was reconstituted only a short while ago, although no substantive evidence, such as statements by an Indochinese Communist party through the medium of the Viet-Nam government radio, has appeared. If you talk about communism as a force in the area, there are sufficient indications that the Communists are attempting to align the activities of the Viet-Nam government within the world Communist framework.

Mr. J. O. M. Broek: How do you explain the fact that the

Soviet Union never raised the question of Viet-Nam in the United Nations, while, of course, on Indonesia the U.S.S.R. took a very strong stand?

MR. ISAACS: I would say that the most likely explanation would be the relationship of the French Communist party to this situation. The French Communist party has taken a wholly equivocal stand on the Viet-Nam issue. Right after the war the French Communists still had high hopes of conquering France. The French Communists, Ho Chi-minh told me in 1945, are colonialists first and Communists second. They want to keep their empire intact. Only a month ago I submitted a list of questions to Ho by radio and asked him whether he thought the French Communist party had effectively championed the cause of Viet-Namese independence. He replied evasively: "It is the duty of all Communist parties in colonialist countries to champion the cause of independence movements." My next question: "To your knowledge, has the French Communist party done anything to hinder the war in Indochina?" His flat answer was "No."

I think the strategy has been to keep Indochina within the French orbit in the light of the possibility that it would be a part of a Communist-dominated France. In 1945, I know for a fact, the French Communists in Saigon drew up a statement, obviously on instructions from Paris, asking the Viet-Namese Communists to check their intensive effort toward independence because the election was due in France in October and the Communists were going to be victors and everything would be settled satisfactorily between them. The Viet-Namese position has remained very equivocal. To this day Ho Chi-minh does not demand complete independence. He still says he is willing to form part of a French Union if the terms are satisfactory.

MR. SACKS: Soviet materials, written for the edification of Soviet nationals, in discussing the Indochinese situation clearly do not talk of the Viet-Namese movement as a struggle for independence. The books and pamphlets always end with the theme that the struggle in Indochina is an attempt by the Viet-Namese to win a place within the French Union on terms which would allow them independence while maintaining a relationship. There is no effort to explain the struggle in terms of a pure and simple struggle for national independence, to break away from the French Union. It is a question of the democratic elements in France reaching some reasonable solution of the problem and dealing with the Viet-Namese.

MR. ISAACS: I might add one further point. The Viet-Namese have been very leery of having their case brought before the UN. They have steered clear of it. They maintained this policy consistently up until March, 1949, when in the first effort of its kind they formally applied for admission to ECAFE. At the meeting I attended in Bangkok, they applied for admission as an associate member on the same basis as Indonesia—the first time the Viet-Nam government had shown any interest in the UN.

MR. SARKAR: How far was communism raised to the present position in international prestige by England and America during World War II? To what extent did it become a world force on account of the propaganda done in favor of Soviet Russia by the Allies after 1941?

MR. ISAACS: It is an ironic fact that many Malayan Communists—all Chinese—were trained and armed by the British as an anti-Japanese measure during the war. Arms were dropped to them and were cached in the jungles. The leadership of the Communist guerrilla movement in Malaya today is virtually a creature of the British in a technical sense. The same thing was true in Burma, as the British have since also had occasion to regret.

MR. SACKS: One of the characteristic features of the war period was the fact that, in their effort to create an anti-Japanese base, it was necessary for the Allied armies to utilize such forces as they could find in the area. In many cases, because the Communists did have a clandestine apparatus that had maintained itself for a long time, they were the force that was used to conduct and carry on guerrilla warfare. The importance of the Communists in the area does not arise merely from the fact that the Communists were given arms. That was just an additional weapon in the arsenal that was provided them by the conditions that existed in the area. They had previously functioned in the nationalist leadership and won much prestige and authority as fighters for national independence in their own right.

MR. THORNER: I wonder if Mr. Sacks would supplement his analysis on one point, and that is: Where in the sequence he has given us do the Bombay naval uprising of February, 1946, the severe strike in September, 1946, on the South Indian Railway, and the agrarian movements of 1946 and 1947 in four different areas fit in?

MR. SACKS: I think that when the war ended, given the way in which the Communist movement internationally and the Soviet Union were working within the framework of this Allied struggle, there was a certain amount of general leeway for the various Communist movements. The Cominform itself stated in 1947 that the reason it was set up was that a number of difficulties had arisen in the relationships between Communist parties. They had not been co-ordinated sufficiently and were going to be co-ordinated from then on.

Actually, the Indian pattern does display some differences in 1945 and 1946. The Indian party reacted in a rather radical fashion to solve things by guerrilla warfare, as in the Hyderabad situation. When the Indian party actually met and discussed these questions, it was set straight by adopting the line of Joshi. Agreement was reached, and there was a change leading to support of Nehru in the whole period up to the end of 1947. The Communists adopted a very conciliatory attitude and collaborated with the nationalist leadership. In February, 1948, at the same time that the youth conference met in Calcutta, the Indian Communist party also held meetings. A difference of opinion arose, and a new line was adopted. An opposition policy was taken toward the Indian government, as I have indicated. India does not follow the pattern exactly, but, when there is pressure from the international Communist movement, there is at distinct intervals the regulation of the line along the general pattern.

MR. A. C. S. ADAMS (British consul, Cincinnati): I would just like to say that I go along with Mr. Isaacs in his opinion that the Communists will not have to fight for it in Southeast Asia, but I do think it would take them quite a time. The populations of South Asia are largely peasant ones, and certainly, judging from the population of Siam, which I know better than the others, it takes a long time to sell the Siamese peasant any idea. I don't thereby minimize the Communist long-range risk there, but I just want to try to put it into relation to the peoples whom it would concern. The Siamese, as far as I know, don't have any genuine, simon-pure communism. They certainly have a Chinese Communist population in their country, and the Chinese population is relatively so large—it may be as much as 4,000,000 out of the 17,000,000 or 18,000,000 of the whole country—that it could form an *imperium in imperio;* but even among those Chinese, most of whom have been settled in the country for a long time and have a stake there, I should say that the possible Communist element is a small and recently immigrated one. It may be paralleled by the Communists in Malaya, I imagine. I believe that the authorities in Malaya reckon the active Communist leaders of the present troubles number between 500 and 1,000, and they, we are told, take good care not to expose themselves to the risks of capture, wounding, or shooting.

MR. SOEDJATMOKO: I think that with regard to communism two factors should be borne in mind: the internal situation in the countries in South Asia and the effect of the approach of the Western countries toward the political and economic problems there. As to the internal political situation, it should be remembered that the Communist parties in their propaganda in a great number of the countries in Southeast Asia have made use not of social slogans but of purely nationalistic ones.

That is especially true in those areas where social tensions were not too acute, as, for instance, in Indonesia, where, because of the absence of landlordism, no acute peasant problem exists. It is understandable that, in those areas where the struggle for political independence was still the main issue, this was the approach with the greatest appeal. Especially so in those countries where the policy of negotiation with the former colonial ruler did not bear fruit as a result of the unwillingness on the part of the former ruler to implement its agreements, as was the case in Indonesia. And wherever a mood of political nationalist frustration set in, it resulted in a tendency to look away from a policy of conciliation and away from the Western powers, away especially from the United States, and to look toward Russia as the only hope for the fulfilment of the nationalist aspirations.

And this is the point I would like to stress here. In the course of our discussions we have been dealing with South Asia in a way that would indicate that these countries are already free in pursuing their own course. It should not be overlooked that colonial warfare is still going on in two of those countries. It is impossible under those circumstances to try to take stock of the political potentials in those areas and to base any political strategy on such an analysis. The colonial problem will have to be solved first.

Coming to my second point, concerning the effect of the approach of the Western countries with regard to that area, there seems to be too great an inclination on the part of the Western countries to approach Southeast Asia merely in terms of anti-Communist strategy. I think that is a serious mistake. An approach in terms of anti-Communist strategy would only tend further to polarize the political elements in that area, and it would bring about the complete disruption of whatever amount of coherence there is actually and potentially in those areas. Several countries would not survive such a polarization. The only fruitful approach would be one of complete acceptance of the general temper of the political feelings there, and that is a complete acceptance of the fact that the political movements in that area are left of center, and certainly left of what is considered the center in American political life. There seems to be some difficulty on the part of the American public in realizing such a need; consider the difficulties they have had in coming to an acceptance of socialism in western Europe. But that is the only possible basis which I see.

MR. FURNIVALL: I do most emphatically agree with what Mr. Soedjatmoko has just said. If you regard communism as subservience to Russia and the belief in violence, that is confined to a very few leaders of the movement. In communism there are some constructive elements that are very necessary, certainly in Burma, and I imagine in a good part of the rest. There is necessary a reintegration of rural life, which requires strong leadership under a strong government. What communism there is in Burma derives its strength from the rural population, which wants not communism but *communalism*, which is common to socialists and to a very large extent to the conservative element.

MR. SACKS: I would like to indicate that the most distinctive thing to me, as far as the Communists in South Asia are concerned, as well as their greatest asset, is their recognition, which is new, of the linking-up of their own future with that of an agrarian movement in the area. That means that they are no longer addressing themselves solely to a small Westernized political group. They are evidently interested in sponsoring a revolutionary peasantry or at least in trying to utilize or spread the things they have learned in China throughout South Asia. I think that is a distinctive feature that emerged in part in the Hyderabad situation in 1946 and 1947. The character of this agrarian movement, I think, is in part visible in the Burmese situation. I think it is also in part apparent in the attempts which the Communists are making with respect to the guerrilla movements in Indochina, in Malaya, and in the Philippines.

It is well to keep in mind that the Communist reorientation toward the great bulk of the population in the area is an attempt to utilize local customs at the village level and to revolutionize them. This itself constitutes an important factor for change. It leads to the necessity for radical solutions that we are discussing. Great efforts have to be directed toward the agrarian problem itself if we wish to stop the authoritarian answer to the problem from becoming the only dominant and clear one.

PART V

AMERICA'S STAKE IN SOUTH ASIA

A POLICY FOR THE UNITED STATES

By Harold R. Isaacs

IN THE last three years the great opportunity which the United States did have, the tremendously favorable political climate which existed for some kind of bold new intervention by the United States in the affairs of Southeast Asia, has largely been dissipated. Friendliness toward America and hopes of American dollar intervention are now increasingly confined to rather small groups of self-seeking politicians or aspiring capitalists, who think that, if they can get their cut of the American pie, they will be able to profit from it enormously and strengthen themselves militarily. That would be particularly true of leaderships like the one now in Siam, where a small clique of politicians and generals is in power. They dream of enjoying American aid on the basis of the Communist menace, and they go to considerable lengths to drum up this Communist menace in the hopes of arousing American interest.

In general, there is among more thoughtful people in South Asia a feeling of complete frustration with regard to the United States. They were acutely conscious in these years of struggle that they were in the midst of great changes. They actually believed that the United States, which was not directly identified with the imperialist structure of the past, with its immense power and capacity and with its new democratic idea (which meant something to all people at almost all levels), was going to be a dynamic force, that it was going to introduce a new era, and that it was going to make possible a real start at the big job of reconstruction.

That belief was, unfortunately, an illusion. The United States in 1945 could have identified itself with the nationalist revolutions, at least to the extent of preventing the forcible return of the old colonial masters to the areas that had been held by the Japanese. It could have taken the position that the war had created new *de facto* situations that had to be recognized, and it could have sponsored negotiations for fixing the new relationships between the ex-rulers, i.e., the French and the Dutch, and the new nationalist leaderships which had taken power in Indochina and Indonesia. Instead, the United States reverted to recognition of the old "legalities." It accepted the position that French and Dutch "sovereignty" had to be restored in the colonies before the colonial system could be revised. It stood by passively while American military equipment and Japanese troops were used in cynical and brutal attacks on the nationalists both in Indochina and in Indonesia. As a participating ally in the Southeast Asia Command, the United States accepted responsibility for shoehorning the French and Dutch back into footholds and for starting the colonial wars which have continued intermittently ever since.

That was the critical time. Those were the critical decisions. It may be that their effects will prove to be irretrievable. In any case the myth about the United States had been one of the major political factors in the objective situation. The spiking of that myth was, by the same token, a major political development. It has gone on progressively in the last four years. The result is that today even those South Asians who most ardently desire to enter into a partnership with the United States are disappointed, baffled, and confused. The Communist description of the United States as an imperialist power supporting its own imperialist satellites against the nationalist movements has won wide acceptance and is not easy to refute. But it would be a mistake to think that the negative attitudes about the United States are a mere product of Communist propaganda. The Communists are simply able to exploit the facts and feelings apparent to everybody, which are shared in no small measure by the most moderate nationalist leaders.

There is now also a strong feeling, which Mr. Soedjatmoko has reflected for us, that any American interest in the area at the present time or in the immediate future will be determined purely by considerations of anti-Communist strategy, i.e., that any new interest or initiative by the United States in the area is directly due to the Communist victory in China.

People are extremely cynical about this now, and it seems quite likely that their cynicism will be justified. It would not be surprising if the State Department did not now start casting about desperately in South Asia in search of anti-Communist allies. It will look for stooges that it can prop up. I submit that, if the United States develops such a policy in South Asia, its defense there against the Communists will be just about as effective as that wooden fence that was built around Shanghai during its last weeks under Nationalist control. Given the present political climate and the total situation in Southeast Asia, a policy based upon armed anticommunism alone will lead only to new bankruptcy. If it should ever come to actual war in South Asia, the United States would find itself with even less effective support than the British, French, and Dutch found against the Japanese.

Mr. Soedjatmoko is entirely correct, in my opinion, in stressing that the American approach to the area has to be based on more than military or strategic considerations. I found throughout South Asia that, apart from the most cynical little groups of ambitious politicians, virtually every articulate person is determined to keep clear of the cold war between the United States and Russia. Nehru's policy of neutrality as between the power blocs gets a big response everywhere. People do not want to get sucked into another war between the powers. They have had their fill of such wars. They hope that they can find a non-Communist road for themselves by their own means. This, to be sure, is not an easy position to maintain in the present state of world politics, and, since most of the nationalist leaderships are not ready for bold social programs in their own countries, there is a strong impulse to fall back on naked force.

What, then, could an enlightened American policy be? This is a formidable question. There is no easy answer. In the first place, any new American initiative will have to be able to overcome the suspicion and distrust engendered by American acts in the area since the end of the war. This will make any policy more difficult to carry out, in contrast to the relative ease with which bold initiative could have been taken in 1945. It may actually be impossible. But I still believe, somewhat grimly, that there is still time, still a surviving opportunity.

As Mr. Soedjatmoko has suggested, the first prerequisite is a political settlement. The American failure to help put an end to colonial rule is the main source of the distrust of American motives. Verbally, the United States has spoken for equitable settlements and expressed sympathy for nationalist aspirations. It has not, up until now, effectively translated these pious expressions into active policy. One result has been to worsen the situations in the two countries directly affected, i.e., Indochina and Indonesia, and to make settlements on desirable terms more difficult.

In general, the American attitude has been conditioned by the needs of American European policy, an unwillingness to upset the applecart of the Atlantic community plan in order to deal more satisfactorily with the colonial problem. A corollary to this has been the conviction held by many influential people in the State Department that only the foreign rulers in these countries could hold the front against the Communists. Both these ideas have, latterly, been compelled to give way to the realities. It has become plain that the Asian problem could not wait. China has taken care of that. It has also become plain that an American European policy that loses the friendship and support of millions of Asians is self-defeating.

As a result, the halfhearted pressure applied on the Dutch has grown a little stronger. The Dutch "police action" in December, 1948, evoked strong American opposition. But the opposition was not strong or consistent enough. Negotiations for a settlement are taking place now amid conditions of serious division and hardship in Java. It is extremely late in the day, but stronger American pressure might possibly still retrieve enough ground to help the Indonesians win real political power from the Dutch and force Dutch military withdrawal from the archipelago.

In Indochina the initial failure of the United States to support the nationalist movement has helped the Communists in that movement to win strong and perhaps dominating positions. The French have traded shrewdly on the Communist issue to avoid the kind of pressure that has been applied on the Dutch. But, at the same time, they have failed, after nearly four years of intermittent warfare, to re-establish any significant degree of control over their colony. Defeated politically and all but defeated militarily, they attempted still another experiment in establishment of a puppet regime, this time under the former emperor of Annam, Bao-Dai. American support for Bao-Dai was solicited and half-withheld only because of the unanimous testimony of observers in the field that he has no chance of succeeding and that the future in Indochina lies in the hands of Ho Chi-minh, the Viet-Namese nationalist leader. Ho, a former Communist, still maintains an equivocal position in international politics, has shown signs of distrusting both Moscow and the Chinese Communist leadership, but will undoubtedly now deal with both of them and eventually lead Indochina into the Communist Asian sphere. Future American policy, as in regard to China, will depend on the future evolution of intra-Communist relationships, about which little is known. But it does seem plain, in any case, that Viet-Nam will gravitate only toward strong poles and that its future will depend still in some degree on whether any new center of polarization is created in South Asia.

It is in this respect that American initiative is still clearly possible. Once again it is a question of whether there is a willingness to take bold steps, to think in new terms, and to bring South Asia into a new international structure based on rationalized common effort. We can start by orienting ourselves to South Asia as a region. Much has been said here to dispute the practicableness of a regional approach. But I can only revert to the statement that the need for it is there, and it is urgent. Antagonisms, differences, even conflicts, tend to iron themselves out sufficiently when there is a common aim and a common need. It is not a matter of accommodating ourselves to old prejudices but of opening new paths.

South Asia's countries must likewise move far along this road. They have to develop a concept of mutual relations that goes far beyond the inadequate machinery of exchanging ambassadors and ministers between separate nations. It would make much more sense, I submit, to begin, right now, to set up a radically different structure. Each country could have a minister for South Asian affairs. Each of these ministers would be a member of a council for South Asia, uniting all the countries concerned. This council could employ foreign technical experts and work in co-operation with the specialized agencies of the UN.

Such a council could draft regional plans for dealing with such common problems as food, transport, education, health, agricultural services. It could establish machinery for carrying out these plans. The scope is almost unlimited. It is really restricted only by the extent to which these nations are willing to go in pooling their resources and their problems. Working with such a council, possibly through the UN or in a more direct relationship, the United States could certainly provide technical assistance of every kind, participate in many of the projects, and make available sufficient capital to get these regional projects under way. These sums need not be astronomic. South Asia is a region rich with products that the West has exploited for decades and centuries. It has sources of internal wealth which can be applied to such programs, provided that these new countries are not required to shoulder staggering burdens of compensation to pay off the old rulers and old owners. In any case, political returns in the shape of returning stability, of common effort attracting the vigor and resources and vitality of the people, of creating a new center of polarization, would be immeasurable in dollars. A small fraction of America's present military budget diverted to these purposes would buy more real American security than any quantity of armaments that will be obsolete and useless almost before they are delivered.

Incidentally, to anticipate an obvious question, I certainly believe that Viet-Nam could and should be included in this program, whether or not it is under Communist domination or threatened with it. I believe such an organization as this would strengthen the hand of the left-of-center elements in every country—and these are the only elements which can possibly carry out the projected program. It would tend to disarm the Communists politically because it could effectively bolster the kind of revolutionary change that the situation so urgently requires without surrendering to totalitarianism. Action along these lines is one remaining means of making a start, of beginning to prove that there *is* an alternative to the totalitarian method, and a better one at that.

Obviously, this is contingent upon a world-wide policy designed to prevent the outbreak of war, as distinct from a policy that is based on preparation for war. This is a crucial distinction and colors all policy thinking. If the calculations are for a war in the more or less near future, then obviously all bets are off, and the outlook is filled with all forms of defeat and no forms of victory. I think that we have to travel another road. There is a real struggle to be waged against expanding Soviet totalitarianism. But it will only serve totalitarian ends if we allow ourselves to be drawn into a military contest. I think the answer to totalitarianism is the effective reorganization of the world, or at least of those areas still accessible to new experiments. A political and economic offensive of this kind is the only way to disarm and push back the expanding Soviet totalitarian power. It is the only way to neutralize the development of indigenous Communist movements, which are and always will be the major weapon in the Soviet arsenal. It means that these countries will be embarked on a heroic program along new lines. It will call for "Hungry Forties" and Hungry Fifties and Hungry Sixties for a great many people, including ourselves. It will mean bold use of scientific methods. It will mean applying to these purposes of peace at least as much vigor and sacrifice and technical genius as were applied to the purposes of war.

There has been mention here of Point Four, President Truman's program for technical assistance to backward countries. We do not yet know much about this program or what it is intended to be. But the form it seems to be taking strongly suggests how little we appreciate the real magnitude of the problem. It appears to be based on the idea that private capital can be encouraged to do the job, with guaranties both on the American end and abroad, to protect investors against loss of their investments. This is like trying to put out a big fire with a cup of water. Private capital has been unable to carry out a single major social task in our time on the basis of so-called "free enterprise." Where such tasks are involved, it has demanded and has been given guaranties and protection and subsidy to an extent that virtually eliminates the investor's risk. This is a pretty costly way of keeping a system going. Private capital, as such, could not swing the recovery of Europe. It certainly cannot do the job in Asia.

It seems to me that we have to start from new and different premises. Whether we like it or not, we are in an era of statism. The problem is to create a statist system based on expanding human freedoms in opposition to a statist system based on human enslavement. We have to be done with the old shibboleths, the old categories, the old ideas. They are bankrupt and unproductive. An immense vacuum exists in the world. It has to be filled with new concepts, new approaches to society's problems. If we abdicate to the totalitarian power in advance by stubbornly clinging to the past, we can blame only ourselves for the inevitable outcome. Our opportunity is slipping away from us. But it is still within our grasp.

EXCERPTS FROM ROUND-TABLE DIS-
CUSSIONS ON POLITICAL FORCES
AND AMERICA'S STAKE

MR. WERNER LEVI: I cannot agree with the whole analysis by Mr. Isaacs. I want to make a few remarks as the devil's advocate on the proposals he has made and to question some of the positive suggestions he has made.

First, it seems to be generally taken for granted here that the creation of an area including India and the southeastern nations is necessarily desirable from the United States standpoint. That may be so for the moment, but whether in the long run it is in our so-called "national interest" or from the standpoint of power politics to have a huge, very powerful bloc established there under the leadership of one very powerful nation I am not sure. Second, the question has always been in my mind whether the Southeast Asiatic nations would accept such a council as Mr. Isaacs suggests when India is in it. I still say that the only concrete evidence of anything driving toward regionalism politically in that area is the fear of India and the fear of China. If it is true that the drive toward regionalism in that area is stimulated and provoked by fear of the power of either India or China, I can hardly see how they would voluntarily or gladly join some such council. All the talk that I have heard from the Southeast Asiatic nations was for some sort of regional organization with the exclusion of India, quite specifically with the exclusion of India, as well as China, of course. So I am just wondering about the feasibility of that suggestion.

Furthermore, there is also the rivalry between India and China for leadership in Asia, and from the purely, shall we say, power political standpoint I am wondering whether some of the Southeast Asiatic nations that are situated closer to China than to India would consider it wise to get off the fence, join a bloc or organization in which India has leadership, when they know that this obviously will provoke resentment on the part of China.

We do know that after the war China was greatly interested in having some sort of influence over Indochina and that there were even invasions of Burma from China. Certainly, there are numerous indications that China has expansive intentions, and I, for one, believe that, whether the Nationalists or the Communists are in control of China, that aspect of the foreign policy will remain the same; as a matter of fact, I could imagine that, if the Communists take over, the expansionism actually will be increased.

Then United States loans to this region on a governmental basis are bound to have strings attached also; at least, I doubt whether loans can be granted in a completely altruistic manner. I think altruism is too much to ask in international relations. If the United States even on a governmental basis makes loans, it will tie them in with some sort of political policy, which to me seems to be at the moment to maintain the absolute control and power that we have over both the Pacific and the Indian oceans, and we will not do anything that might strengthen any actual or potential rivals to that power position. This would lead back to the first point that I made.

We might very well consider—not in the near future but nevertheless at some future day—the possibility of a rival to our position developing there. From that standpoint I think it would be impossible to expect any government, whether the United States or any other, to make loans without any reciprocity or anything to expect in return.

That is really the dilemma in this whole discussion of the economic aspects, too. It seems to me that we have been somewhat in a vacuum here because we assume, at times at least, that our interest would be to put these nations on their feet, with no particular expectation on our part. I wish it could be done, but I doubt that it can. Economics in the world today has changed to power economics, no matter what we may have told the other nations and ourselves. I may quote Professor Morgenthau, who once said: "We have become the prisoners of our own propaganda." That is very applicable to the area in which we deal.

Furthermore and finally, I have yet to see any constructive requests from any of the peoples of Southeast Asia concerning what we could lend the money for. To be sure, they have asked us for money, but that is about as far as they went. Mr. Soedjatmoko criticizes us for ignoring the socialist forces. I am in perfect agreement with that, but I think that these forces also are under the obligation to give us some really constructive ideas on what they are planning to do with the funds that they get from us.

MR. BROEK: We can for good reasons discuss South Asia as a unit when we think of the present-day problems, but Southeast Asia lies, after all, between these massive and potentially powerful blocs of China and India, which dominated Southeast Asia before the Europeans came and may do so again in the future. I have sometimes compared Southeast Asia to the Balkans in Europe, in that you have here an area consisting of some half-dozen relatively small countries (with many minorities) under pressure of more powerful neighbors. It is for that reason that I think we should keep an eye on potential points of friction. It is therefore particularly important to consider how the countries of Southeast Asia can be strengthened.

As for Southeast Asia, I see three possibilities. It may come under the guardianship of India; I do not think, however, that the peoples of Southeast Asia would receive the necessary assistance in capital and technology; neither do I think that they would welcome a domination by India. Another possibility is that China by way of communism will gain a predominant position. There is a strong anti-Chinese feeling in this region. The Western countries certainly should oppose Communist-inspired regimes in this area. The third possibility is that the West give help to these countries of Southeast Asia, building up their strength by developing their economic and political effectiveness.

What interest does the West have in South Asia? The West, as I think of it, is essentially the "Atlantic community." The interests are partly ideological, partly economic, and partly strategic. Ideologically, it is the struggle against communism. The majority of the leaders may not want the Russian form of communism, but—as in China—a political vacuum or economic chaos may open the door to seizure of power by Communists.

Material assistance, not piecemeal or to a few selected countries but strong support on a regional basis, is necessary. Private capital is not likely to be available, or only on onerous terms. The assistance will have to come through government loans, inevitably mainly from the United States. Some kind of Marshall Plan may be necessary. Thus a situation facing the United States in Europe repeats itself halfway around the world in Southeast Asia. At the same time we should support governments that appear to have the power to insure order, even if they have strongly socialist tendencies. Most of the present governments tend in that direction, and they are in fear of being pushed aside by Communist groups. If they now receive the necessary help on a liberal basis, I think that co-operation between the West and the former colonial countries, on a broad regional basis, can be re-established to their mutual benefit. Several of us here have raised the point that Southeast Asia may sink into anarchy, but I feel very strongly that we should do everything possible to avert such a disaster.

As to the economic significance of South Asia to the West, most of this is rather obvious, but one point should be stressed. Before the war western Europe paid for a good deal of its imports from the United States by profits made on the sale of tropical commodities to America. Although part of this trade is irrevocably lost, there remains a substantial European investment in Southeast Asia. If the United States—for its own protection—wants a prosperous western Europe, these investments should be allowed to produce profits again, a revival that should also benefit the local economies in Southeast Asia.

Strategically, South Asia, through its location, controls the links between the Pacific and Indian oceans. With all seapower gathered in the Atlantic community, this fact seems less important than before; but if South Asia, or at least Southeast Asia, should fall into the sphere of influence of the Soviet Union, the consequences for the West would be quite serious.

And what about the strategic commodities? Here I think it is clear that Southeast Asia no longer has the position it once had. This is so because of the competition of other areas and of synthetic materials. But we have not yet reached the point—if we ever do reach it—where we can do without its products. Natural rubber and quinine are still valuable. Consider also the manganese from India, the tin from Malaya and Indonesia, and the vegetable oils and fats.

Altogether, then, it appears that the West has still a considerable stake in the region. That is all to the good. If substantial and sustained help is going to be given, it will not and cannot be done as charity, on a purely humanitarian basis. It will have to be done as a business deal, be it a farsighted business deal. I may end up by saying once more that the time is now and not later. The present circumstances are favorable. The local governments of the area feel the pressure of communism, and the West—after the experience of China—should realize that a determined stand must be made in the remainder of Asia. These considerations should lead to a new relationship in which the Atlantic community and South Asia are partners in a common enterprise.

MR. HOLLAND: To consider further the problem of the place of this part of the world in United States strategic priorities, my impression is that Southeast Asia and the Indian Ocean generally, in fact—even the South Pacific—have now a much lower place in the scale of priorities than they had at the beginning of the second World War. Part of that is just another way of saying that the experts are now more concerned with an air war over the top of the world. Compared with such areas as Alaska at one end of the scale and the Middle East on the other, this in-between area of India, Southeast Asia, even the off-shore islands of East Asia including Japan, now appears to have a much lower scale in the priorities.

MR. ISAACS: The fact that Southeast Asia today has low military priority is an advantage from the point of view of the possible effort we can make to shape a better society. It is not necessary in Southeast Asia to count benefits in terms of immediate strategic value. This gives us a chance to think about Southeast Asia in nonmilitary terms, to help in a program out there that will increase productivity and serve the general well-being of the people there as well as ourselves. It is an opportunity that we are letting slip—to begin thinking in world terms, to become world citizens in a truly new sense of the term.

But I would like to offer one reservation to the reported military attitude: It seems to me quite possible that the day might come when the Southeast Asian peninsula will acquire in the minds of our military people approximately the same role as the Aegean peninsula, a toehold on a continent. That may well happen. It may happen to our State Department people even without military pressure. The danger is that we will pursue in Southeast Asia the same kind of policy that has been followed in Greece, and with even less effective results. The whole experience of the war should have taught us that military decisions without effective political and social changes are of small use in the long run.

RAPPORTEUR'S REPORT OF ROUND-TABLE DISCUSSIONS ON POLITICAL FORCES AND AMERICA'S STAKE

By WILLIAM L. HOLLAND[1]

IN THE true sense the word "politics," as we should here understand it, really involves the sum total of all the factors that come to bear on the decisions made by the leaders of nations, and they certainly affect, therefore, the cultural and economic aspects that have been discussed. For that reason I am arbitrarily going to confine myself to what you might call the dregs of those aspects. That, in fact, means that I will be dealing largely with certain aspects of internal administrative and governmental problems, on the one side, and then with some of the more noteworthy aspects of international conflicts or communities of interest which have been brought out in the discussions, and, finally, a few words on some of the more specific political implications of these factors for American policy and for the foreign policies of other nations outside South Asia.

Running throughout our discussions on the political or economic level has been the unresolved question of, first of all, whether we are dealing with one or two regions or even whether, if broken down into two, you have really general agreement on the validity of the regional concept. That has been discussed from various points of view. There is a number of theoretical and logical doubts which have been expressed about the validity of the concept either for South Asia or for Southeast Asia. One of the obvious points is, of course, that the disparity in power between India, on the one side, and Southeast Asia, on the other, is so great as to raise some doubt as to the notion of a "region" even in political terms. Perhaps even more important is the fact that both parts of the region—India, on the one side,

1. Secretary-general, Institute of Pacific Relations.

and Southeast Asia, on the other—do not look merely within their own boundaries for the major solution of their problems. Both look outside: India, because it regards itself increasingly as a world power and because in any case it has to look to the West, and Southeast Asia, certain parts of it at least, because the historic ties have been until very recently with the Western world. In the case of the Philippines that still remains true in a notable degree.

It is further to be noted that, despite these theoretical and logical doubts about the validity of the regional concept, certain practical events have greatly increased the evidence that there is the consciousness of regional identity. As Mr. Isaacs pointed out, that was perhaps first symbolized in the calling of the Asian Relations Conference in 1947 and then further intensified by the holding of the Delhi Conference on the Indonesian issue.[2] But there I think it should be noted that the initiative in both cases came, not from the region as a whole or even from a group of the main countries there, but almost entirely from India and that an important aspect of the Delhi Conference was the fact that it was extended beyond the region to include Australia and New Zealand and that perhaps contributed a good deal to its international significance.

I pass now to a brief review of the more important internal political factors. We have heard a good deal already of the numerous differences which exist within the countries of Southeast Asia, and that, of course, is true in the political sphere. I need not take the time to detail them all here. Perhaps as illustrations we might point to the fact that, though in all areas there has been up until recently an acute concern with the throwing-off of external Western political control, the actual methods adopted have differed markedly among the different countries. Therefore, you have a totally different political climate in such countries as the Philippines, India, or Pakistan, because of the way in which their aspirations toward independence have been handled by the United States and Britain, from that in Indonesia and Indochina, because of the less statesman-like way in which these same tendencies have been treated by Holland and

2. See the paper of Harold Isaacs, pp. 161–73 of this volume.

France. Moreover, because of historical accident, as Mr. Embree has noted, Siam, having been independent, has not manifested its nationalism in quite the same forms as the other countries, and that has a very real bearing on the nature of the internal political development there.

I now turn to see what principal common elements exist within the internal political situations in the countries that we are considering. In all there is, even on the political level as distinct from the economic, a noteworthy preoccupation with socialism as a general political doctrine, however it may be defined in practice. The same is true of nationalism, involving, as I have already said, a considerable concern with the elimination of either actual or recent vestiges of external forms of control, whether those are explicit in the form of actual sovereignty or indirect in the sense that a country like Siam feels itself to be to some extent under pressure from other nations, as, for instance, Great Britain in recent years.

Second, in all these areas—I regard this as a central problem —there are serious administrative deficiencies, which means that the technical level of governmental administration constitutes a very serious problem, all the more so because the problems that have to be grappled with by the new administrators are so acute and the margin in which mistakes can be made is such a very narrow one.

That leads us to the next common element. In all these areas there is appreciable danger of undemocratic trends, partly because in some cases the tradition of democracy, at least in the Western sense, was never deeply rooted. Even where it has been implanted, as in India, Pakistan, and the Philippines, it is too early to say that it has taken deep and healthy roots. But, throughout, the lack of parliamentary tradition and the weaknesses of the educational system mean that the aspirations toward political democracy are in danger always of being subverted. That danger is probably most serious in a country like Siam, and perhaps in Burma. It is less serious for the moment in areas like the Philippines, India, and Pakistan, though we have seen some of the rather serious tendencies in those countries which may offset the trend toward democracy.

〖 237 〗

A tendency in all these areas is for the real control of power to gravitate into the hands of rather tough party or military factions. That is perhaps all the more important because in a number of areas those factions for the moment hide behind more liberal, or more lenient, political leaders. The most noteworthy example of that is in India today in the contrast between the personalities of a man like Nehru and his rather tough henchman, Patel.

Throughout the area I think that a significant political problem also arises from the existence of minority problems, some of them being aggravated by the fact that the minorities are alien groups and not merely internal minorities. As we see in Burma, the fact of even internal minorities constitutes a very real problem, and we have had discussion on the significance of linguistic and regional minority groups in India.

Next I would stress, although it has been mentioned in the economic sense already, the absence or very great weakness of a middle class or of a modern business class. This is complicated by the fact, as we have already noted, that the middle class in many parts of Southeast Asia has been alien, either Indian or Chinese. A notable exception perhaps is India, where there is much more of a middle class and where, consequently, there is already in evidence a decided conservative trend, not merely, I suspect, in the economic sphere but in certain aspects of politics as well.

Next it might be noted that all areas here are affected in considerable degree by Communist movements, though those movements are of varying strength. The Communist movement has very strong internal roots, largely based on the fact that it has been able not only to exploit traditional social and economic evils but also to link them up to the problem of external colonial control and, furthermore, to play upon the rivalries on the world scene between Russia and the other Western powers. It is noteworthy, therefore, that communism has shrewdly exploited the nationalist appeal, even, as Mr. Isaacs pointed out, to the absurd extremes of appearing at times to favor nationalism and nationalist independent movements at the expense of what might seem to have been rather desirable co-operative regional movements, even on the economic level. It is significant, since we often tend to make the mistake of assuming that communism is a uniform phenomenon which operates the same everywhere, that there are appreciable variations in the South Asian Communist movements. As Mr. Milton Sacks brought out, in the Indochinese movement it leads a coalition.[3] In India for various reasons the Indian Communist movement has had to go through certain devious phases, some of which were undoubtedly forced by developments on the Indian political scene.

Throughout the region, despite the aspirations toward democracy and despite the genuine efforts of countries like Pakistan and the Philippines and India to adopt the orthodox parliamentary forms of government, actual leadership remains in the hands of very small minorities. On the other hand, it should be noted that these elite groups are significant and, from the point of view of the outside world, are the only groups that probably can be dealt with by foreign governments. The minorities, though small, are, in fact, able to mobilize considerable emotional and other support from the mass of the people. The obverse of that—the dangerous aspect of it—is, of course, the risk that these small minorities can rather easily move in the direction of the establishment of oligarchies or personal dictatorships and police states.

That is a real danger because there exists in all these countries what might be called, as it was in China, the fact of an uncompleted social revolution. Nowhere in this area can it be said that even the mildly socialist and nationalist governments which have come into control or are aspiring to control have worked out far-reaching plans for dealing with some of the survivals of medieval or feudal or at least precapitalist social and economic institutions, which certainly determine a great deal of the political climate of the country. That is obviously true in such matters as the failure to enforce drastic land reforms or to curb the important political influence exerted by moneylending and merchant groups. That failure has its implications, in that it provides the Communists or other extremist leaders with a very convenient rallying cry. Even though a Communist move-

3. See the paper by Milton Sacks, pp. 202–10 of this volume.

ment itself could not perhaps put forward any very effective positive program of its own for dealing with these intractable economic problems, it has a very effective political weapon in simply calling for the overthrow of these obvious and age-old evils, and, as the example was cited, you don't have to work out a new, a perfect, system of agricultural credit; it is sufficient to call upon the peasants to stop paying rent to the existing landlords.

That is perhaps best summarized in a statement which was made that throughout the area the mass of the people, though often described as inert and unorganized, are nevertheless in a process of change, confused change but very real change, and that the one thing they are sure about is that they want some kind of change—almost any kind. In that sense, to talk of restoring something of the old stability of the prewar system is unreal because certain vital elements in the old system have gone forever. Certainly, those vital elements depended directly on the fact of foreign control or of foreign economic participation, and for the most part those have broken down or disappeared. In that sense the djinn is out of the bottle. To make an outrageous pun, one of the ironies is that the Dutch, who ought to know most about gin, are least willing to recognize the fact and persist in the futile attempt to put the djinn back into the bottle.

Finally, I would allude to what was briefly mentioned but which I think to be a matter of great significance. That is the present, and even more the future, role of the military in these areas, all the more because throughout the area one of the significant political facts has been the wide and uncontrolled distribution of arms into the hands of the people and the fact that even among the so-called "armies" of the area the military organization is so loose that it has proved very easy, whether in Burma or in Indonesia, for small armed groups to break off, to constitute a serious threat to security and political stability, even against the wishes of the nationalist leaders. However much we may discount the charges of the Dutch about the irresponsibility of the Indonesian leadership, the fact remains, as we have seen in Burma or in the Huk movement of the Philippines, that the existence of arms and the lack of any tightly controlled system of military organization constitute a serious political problem.

In the few remaining moments I want simply to sketch very briefly certain of the international aspects of the political side of our discussions. First, I would stress the fact of the disparity between the power of Southeast Asia as a whole, on the one side, and the nations of Southeast Asia and to some extent India and Pakistan, on the other. While it was not discussed at length here, it is worth noting that in the minds of a good many of the peoples of Southeast Asia this gives rise to certain anxieties which can be crudely expressed as the fear of a certain type of Indian expansionism or even imperialism, the risk of that being all the greater because India has, in Malaya and Burma, colonies of its own nationals who might conceivably provide an excuse for intervention. Notably it was mentioned that, though there has been a change in administration in China, the Chinese Communists have already expressed concern for their groups overseas. That is most significant in the case of Malaya, where almost all the leadership of the Communist insurrection has been Chinese.

It was noted also that in terms of power structure, if we are trying to think of this area as a region, it is very difficult to envisage it as an effective, functioning area unless we bring into consideration such outside areas as Australia as one of the so-called strategic "pivot" areas, and possibly even Japan, looking ahead and thinking of power in terms not merely of military power but of a complex of industrial and commercial power.

The question has been raised of who could "impose" regionalism in view of the great strength of nationalist sentiment here? That constitutes one of the very serious problems and is at the back of the notion which has already been expressed by Mr. Thorner on the economic side, namely, the perhaps inevitable tendency toward some kind of system in which a great degree of Indian predominance or leadership would have to be recognized. The only alternative would be some new type of regional organization in which, with the guaranty of the outside powers, there would be a sort of treaty of neutrality, in other words, an attempt to hold the ring and prevent Southeast Asia from becoming an arena for international rivalries. That, in turn, would require a much greater degree of self-control and statesmanship than most of the outside powers have been willing to show so far. In fact, the real danger is rather the reverse, as was noted this morning; that the great outside powers, particularly the United States and Britain and Russia, because of their ability to give economic aid, might couple that aid with political demands in the attempt to fight the cold war and extend the battle over Russian Communist influence into that part of the world.

I suggest that this concept of international co-operation for a guaranty of the neutrality or the protection of the area from external aggression is something that deserves more attention than we were able to give it here. In that connection we must note that American policy today is double-faced. It is full of serious contradictions because of its apparent decision to give priority to the strengthening of western Europe and that has, in turn, led to a decided reluctance to go ahead with any immediate plans for a Pacific pact, despite the effort of the Australians to push that idea. We saw from General Romulo's remarks how the United States has lost in Asia much of the good will it had at the end of the war, how any attempts which it might make now to propose regional schemes involving direct American political and military support would, in fact, be suspect and rendered difficult because of that very fact.[4] I would suggest, however, that we tended in some of those discussions to overlook the fact that power does continue to exist in this part of the world. It cannot be wished out of existence, and this part of the world may become an arena for conflict of world power systems. The important thing, I assume, is to devise means for canalizing those power systems so that they will not meet in head-on collision in this part of the world.

That leads, then, to some of the implications of our discussions for the United States and other nations. The remark which was made most generally and which seemed to command a great deal of support was that foreign policies which are based merely on anticommunism and the desire to check either Asiatic Communist expansion or the expansion of Russian power in Asia will not be sufficient. On the contrary, policies based on

4. See the paper by Carlos P. Romulo, pp. 153–60 of this volume.

that idea will rather tend to polarize the political situation in this part of the world and weaken the all-important non-Communist leftist but middle groups. One might therefore conclude that if we were trying to come forward with an exhortation, it would be that the United States and the other principal Western powers ought to give much more attention to the support of the non-Communist leftist groups in South Asia, and that, of course, means that it is dangerous for us to be too obsessed with the mere preservation of stability, recognizing the need for this in certain respects. A measure of upheaval in this kind of situation is perhaps inevitable, and one might even say that it is necessary and desirable. Whether you can have such a thing as "controlled upheaval" I don't know, but it is something which perhaps needs to be kept in mind.

Finally, since we have been concentrating so much on a particular area here, I think we must conclude with a slightly chilling thought that, by all the current evidence, this part of the world for the moment is not one of the top priorities in United States over-all foreign policy. It may become much more important, but for the present it does not rate with western Europe or even, let us say, with the Middle East in United States over-all strategic concerns. That fact has a very real bearing on the urgency of American Far Eastern policy-planning.

Quite naturally here we tend to think simply of South Asia and the United States, and that relationship certainly is important. On the other hand, we must remember that there are other important parts of the world which can influence South Asia, and the most notable of those, I suppose, is still the British Commonwealth. I conclude by simply noting the fact that here is one case where, as a result of the recent decision of India to remain even symbolically within the Commonwealth, the international situation in Southeast Asia remains, therefore, one in which other Western powers can still be of considerable influence and can, in fact, decidedly influence American policy. Finally, I would note that the one functioning regional organization with some degree of executive power has been one within the British Commonwealth system, namely, the very small but quite important Southeast Asia organization set up under Lord Killearn and Mr. Malcolm Macdonald.

APPENDIX

LIST OF PARTICIPANTS, TWENTY-FIFTH HARRIS INSTITUTE

PARTICIPANTS

ADAMS, A. C. S., British consul, Cincinnati (formerly assigned to British Embassy, Bangkok)

BARR, R. O., Standard–Vacuum Oil Company

BEKKER, KONRAD, economist, Division of Research for Far East, Department of State

BOBRINSKOY, GEORGE V., associate professor of Sanskrit, University of Chicago

BRODIE, HENRY, special assistant to the chief, Division of Research for Far East, Department of State

BROEK, JAN O. M., professor of geography, University of Minnesota

CHARTRAND, CHESTER R., acting chief, Near East and African Area, Public Affairs Overseas Program Staff, Department of State

DAVIS, KINGSLEY, director, Bureau of Applied Social Research, Columbia University

DU BOIS, CORA, chief, Southern Areas Branch, Division of Research for Far East, Department of State

EGGAN, FRED, professor of anthropology, University of Chicago

EMBREE, JOHN F., associate professor of sociology, Southeast Asia Studies Program, Yale University

ESPENSHADE, EDWARD, associate professor of geography, Northwestern University

FURNIVALL, J. S., adviser to the government of the Union of Burma

GINSBURG, NORTON S., instructor in geography, University of Chicago

HALPERN, A. M., social scientist, Rand Corporation.

HAYES, FRANK, reporter, *Chicago Daily News*

HOLLAND, WILLIAM L., secretary-general, Institute of Pacific Relations

HOSELITZ, BERT F., associate professor of the social sciences, University of Chicago

HUGHES, EVERETT C., professor of sociology, University of Chicago

ISAACS, HAROLD, associate editor, *Newsweek Magazine*

JANOWITZ, MORRIS, instructor in the social sciences in the College, University of Chicago

JOHNSON, D. GALE, associate professor of economics, University of Chicago

KATTENBURG, PAUL, instructor in political science and research assistant, Institute of International Studies, and Southeast Asia Program, Yale University

LEVI, WERNER, associate professor of political science, University of Minnesota

MANDELBAUM, DAVID, professor of anthropology, University of California

MERRIAM, CHARLES E., professor emeritus of political science, University of Chicago

METZLER, LLOYD A., professor of economics, University of Chicago

MORGENTHAU, HANS J., professor of political science, University of Chicago

MORRIS, CHARLES W., lecturer in philosophy, University of Chicago

O'FLAHERTY, HAL, director, *Chicago Daily News* Foreign Service

PELZER, KARL J., associate professor of geography, Southeast Asia Program, Yale University

PERLOFF, HARVEY S., associate professor of the social sciences, University of Chicago

PIPLANI, B. M., Food and Agriculture Organization; deputy secretary, Ministry of Agriculture, Government of India

POLEMAN, HORACE, chief, South Asia Section, Orientalia Division, Library of Congress

PURNELL, LEWIS M., foreign service officer, Department of State

REUBENS, EDWIN P., assistant professor of economics, Cornell University

ROMULO, CARLOS P., Ambassador, Philippines representative to the United Nations

SACKS, MILTON, foreign affairs analyst, Division of Research for Far East, Department of State

SARKAR, BENOY, professor of economics, Calcutta University

SCHULTZ, THEODORE W., professor of economics, University of Chicago

SCOTT, ARTHUR P., professor of history, University of Chicago

SOEDJATMOKO, member, Indonesian delegation to the UN Security Council

TALBOT, PHILLIPS, senior associate, Institute of Current World Affairs; visiting assistant professor of political science, University of Chicago

THORNER, DANIEL, research assistant professor of economic history, Department of South Asia Regional Studies, University of Pennsylvania

TYLER, RALPH W., dean of the Division of Social Sciences, University of Chicago

VANDENBOSCH, AMRY, professor of political science, University of Kentucky

WILSON, JOHN A., professor of Egyptology, University of Chicago

WRIGHT, QUINCY, professor of international law, University of Chicago

ZIERATH, F. R., Colonel Plans and Operations Division, General Staff, United States Army

INDEX

INDEX

Indonesian proper names are spelled in the orthography current before independence.

Acculturation, 51
Accumulation of wealth, 66, 67
Adat law, 33, 54, 200
Agrarian legislation: in Indonesia, 113; in Philippines, 117
Agriculture, 85, 117–18, 135–37, 144; in Burma, 65; in India, 89–90, 92, 94–97, 105; in Java, 70, 109, 177–78; in Siam, 114
Alimin, 206
Asian Relations Conference (1947), 30, 35 ff., 38, 50, 158, 166, 207, 236
"Aslia," 34, 205

Bajpai, Sir Girja Shankar, 168
Balance of payments, 121 f., 135, 139–40; of Burma, 80
Bangkok Conference of ECAFE (1949), 170, 212
Bao-Dai, 56, 225
Barr, R. O., 55
Bauer, P. T., 114
Berg, Cornelius C., 46
Bilateral trade agreements, 141
Birth control, 104
Boeke, J. H., 177, 178
Bombay Plan, 149
British policy in South Asia, 6, 169
Buddhism, 37, 40, 41; in Burma, 4–5

Capital, 64–65, 67, 140, 143, 149; in agriculture, 94, 96
Capitalism, 67 ff., 177, 192; opposition to, 180 f.
Caste, 79
Chase, Stuart, 53, 54
Chiang Kai-shek, 56
China, 155 ff., 164; ascendancy in Asia, 229–30, 231, 241
Chinese in Southeast Asia, 35–36, 37, 110, 164, 180, 182, 215, 238
Christian missions, 8, 46, 78
Christianity, 37, 57
Civil strife: in Burma, 13; in Indonesia, 180–81, 236–37

Class structure, 77, 171–72; in India, 144
Cold war, 148, 153, 163, 170, 223, 227, 238
Colonialism, 32, 143, 146, 159–60, 190–91, 216
"Communalism," 21, 217
Communism, 10, 20 f., 146, 154–55, 158–59, 202 ff., 216–17, 238–39; in Burma, 13, 18, 206, 217; Chinese, 155, 159, 224; in India, 204, 207, 214, 239; in Indonesia, 183–84, 186, 191, 204, 206, 209, 215–16; in Malaya, 215; opposition to, 223; in Siam, 215; in Viet-Nam, 205–7, 211–12, 225
Communist International, 202, 203, 207, 214
Constitutional reform, 237; in Burma, 9, 10, 16
Covarrubias, Miguel, 54
Crop yields, 93–94, 111–12
Cultivators' Union (Burma), 18
Culture, 54, 55, 58–59
Culture areas, 52
Custom as a force of social cohesion, 6, 7, 13, 55, 69, 75

Democracy, 20, 69, 155, 221, 239; versus totalitarianism, 173, 237
Density of population, 87–89, 91, 102–3, 117
Disintegration of native culture, 7, 14, 75, 143, 179 ff., 200, 240
Disunity in Southeast Asia, 53–54, 146, 225, 229, 235, 241–43
Dual economy, 70–71, 192
Du Bois, Cora, 55, 57
Dutch policy in Indonesia, 70, 74, 109, 176 f.

Economic Commission for Asia and the Far East (ECAFE), 30, 83, 137, 170, 212
Economic motives, 73 f.; in South Asia, 63–64, 73 f., 145; in the West, 73–74
Economic planning, 105, 135 ff., 144–45, 149

Economic structure, 14, 32–33, 73–74, 76–77, 143, 175, 239–40; of Indonesia, 178–79
Education, 30–31, 188; in Burma, 78
Eliot, T. S., 48, 59
Elite, 58, 172, 221
Embree, John F., 237
'Ethical" theory of colonialism, 189, 191, 199
Exports, 120–24, 127–30; from Indonesia, 114, 196

Farm size: in India, 93, 96; in Philippines, 117
Financing of economic development, 137 f., 149
Food consumption, 136
Foreign investments, 80–82, 137, 140–41, 226, 232; in Burma, 16, 80; in Indonesia, 176–77; by United States, 147
Foreign trade, 119 f., 134; in food, 127, 130, 132, 135; of India, 98; with Japan, 123, 131, 132, 134, 140; with United Kingdom, 123, 130–31; with United States, 123, 130–31, 132–33, 135
French policy in Indochina, 211–12
Furnivall, J. S., 52

Geographical factors, 28

Hatta, Mohammed, 34
Hill tribes, Burma, 4, 8, 65–66
Hinduism, 27, 37, 39–40, 79
Ho Chi-minh, 34, 165, 205, 206, 211, 212, 225
Hobson, John A., 176
Huxley, Aldous, 57
Huxley, Elspeth, 118

Illiteracy, 35, 188
Imperialism, 16, 142, 167, 176, 196, 203, 207–8, 222; Japanese, 154; in United States, 230
Imports, 120–24, 130–31; into Indonesia, 196
Independence, 162, 212; of Burma, 11–12, 16–17; of Indonesia, 47–48
India, 24; ascendancy of, in Asia, 229–30, 231, 241; cultural impact of, 39–40
Indians: in Burma 6–7, 17, 37, 41, 74, 110, 238; in Malaya, 41
Individualism, 48, 74
Industrialization, 117, 137 f., 143 f.; in India, 97 ff., 104–5; in Indonesia,

181–82; and population pressure, 100 f., 106
Inflation, 134, 138
Intellectuals, 190, 193
Intra-regional trade, 121–23
Isaacs, Harold, 53, 58, 59, 211, 236, 238
Islam, 27, 37, 42, 45–46

Japan, 9, 10 ff., 33, 157, 162–63; occupation by, 11 ff., 14–15; resistance against, 213
Joshi, P. C., 214

Karens, 4, 8, 19, 78
Keynes, John M., 176
Killearn, Lord, 243
Kipling, Rudyard, 77
Kroeber, Alfred L., 59

Labor movement, in Indonesia, 182, 186–87
Labor unions, in Indonesia, 185
Laissez faire, 68, 76, 175–76, 227–28
Land tenure, 79, 96–97; in Burma, 18; in India, 92; in Philippines, 111
Language, 29, 30–31, 41, 45 f., 56; English, 30–31, 50; Urdu, 30–31
"League against Colonial Oppression," 186, 204
Linggadjati Agreement, 206
Lynd, Helen M., 53
Lynd, Robert S., 53

Macdonald, Malcolm, 243
Madjapahit, 40
Maffry, August, 139
Mahabharata, 40
Malakka, Tan, 34, 205, 206
Malayan language, 29, 41, 45 f., 56
Mandelbaum, David, 52
Marsman, Jan Hendrik, 48
Marx, Karl, 75, 76
Mexico, 53
Middle class in India, 144, 238
Migration, 35, 104, 192
Mill, John Stuart, 64, 72
Morgenthau, Hans J., 230
Münzenberg, Willi, 204

National character, 51, 57 f.
National income, 136; of India, 149
Nationalism, 21 ff., 36, 49, 51, 146, 161 ff., 202, 237; in Burma, 9–10, 16; in Indo-

nesia, 47 ff., 199–201, 215–16; in Malaya, 164; in Philippines, 153–54; in Siam, 55
Nationalization, 79–80
Nehru, Pandit Jawaharlal, 34, 39, 147, 167–68, 169, 204, 214, 223, 238
New Delhi Conference on Indonesia (1940), 30, 34, 158, 166, 236
Nguyen, Van Tao, 211
Nu, Thakin, 37

Onn, Dato bin Jaafar, 34
Osmania University, 30

Panchatantra, 40
Pan-Malayan League, 34
Pantun, 47
Partai Nasional Indonesia, 181, 186, 187
Patel, S. V., 238
Pendidikan Nasional Indonesia, 193
People's Volunteer Organization (Burma), 18
Plantation agriculture, 70, 112–15, 178–79, 184
Plural society, 7 ff., 14 f., 76–77, 199
Point Four program, 35, 118, 139, 148, 227
"Police action" in Indonesia, 156, 166, 167, 224
Population, 87 f.; in India, 88 f., 90, 143; in Pakistan, 88 f.
Population pressure, 72, 100 f.
Poverty, 87 f., 108 f., 115, 175, 194
Prices, 119–20, 234 f., 135, 197
Pridi, Panomyong, 34, 166
Productivity of labor, 64, 101, 115; in agriculture, 112
Public finance, in Indonesia, 197–98
Public opinion, 58

Racial minorities, 28–29, 76, 79, 238
Ram, Sir Shri, 38
Ramayana, 40
Ranneft, J. W. Meyer, 196
Redfield, Robert, 53
Regionalism, 34–37, 42–43, 50, 84, 145, 157 f., 165 f., 207, 209–10, 225 f., 229, 235, 241–42
Religion, 4–5, 37 f., 56 f.
Rice, 127, 130, 132
Romulo, Carlos P., 34, 169, 242
Rubber, 114, 116
Rural indebtedness, 8, 110, 177–78; in India, 92, 96
Ruskin, John, 64

Sacks, Milton, 238
San, U Aung, 34
Sarekat Islam, 179–80, 183–84, 186, 187, 193
Saving, 82, 101, 139, 149; forced, 82
Scientific research, 116
Scripts, 29
Seafaring, 42
Semaoen, 183
Sjahrir, Soetan, 34, 37, 166, 175, 191, 200
Skilled labor, 83
Slauerhoff, Jan, 48
Smith, Adam, 67, 78
Sneevliet, 183
Socialism, 21, 69, 144, 230–31, 237; in Burma, 18; in Indonesia, 37, 180, 191–92
Soedjatmoko, 56, 68, 222, 223, 224, 231
Soekarno, Achmed, 34, 165, 181, 207
Soerabajasche Studie Club, 192–93, 196
Songgram, Phibun, 58, 166
South Seas Communist party, 204
"Southeast Asia League," 34, 166, 207
Sovereignty of nation-states, 162–64
Srivijaya Empire, 40
Statistical data, lack of, 87, 149–50
Sterling balances, 139 f.
Strategic position of South Asia, 233–34, 240
Strikes, 182, 184–85, 214
Suikerbond, 181

Tagalog language, 30, 48, 56
Tagore, Rabindranath, 38, 40
Taruc, Luis, 34
Taxation, 117, 138, 194
Technical training, 31–32, 81, 85, 115, 139, 232
Terms of trade, 124 f., 196
Textiles, 129
Tjokroaminoto, 184
Totalitarianism, 10, 105, 144, 172–73, 237
Tran Van Giau, 207
Triangular trade, 121
Tropical economy, 7, 71
Trotskyism, 206
Truman, Harry S., 118, 139, 227

Unemployment, 81–82; in Burma, 18; among intellectuals, 190; rural, 92
Union of Soviet Socialist Republics, 9, 10, 36–37, 170–71, 204–9, 211–12, 216, 242–43

United States policy in South Asia, 156–57, 221 ff., 231–33, 242–43.
Universities, 31–32
Upanishads, 40
Urbanization, 143
Usury, 110

Vedas, 40
Viet-Nam, 57, 168–69
Volksraad (People's Council), 198

War, destruction by, 134
Waste of resources, 66
Western influence, 13 f., 20, 27, 33, 53, 78, 83–84, 177, 231
Women, status of, 35
World Federation of Democratic Youth, 208
Wright, Quincy, 53, 54

[PRINTED IN U·S·A]